Green Bay
PACKERS
THE COMPLETE ILLUSTRATED HISTORY

Green Bay
PACKERS
THE COMPLETE ILLUSTRATED HISTORY

Don Gulbrandsen

Foreword by LeRoy Butler

Voyageur Press

For Tari and Kendal,
my favorite Packers fans

First published in 2007 by Voyageur Press an imprint
of MBI Publishing Company LLC, Galtier Plaza, Suite
200, 380 Jackson Street, St. Paul, MN 55101 USA

MBI Publishing Company titles are also available at
discounts in bulk quantity for industrial or sales-
promotional use. For details write to Special Sales
Manager at MBI Publishing Company, Galtier Plaza,
Suite 200, 380 Jackson Street, St. Paul, MN 55101
USA.

To find out more about our books, join us online at
www.voyageurpress.com.

Library of Congress Cataloging-in-Publication Data

Gulbrandsen, Don.
   The Green Bay Packers : the complete illustrated
history / by Don Gulbrandsen.
       p. cm.
   ISBN-13: 978-0-7603-3139-2 (hardbound w/ jacket)
   ISBN-10: 0-7603-3139-1 (hardbound w/ jacket) 1.
Green Bay Packers (Football team)--History. 2. Green
Bay Packers (Football team)--History--Pictorial works.
I. Title.
   GV956.G7G85 2007
   796.332'640977561--dc22
                                    2007006297

Designer: Ian Hughes, Mousemat Design Limited
Copyedited by Joel Marvin

Special thanks to Mary Jane Van Duyse Sorgel and
David Goessl for generously providing information
and photographs for this book.

Photographic credits are identified with the captions.

Printed in China

CONTENTS

FOREWORD
BY LEROY BUTLER

I first realized that playing in Green Bay was going to be a special experience when I flew into town after getting picked by the Packers in the second round of the 1990 draft. I'd had a good career at Florida State, and people expected big things of me in the pros, but I was surprised when about a thousand fans greeted me at the airport to welcome me to town—during the off-season on a weekday afternoon, and the team hadn't been that good!

But showing up at the airport to cheer a rookie player is not unusual in Green Bay, where following football is a year-round thing. There aren't any other pro sports teams to cheer for, so people put all their energy into the Packers. Their lives seem to focus on Lambeau Field, even when there aren't any games. "Where are you going for dinner?" "Lambeau Field." "Where are you hanging out this weekend?" "Lambeau Field." And so on.

Occasionally you'll hear two people talking and the conversation will go something like, "You don't have Packers tickets? Well, you'd better get on the waiting list. I'm almost up to number 10,000…" It doesn't matter if they don't have a realistic chance of getting to the top of the list. Just being *on* the list makes them a part of the team. Those fans that are lucky enough to have tickets know just how special the experience is. They feel *privileged* to see a game.

During my first winter in Green Bay, I learned that the fans are more than crazy about football—they are good people. I was driving my Nissan 300ZX on Highway 41 in a snowstorm. It was a nice-looking car, but it was not made for winter driving and pretty soon I slid off into the ditch. It was 10 degrees and I was a mile

from the nearest exit. I got out of the car and thought, "What am I going to do?" I was about to start walking when this big truck pulled over and two guys wearing Packers jackets hopped out. "Hey, you're LeRoy Butler!" The next thing I knew, they hooked a chain to my car, dragged it out of the ditch, and jump-started it. Before they left, one of the guys turned to me and said, "LeRoy, if you're going to play and live in Green Bay, you need to get yourself a 4×4." I listened to his advice and traded in my fancy car for a truck!

When you live in Green Bay, people go out of their way to welcome you to town. Neighbors bring you brownies and they bring over their kids to play with your kids. They also want to introduce you to Wisconsin food. I'm from Florida, so when I came to Green Bay I didn't know anything about bratwurst. People couldn't believe that, so they made sure I experienced an authentic Wisconsin meal by bringing over brats, cheese, and beer. (I don't drink, but a lot of people think beer is an important part of an authentic Green Bay meal.)

One of the great Packers' traditions is riding kids' bikes to and from the practice field during training camp. I rode the same kid's bike for eight or nine years; it was fun because I got to watch him grow up over that time. The thing is, this kid took the responsibility of having a bike waiting for me every day *seriously*—he treated it like a job. He even arranged to have another kid in his place, waiting with the bike on days he couldn't be there.

Even though Green Bay fans are serious about football, they aren't star-struck like people in other cities. They live almost side-by-side with the players and they see them at the mall, and that changes how they treat you. For one thing, they are not afraid to talk to you about the team—and they know *everything* about the Packers. I remember being on a flight and an 87-year-old lady told me a lot more about defensive coordinator Fritz Shurmur than I knew about him!

But even if they aren't afraid to talk to you, Green Bay fans are more respectful of you and more protective of you than people in other cities. They know not to bother you when you're eating in a restaurant and give you privacy when you need it. They are also quick to jump to your defense, and will not tolerate bad-mouthing the Packers. "Don't talk that way about MY players or MY team." A word that Green Bay fans often use when they talk about the Packers is *love*. "We love you guys!" fans will yell at you before games—and you know they really do love you.

Experiences like this made me want to stay in Green Bay. Much has been made about the fact that I played my whole career for the Packers and that I turned down offers from other teams, but when people treat you so well, you don't want to disappoint them. I even felt guilty when we lost. I remember losing the 1995 season opener to the Rams. It was a frustrating loss, but after the game 10,000 fans were still there cheering the team, "Go Pack Go!" They knew we weren't going to win every game and wanted to show that they were still behind us. It made me feel great inside and the fans' support helped push the team to win 25 straight home games starting later that season.

My favorite time to be a Packers' player was before games. I would park outside Lambeau Field and walk into the stadium through all the tailgate parties. People would offer words of encouragement, food, or even to look after your car during the game. After suiting up and walking onto the field, I'd look around and see everybody dressed up in green-and-gold, little kids with their faces painted, and five hundred people wearing my No. 36 jersey. I liked to walk around and talk to the fans, slap hands with kids, maybe give away my gloves.

One day, this pre-game ritual ended up having a long-term effect on my life. It was before that sloppy January 1997 playoff game against the 49ers—a big game. I looked around and saw Steve Young and Jerry Rice warming up, but I still wanted to go talk to the fans. One woman wearing a No. 36 jersey with a pink ribbon on it caught my eye. I jokingly asked her, "Why are you messing up my nice jersey with that ribbon?" She went on to explain that it was a tribute to women suffering from breast cancer and she shared some statistics with me. I was shocked; I didn't realize how many people had the disease. She told me, "Not enough people know about this. You could help get the word out."

The experience hit me hard. At the time I had two daughters (I now have four), and I couldn't imagine them

suffering from breast cancer. Also, it dawned on me that right before a big game, this fan cared more about helping other people than about football. I realized that's what being part of the Packers was all about, and I knew that I had to do something to help fight this disease.

Today, the LeRoy Butler Foundation for Breast Cancer raises money to educate the public about the disease, and to provide financial assistance to women who are fighting breast cancer. I'm proud to do my part in the fight against breast cancer, but I'm only putting into action lessons that I learned from the very special fans of the Green Bay Packers.

LeRoy Butler played for the Packers from 1990 until his retirement after the 2001 season. He was a standout safety, a defensive leader on Green Bay's Super Bowl teams, and one of the most popular players in Packers history. Many remember him as the originator of the legendary "Lambeau Leap." Butler was named All-Pro four times, played in four Pro Bowls, earned a spot on the NFL's 1990s All-Decade team, and was inducted into the Packers Hall of Fame in 2007.

If you want to help in the fight against breast cancer, please contact The LeRoy Butler Foundation for Breast Cancer. The foundation sponsors fund-raising and educational events throughout the year and also offers a variety of merchandise for sale. Money raised is used for research, financial assistance, treatment costs, and public education on breast cancer. For more information contact:

The LeRoy Butler Foundation for Breast Cancer
P.O. Box 130, Galesville, WI 54630
Phone: (608) 582-4916 • E-mail: info@leroybutler.org
Web Site: www.leroybutlerfoundation.org

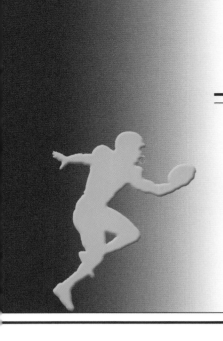

INTRODUCTION

Lambeau Field, the home of the Green Bay Packers, has been described as a "shrine to football." Thanks to numerous expansions and upgrades—the most recent in 2003—the 1950s-era facility remains one of the best in the NFL.
Tom Hauck/Allsport

Titletown USA. The Green and Gold. The Frozen Tundra. The Lambeau Leap. The Ice Bowl. The Cheeseheads. The Pack is Back.

These nicknames and catch phrases are indelibly etched into the lexicon of American sports. Start reading this list to any casual fan and most will quickly identify the team being described: the Green Bay Packers. No other U.S. sports franchise, save baseball's New York Yankees, has achieved the mythical status afforded this National Football League team from Wisconsin. While the preeminence of the Yankees—the richest team, located in America's leading city—is understandable, the appeal of the Packers is less

obvious. The team is headquartered in the country's smallest city with a major-league sports team. In fact, Green Bay, Wisconsin, has a population of only 102,000 and ranks as merely the 92nd largest television market, unheard of for a sport that derives much of its revenues from broadcasting. While the Packers have enjoyed periods of success (some might argue dynasty-like dominance), they have also suffered through several multiyear droughts that saw them hovering for long periods at or near the bottom of the NFL standings. And though they are stable today, the Packers have skirted on financial thin ice several times in their history, narrowly avoiding failure thanks to the amazing loyalty of their fans and a little luck.

Despite this questionable pedigree, no other professional sports team—not even the aforementioned Yankees—generates as much fan passion as the Green Bay Packers. Consider some of these amazing numbers:

- According to the Harris Poll, the Packers were the No. 1-ranked NFL team among football fans for the years 2002–2005, before finally slipping to No. 4 in 2006 after their disappointing 2005 season.
- As of 2006, the Packers had sold out their season tickets for 45 straight years. The 28,000 season-ticket holders represented all 50 states plus Canada, Japan, and Australia.
- There are currently 71,500 names on the waiting list for season tickets, which likely represents a wait of several decades. Many fans are adding their newborn children to the list, hoping that today's infant Packer fans will be rewarded with season tickets by the time they retire.
- The Packers have ranked at or near the top of licensed merchandise sales for the past decade—which, according to some experts, is the best way to rank the popularity of NFL teams.

These very big numbers become especially impressive when you take the time to visit the Packers' very small hometown.

Green Bay's Austin Straubel International Airport is a far cry from LAX or Chicago O'Hare. With only a dozen gates, sparse crowds, and lots of friendly faces, the airport quickly clues you in to the fact that you have left the big city and entered the warm confines of Middle America. In departing the facility by car on Airport Drive, you might be struck by the massive casino located just across the street, but not much else stands out aside from the relatively light traffic. Turning onto Oneida Street takes you through a stretch of retail development that could be Any Suburb, U.S.A, but as you swivel your head looking for a skyline, you ask yourself, "Where's the city?" Well, there isn't one, at least not in the densely populated, skyscraper-centered sense that most of us think of cities.

Suddenly, the real object of your search appears on the left, on the corner of Lombardi Avenue (named after you know who): Lambeau Field (named after that other famous coach), the home of the Green Bay Packers, and the place the legendary NFL coach and television announcer John Madden has described as a shrine to pro football. The stadium itself is relatively unassuming as far as NFL venues go, a traditional bowl that brings to mind a college football stadium. In fact, from the outside, the stadium actually looks rather small—in part, because the field sits below ground level, allowing for lower-profile stands. Lambeau's most

eye-catching feature is a new atrium, built during the stadium's latest renovation, completed in 2003. The atrium features restaurants, the Packer Hall of Fame, and ample rentable space that has become popular for weddings and other big parties.

As you behold Lambeau and its environs, you are quickly struck by the fact that the stadium is surrounded on several sides by residential neighborhoods. Quiet, tree-lined streets populated with modest homes radiate from Lambeau and its surrounding island of asphalt for parking (and tailgate parties). While most pro sports teams have built stadiums on vast tracts in either distant suburbia or on wastelands reclaimed from blight near downtown, the Packers' home seems to have popped up on an unassuming street corner, sited in the middle

Even other teams grudgingly admit that Green Bay fans may be the best in the NFL—they are a loud and loyal force at every Lambeau Field game, giving the Packers an unquestioned home-field advantage.
Scott Boehm/Getty Images

Tailgate parties over, Packers fans stream into newly renovated Lambeau Field to watch the October 5, 2003, contest with Seattle. Green Bay crushed the Seahawks 35–13.
David Stluka/Getty Images

The "cheesehead" has become the universal symbol of loyalty to the Green Bay Packers. This fan shows off her fashionable foam headgear during an October 31, 1993, victory over the Bears at Lambeau Field.
Jonathan Daniel/Allsport

of a neighborhood much like a new high school or church—and herein lies the secret to the Packers' mystique.

Today, Green Bay is the quintessential Middle American community, but its earliest roots are French. The city is located on an arm of Lake Michigan that the French called La Baie des Puants—the Bay of Stinking Water. Explorer Jean Nicolet established a trading post on the site in 1634. A Jesuit mission followed seven years later, a fort was built in 1717, the town was incorporated in 1754, and the British took control of the area in 1761. The new owners gave Green Bay (the body of water and the town) the much more pleasant name we use today. Though the region officially became part of the United States after the Revolution, the British maintained control of the region until after their defeat in the War of 1812.

Starting in the middle of the 19th century, Green Bay and its environs became a magnet for a variety of European immigrant groups attracted by fertile farmland, timber, and jobs in the paper mills and meat-packing plants that became established in the community. Scores of settlers from Belgium, Germany, Scandinavia, Poland, and other countries endowed the city with the traits it maintains today. Green Bay is a hardworking, no-nonsense town, packed with church-going, family-oriented people. Crime is low and everybody seems to know everybody else. Some people think it's a difficult place to move to from the outside, but most new residents admit their reserved neighbors, while tough to get to know, are always ready to lend a hand if you ever need it.

"Reserved" is not the first word that comes to mind when you wander through the Lambeau Field parking lots on a typical game-day Sunday. The asphalt-covered lots are legendary in the world of sports for the quantity and quality of the tailgate parties that take place here, some starting hours before kickoff—meaning early in the morning on Sundays with a noon kickoff. In this charged atmosphere, hardworking Green Bay reveals its fun-loving side, which it satisfies with copious quantities of bratwurst and beer, along with an intense devotion to the Green Bay Packers. Maybe "devotion" isn't a strong enough word, which becomes evident as you gaze upon thousands of fans covered with green-and-gold clothing, along with various cheese-colored chunks of foam and other Packers paraphernalia. Love? No, obsession.

This level of team worship on such a wide scale is not evident for any other major-league franchise—and a person needs to live for a time in Wisconsin (because the fever spreads far beyond Green Bay) to fully understand it. Nowhere else in the country are fans of every color, age, or socioeconomic status so single-mindedly joined together in their interest in a sports team. And nowhere else are they so knowledgeable. Where else in the world would you expect to see a German-American grandmother casually chatting with an African-American teenage boy about their favorite team's needs in the defensive secondary (in the middle of May, no less)? But that's what it means to be a Packers fan—normal barriers between people seem to fall away as they share in the triumphs and tragedies of the team that brings them together.

This class- and color-blind solidarity among

Packers fans extends—amazingly in this era of big-dollar contracts—to the team's players. Though Green Bay fans' love and devotion for their team seems to know no bounds, the small-town blue-collar atmosphere has fostered a unique relationship between stars and fans. Unlike in big cities like New York or L.A. where NFL players rub shoulders with Hollywood moguls and rap stars, Green Bay Packer players live side-by-side with the people that fill the Lambeau seats on Sundays: The running back and the paper-mill worker who cheer his touchdowns both shop for groceries at Pick-N-Save; coaches send their kids to the same schools as those attended by the kids of the UPS driver that delivers packages to the team offices; and the wide receiver smiles to acknowledge the "Keep up the good work!" from the gray-haired lady walking by his table as he catches dinner at Brett Favre's Steakhouse, just a few blocks from Lambeau Field.

The reality is that Green Bay exists in a time warp. The team, the players, the stadium, and the fans existing as part of one tight-knit community is a phenomenon that harkens back to the earliest days of professional sports, before TV and licensing agreements, free agents and salary caps. It's a journey back to a time when the local football team consisted of a bunch of guys with day jobs and a love for the game and who enjoyed getting muddy and bloody on fall weekends. That's how the Packers started out, just like every other team in what became the National Football League. But for some reason, while all those other teams morphed into privately owned franchises (and toys for very rich boys), Green Bay managed to keep its football team in the hands of its citizens—and the story of how that transpired is one of the most fascinating in pro sports.

There is nothing like the game-day atmosphere at Lambeau Field, even during the preseason. Here, Packers fan celebrate during an exhibition contest against New England—a rematch of the previous year's Super Bowl—on a warm July evening in 1997. The Packers won this game, too, 7–3. *Getty Images*

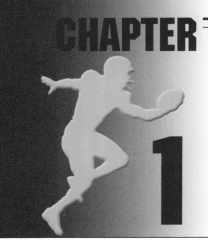
1919–1929: FULFILLING CURLY LAMBEAU'S DREAM

Opposite: **Before helping launch the Packers, Earl "Curly" Lambeau was a star player at Green Bay East High School and played a year for legendary coach Knute Rockne at Notre Dame. Lambeau's focus on passing forever changed the game of football.**
Pro Football Hall of Fame/WireImag.com

The history of the Green Bay Packers can be traced back to one man: Earl "Curly" Lambeau. Though in recent decades fan adulation has focused more on other Packer stars, including quarterback Brett Favre and most notably legendary coach Vince Lombardi, it is undeniable that there would not be a pro football team in Green Bay without the vision and determination of Curly Lambeau. When the team honored its founder and first coach after his 1965 death by naming its stadium Lambeau Field, the egotistical Lombardi was reportedly offended, thinking that *he* was the coach who deserved

the honor. If that was truly the case, "Saint Vince" probably had not spent enough time studying Packer history. If he had, he would have quickly realized that without Curly Lambeau Green Bay would have been just another unassuming Midwestern factory town.

THE FUTURE COACH FROM A FOOTBALL-CRAZY TOWN

One thing to understand about Green Bay is that Curly Lambeau and his Packers did not introduce football to this Wisconsin city—the town was already

Right: **Green Bay was football crazy prior to the start of the Packers. This portrait shows an amateur "town team," possibly in 1917 or 1918. The third player from the right end appears to be Packers founder and coach Curly Lambeau.**
GreenBayAntiques.com/The Oneida Archive

football-crazy before the pro game arrived. In the first decades of the 20th century, the game was a popular pastime, both to play and watch, among the city's rough-and-tumble blue-collar workers and their children. The city had an organized school league and a heated football rivalry between East and West high schools. Green Bay sent a regular stream of talented players to the college football ranks, by far the most popular wing of the sport in this era and for several decades to come.

It was in this football-loving environment that Earl Lambeau grew up. He was born in Green Bay on April 9, 1898, the first of four children; he earned his nickname for his luxuriant, wavy locks of dark hair. His parents, Marcel and Mary, were the children of Belgian and French immigrants, respectively, who had settled in Green Bay only a couple of decades earlier. Marcel owned what would become a very successful construction business, but during Curly's youth the family lived in a modest neighborhood just northeast of downtown Green Bay. Lambeau family life revolved around nearby St. Willebrord Catholic Church; even today, Green Bay retains its strong Catholic roots, with roughly 70 percent of the residents claiming affiliation with the church.

Though family, church, and school were important to the young Curly Lambeau, his true love was football, and he showed exceptional promise in the sport early in life, playing games on vacant lots near his house. Despite his skill at the game, Lambeau claimed late in life that as a child he never owned a real football, and played with one he made himself from an old cloth sack stuffed with leaves and sand.

Lambeau started playing organized football in the eighth grade and later became a four-year letter winner at East High School. By his senior year, he was the top player in the city, and a punishing running back who excelled by plowing through, not around, tacklers. What set him apart from many players of his day, though, was his ability to pass the ball. Curly's focus on throwing not only made him a star in high school, it would eventually revolutionize the entire sport of football.

Football in the early years was a very different game than the one played today—in fact, many modern fans would not recognize the game that Curly Lambeau and other players engaged in back before World War I. Though a lot of people assume that football is different primarily because the equipment—pads and helmets—worn by the players has changed so dramatically, the real difference in the game is more closely related to the ball. Back in the early 20th century, the ball was much more spherical and less bullet-shaped than it is today. This shape was a testament to the fact that football is a descendent of what Americans call soccer—what the rest of the world calls football. The plump American football was designed to

This scene offers a rare glimpse of the first year of professional football in Green Bay. The fans have jammed the bleachers at Hagemeister Park to witness a 1921 contest between the "Acme Packers" (in reference to the company sponsoring the team) and an unknown opponent. *GreenBay Antiques.com/The Oneida Archive*

be kicked, handed off, carried, and pitched short distances. Though early rules allowed forward passing, they did not encourage it, and the shape of the ball made it difficult for most players to throw effectively. Curly Lambeau practiced passing religiously, to the point that he could throw better than most, but it was really his vision of what passing could do for the game that set him apart. And it was this vision that he put to work when it came time to establish Green Bay on the pro football map.

IT ALL STARTED ON A GREEN BAY STREET CORNER

After graduating from high school in 1917, Curly enrolled at the University of Wisconsin-Madison but quit after a month when the school dropped its freshman football program. He returned home to

Green Bay to work for a year, but by the following fall, he was playing fullback for Knute Rockne at Notre Dame, working in the same backfield alongside halfback George Gipp. At home in Green Bay over Christmas break, Lambeau contracted a severe case of tonsillitis that required several weeks of recovery. Because he missed so many classes, Curly decided to skip his spring term. Instead, he accepted a job at the Indian Packing Company. By the summer, his $250-per-month salary and a burgeoning relationship with his future wife, Marguerite, made Curly realize that he was probably never going to return to Notre Dame—but he had not given up on football.

One day in early August 1919, Curly Lambeau ran into Green Bay sports writer George Calhoun on a city street. They started with a casual conversation about organizing a city team for the upcoming fall

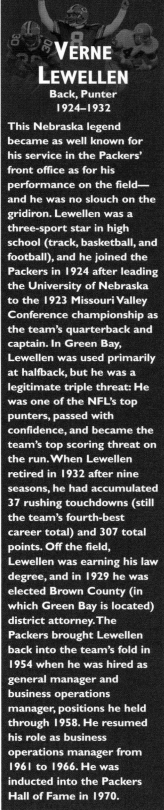

VERNE LEWELLEN
Back, Punter
1924–1932

This Nebraska legend became as well known for his service in the Packers' front office as for his performance on the field— and he was no slouch on the gridiron. Lewellen was a three-sport star in high school (track, basketball, and football), and he joined the Packers in 1924 after leading the University of Nebraska to the 1923 Missouri Valley Conference championship as the team's quarterback and captain. In Green Bay, Lewellen was used primarily at halfback, but he was a legitimate triple threat: He was one of the NFL's top punters, passed with confidence, and became the team's top scoring threat on the run. When Lewellen retired in 1932 after nine seasons, he had accumulated 37 rushing touchdowns (still the team's fourth-best career total) and 307 total points. Off the field, Lewellen was earning his law degree, and in 1929 he was elected Brown County (in which Green Bay is located) district attorney. The Packers brought Lewellen back into the team's fold in 1954 when he was hired as general manager and business operations manager, positions he held through 1958. He resumed his role as business operations manager from 1961 to 1966. He was inducted into the Packers Hall of Fame in 1970.

football season, but they ended up hatching a full-blown plan. Calhoun agreed to run an ad in his paper, the *Green Bay Press-Gazette*, to publicize an organizational meeting for the team, and to provide coverage for the team in the paper. Curly said he would do his own player recruiting and also proposed to ask his employer for financial support. The organizational meeting took place on August 11, 1919; some sources cite this as the day the Packers were born, though nothing official transpired at this get-together. After this first meeting, Curly secured $500 worth of sponsorship from his boss at Indian Packing, Frank Peck, along with permission to use vacant land next to the company's plant for the team's practices.

A second meeting, on August 14, marked the official organization of the new Green Bay city football team. Curly Lambeau was elected captain by a vote of the 25-man roster. A Calhoun article in the next day's *Press-Gazette* revealed details of the "Indian Packing Corporation squad" meeting, including an announcement of its first game on September 14 against Menominee (Michigan). In this same article, Calhoun was the first person to use the nickname "Packers," though the team did not officially adopt the moniker for a couple of years.

The new Green Bay team—also nicknamed the "Baby Blues" because of the blue jerseys worn by the players—was an immediate success. They steamrolled effortlessly through ten weaker teams, outscoring their opponents 565 to 6, until they finally met their match in Beloit the last game of the season, dropping a hard-fought 6–0 decision. Lambeau did it all for the team— he drew up and called the plays and was the team's

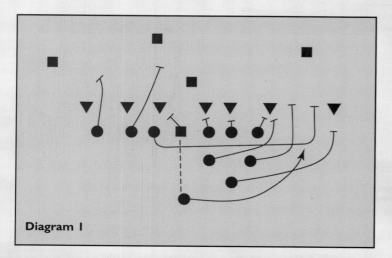

Diagram 1

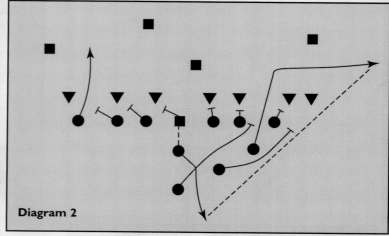

Diagram 2

KEY PLAYS: RUNNING AND PASSING OUT OF THE NOTRE DAME BOX

Curly Lambeau learned everything about running an offense during his one season playing for legendary Notre Dame Coach Knute Rockne (shown at right). After returning home to Green Bay and starting his football team, Lambeau employed Rockne's "Notre Dame Box"—a balanced-line offshoot of the single-wing formation—with great success, and stuck with variations of the formation for a quarter-century. The offense would usually line up in the T formation then shift into different arrangements of the Box. This was in the era before the center-to-quarterback "handoff" snap, so the ball was usually hiked directly to the player in the tailback position. The player generally ran from this position, following the blocking provided by the other backs (see Diagram 1), but could also pass the ball. Lambeau was an early passing-game innovator, and he added a variety of twists to the basic Box. For example, he would have the quarterback line up behind the center (about a yard back), and after taking the short snap, fade back to pass (rules required the thrower to be at least 5 yards behind the line of scrimmage). Sometimes the quarterback would hand the ball off to one of the other backs, while other times, he would fake the handoff and throw a pass, often to the back lined up in the "wing" position (see Diagram 2)—the predecessor of what we today call the play-action pass. John McNally was particularly effective catching passes out of the backfield on plays like this.

principal runner and passer. He was also a defensive stalwart in this era of "two-way" football.

It's important to remember that despite the success of this first "Packers" team, they were not professionals, but rather 25 guys with day jobs who got together for practice three days a week and a game on the weekends. Home tilts were played at Hagemeister Park— a grassy expanse near East High School with a football field chalked out on it. Ropes protected the field from eager fans, who pressed in to get as close to the action as possible. There were no stands and no admission. George Calhoun typically walked around soliciting donations from the spectators; some of the money was used to pay medical bills for injured players. At the end

"Shake hands? That would have been a lie. If I lost I wanted to punch Halas in the nose."
—Curly Lambeau, asked if he shook the hands of his rival after Packers-Bears games

of the first season, the remaining money was divvied up among the players. Reportedly, each received $16.75 at the end of that first year.

Throughout the first season and afterward, Curly Lambeau kept working at the packing plant, which continued its financial support for the team, even after being bought out by Acme Packing Company. Curly's life

GreenBayAntiques.com/The Oneida Archive

Opposite: **Packers tackle Cal Hubbard.**
Bettmann/CORBIS

had been a whirlwind in the last month of 1919. In addition to his job and his commitment to the Packers, the 21-year-old Lambeau had married Marguerite and also been named head football coach at East High School—a job he held for three successful seasons.

Lambeau entered his second season as captain of the Green Bay city team with high hopes. Most of the players returned for a second go-round and fan support was growing by leaps and bounds. Before the season, Marcel Lambeau directed volunteers in the construction of wooden bleachers on one side of the Hagemeister Park field; the roughly 200 seats were available exclusively for ticket-holders. The team set up a ticket office at a nearby American Legion post. Official attendance for the first game, with the Chicago Boosters (which ended in a 3–3 tie), was 1200.

Despite a schedule featuring better teams, 1920 proved to be nearly as successful for the Packers, and they finished with a 9–1–1 record. As with the previous season, Beloit handed the team its only loss late in the season, but even this setback was tempered by the fact that Green Bay had beaten Beloit 7–0 in a game played on Halloween. Still, the Packers were still a prototypical "town team." They continued to work their day jobs, practiced on the grounds of the old courthouse, and showered at the local Elks Club. Volunteers—fans—took care of Hagemeister Park and collected tickets. Yet change was in the air.

While Curly Lambeau remained the centerpiece of the team, another star emerged who would become a force with the Packers for several years. Howard "Cub" Buck was a former University of Wisconsin and Canton Bulldog lineman that the persuasive Lambeau

GreenBayAntiques.com/The Oneida Archive

had recruited to join him in Green Bay. Buck's presence was noteworthy for a couple of reasons. First, he was a big football player for his time—6-feet and 259 pounds—and he dominated play on both sides of the ball. Second, he was the first man that Curly Lambeau paid to play for him. Buck received $75 per game, a handsome fee for 1920 that was roughly equivalent to two weeks' pay in a Green Bay factory. With Lambeau already paying players, and with a growing fan base willing to spend money on tickets, it looked like Green Bay might be ready to make the jump into full-fledged professional football—and the opportunity soon presented itself.

THE ROOTS OF THE NFL

The roots of professional football date back to at least 1892, when Pudge Heffelfinger earned $500 to play for Pittsburgh's Allegheny Athletic Association, but the sport was terribly disorganized. Just getting teams to agree on a standardized set of rules was difficult. A serious attempt to organize a pro

league in Ohio failed in 1904, and it was not until 1920 that another effort along the same lines emerged. Representatives from 11 teams in five different states met in Canton, Ohio—home of the Bulldogs, the preeminent team of the era, and Jim Thorpe, the best player—on September 17 of that year. Gathering in the showroom of a Hupmobile dealership owned by Canton manager Ralph Hay, the team leaders decided to form the American Professional Football Association, even voting to require a $100 membership fee. Nobody ever paid.

The first year of the league was not a successful one. During the course of the season, four more franchises joined, though the APFA members were just as likely to play teams outside the league. No won-loss records were recorded; by the end of the season, three teams claimed the championship. Something had to be done if this venture was ever going to be successful.

At an April 30, 1921, meeting in Akron, Ohio, the teams named Joe Carr president and established league headquarters in Columbus, Ohio. Carr ended up leading the league until his death in 1939, and he provided the discipline

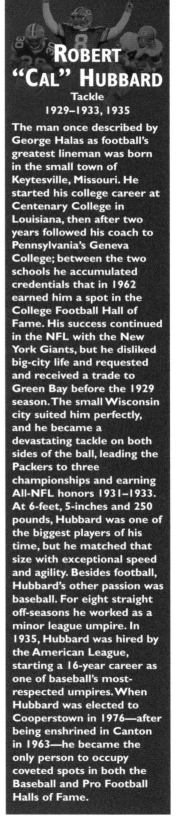

ROBERT "CAL" HUBBARD
Tackle
1929–1933, 1935

The man once described by George Halas as football's greatest lineman was born in the small town of Keytesville, Missouri. He started his college career at Centenary College in Louisiana, then after two years followed his coach to Pennsylvania's Geneva College; between the two schools he accumulated credentials that in 1962 earned him a spot in the College Football Hall of Fame. His success continued in the NFL with the New York Giants, but he disliked big-city life and requested and received a trade to Green Bay before the 1929 season. The small Wisconsin city suited him perfectly, and he became a devastating tackle on both sides of the ball, leading the Packers to three championships and earning All-NFL honors 1931–1933. At 6-feet, 5-inches and 250 pounds, Hubbard was one of the biggest players of his time, but he matched that size with exceptional speed and agility. Besides football, Hubbard's other passion was baseball. For eight straight off-seasons he worked as a minor league umpire. In 1935, Hubbard was hired by the American League, starting a 16-year career as one of baseball's most-respected umpires. When Hubbard was elected to Cooperstown in 1976—after being enshrined in Canton in 1963—he became the only person to occupy coveted spots in both the Baseball and Pro Football Halls of Fame.

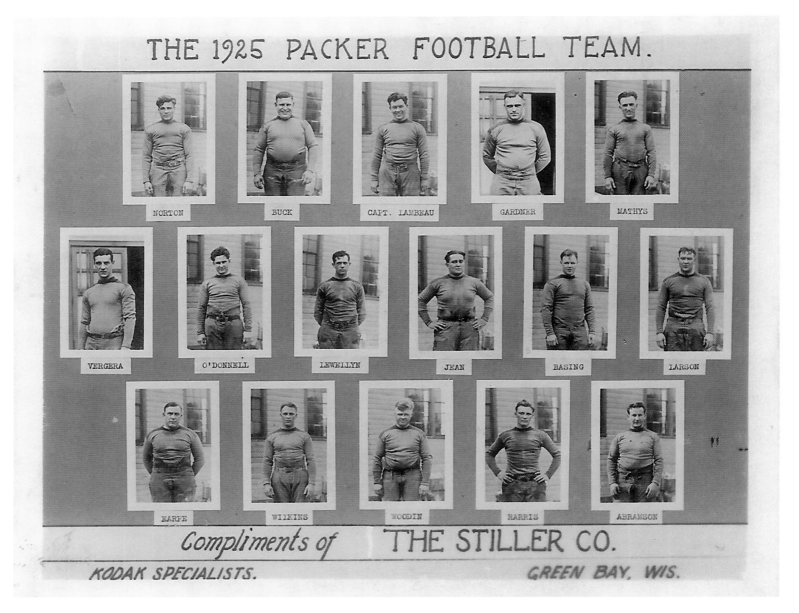

THE 1925 PACKER FOOTBALL TEAM.

NORTON   BUCK   CAPT. LAMBEAU   GARDNER   MATHYS

VERGERA   O'DONNELL   LEWELLYN   JEAN   BASING   LARSON

EARPE   WILKINS   WOODIN   HARRIS   ABRAMSON

Compliments of THE STILLER CO.

KODAK SPECIALISTS.   GREEN BAY, WIS.

The first championship was still four years away, but 1925 was a significant year for the young Green Bay Packers, shown in this team photo created by a local photographic company. It was at the beginning of this season that the team moved into the first City Stadium, built on the site of Hagemeister Park, giving the team greater financial stability and a quality field to play on. *GreenBayAntiques.com/The Oneida Archive*

and sense of organization that until that time was severely lacking in pro football. Through his efforts, the league finally appeared to be a viable entity in the American sports scene.

Back in Green Bay, George Calhoun learned about the April 1921 APFA meeting and approached Curly Lambeau with the idea of submitting a bid for a Green Bay franchise at the next APFA meeting, in August. Lambeau convinced his boss, Acme Packing co-owner John Clair, to send his brother, Emmett Clair, to Akron to present the case for a Green Bay pro football team. Success in the effort was far from guaranteed. Despite receiving the sponsorship of two established APFA teams, the Chicago Cardinals and Canton Bulldogs, Green Bay was the smallest city seeking entry into the

league. Geography and odd numbers were two factors in their favor: In addition to Green Bay, Minneapolis, Minnesota, and Evansville, Indiana, were favorites to join the league, and the trio of newcomers would allow the APFA to form nine-team east and west divisions. Acme Packing was granted a franchise on August 27, 1921; Emmett Clair paid the league's $50 entry fee and took the train home to Green Bay the next morning.

Marcel Lambeau continued to expand the Hagemeister Park bleachers and the team erected a canvas fence around the facility to make sure only paying customers could view the games. General admission was 50 cents. Decked out in their new blue jerseys boldly emblazoned "ACME PACKERS," Green

Bay tuned up for their first pro season by routing four non-league teams by a combined score of 109 to 0. As had become standard when it was just a city team, Curly Lambeau did it all for the new AFPA franchise—off the field he was the general manager and publicity chief, while on the field he was the head coach, star halfback, and principal passer.

On October 23, APFA football made its official debut in Green Bay when the Packers defeated the Minneapolis Marines 7–6 in front of roughly 6000 ecstatic fans. The Packers soon found life in the pro league to be a bigger challenge than their previous

seasons. The team ended up with a 3–2–1 record, good for seventh place in what by the end of the season had become a 13-team league. The Packers dropped their final contest of 1921 to the first APFA champions, the Chicago Staleys, who were guided by the brilliant young player-coach George Halas. The following season the Staleys adopted a new nickname and became the Chicago Bears. The Packers' 20–0 drubbing at Wrigley Field was marred by a legendary sucker punch by Staley guard John "Tarzan" Taylor that broke Cub Buck's nose, fueling a heated rivalry between the teams that still burns strongly even in the 21st century.

SURVIVING THE FIRST CRISIS

Though 1921 ended with every sign that the Packers were

Official Program

Published by the Green Bay Football Corporation

National League

Green Bay Packers

vs.

Milwaukee

Sunday, Oct. 11, 1925

2:15 P. M.

Price 10c

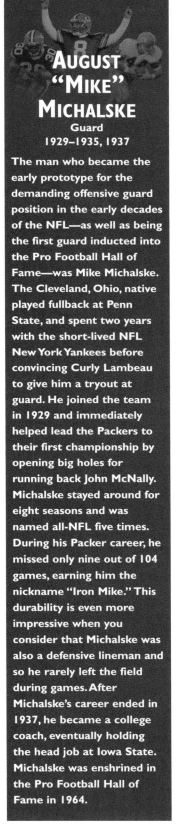

AUGUST "MIKE" MICHALSKE
Guard
1929–1935, 1937

The man who became the early prototype for the demanding offensive guard position in the early decades of the NFL—as well as being the first guard inducted into the Pro Football Hall of Fame—was Mike Michalske. The Cleveland, Ohio, native played fullback at Penn State, and spent two years with the short-lived NFL New York Yankees before convincing Curly Lambeau to give him a tryout at guard. He joined the team in 1929 and immediately helped lead the Packers to their first championship by opening big holes for running back John McNally. Michalske stayed around for eight seasons and was named all-NFL five times. During his Packer career, he missed only nine out of 104 games, earning him the nickname "Iron Mike." This durability is even more impressive when you consider that Michalske was also a defensive lineman and so he rarely left the field during games. After Michalske's career ended in 1937, he became a college coach, eventually holding the head job at Iowa State. Michalske was enshrined in the Pro Football Hall of Fame in 1964.

going to be a success in the new league—which soon re-christened itself the National Football League—a crisis emerged that threatened to make the team's first pro season its last. The APFA/NFL had a rule forbidding the use of players who were still enrolled in college—though it was a common practice, and several collegians took

the field under assumed names in that first season. Curly Lambeau, in fact, had recruited three Notre Dame players, including his former Irish teammate Heartley "Hunk" Anderson, to play in a late-season game. The ringers were recognized and the infraction was reported in the *Chicago Tribune*. Joe Carr decided to make an example of Green Bay. In January 1922, the league revoked the Acme Packing franchise and sent John Clair the $50 franchise fee.

This unfortunate development merely provided the opportunity to add to the increasing legend of Curly Lambeau. Urged on by team supporters, Curly threw himself at the mercy of the league, applying for the franchise in his own name and promising to abide by all the rules. Five months passed and instead of being given a decision, Lambeau was asked to attend a league meeting in Cleveland to present his case for reinstating Green Bay. Curly had the $50 to pay the franchise fee, but he lacked the money for travel expenses and any reinstatement fees that would be required if the application was approved. A friend, Don Murphy, reportedly sold his automobile for $1500 and gave the money to Lambeau in exchange for the opportunity to get on the field with the Packers during a game. (Curly later made good on the deal, letting Murphy play for about a minute during its opening game the next season.) Lambeau traveled to Cleveland and on June 24 was rewarded for his efforts by seeing the team reinstated. Green Bay

Official Program

PUBLISHED BY THE
GREEN BAY FOOTBALL CORPORATION

A National League Game

Green Bay vs. Cleveland

SUNDAY, SEPT. 25, 1927

2:15 P. M.

BENNY. FRIEDMAN

Price

10c

was back in the pro ranks—but the crises were far from over.

Rain ended up being the most intimidating opponent faced by the Green Bay Packers during the team's second NFL season, but Curly Lambeau entered the year with high hopes for the team that was now fully his responsibility. Three newly signed players, in particular, appeared to have great promise: guard Howard "Whitey" Woodin from Marquette University; quarterback Charlie Mathys from Indiana; and center Francis "Jug" Earp from Monmouth College, who played 10 years for the Packers, served as the team's publicity director in the 1950s, and was in the first group of inductees into the Packers Hall of Fame. Despite the new infusion of talent, the Packers lost their first three games and tied their next two tilts.

The team's tepid performance and rainy weather kept attendance down, and as a result, Packer finances were suffering. The November 5 game with the Columbus Panhandlers was critical for the team's bottom line. The Packers finally won a contest (3–0), but it rained and the gate was a disappointment. Even worse, rain insurance purchased by Curly offered no relief because the official rainfall measurement was three-hundredths of an inch short of the policy's payout threshold. The team was in debt and sinking quickly. When Curly was unable to come up with a $4000 guarantee demanded by George Halas, a Thanksgiving Day game with the Bears was canceled, and an exhibition with Duluth scheduled in its place. When the day promised more rain, Curly reportedly considered scrapping the contest—which might have been the death knell for the Packers—but fortunately was talked out of this rash move by a man who was soon to become very important to the team, A.B. Turnbull.

Andrew B. Turnbull was the general manager of the *Green Bay Press-Gazette* and a shrewd businessman, but he was also a devoted Packer fan who dearly wanted the team to succeed. It is said that in the midst of the Packers' 1922 crisis he promised Curly Lambeau that he would personally make sure that the team survived. The Packers' performance picked up toward the end of the year and the team finished its second season with a 4–3–3 record, good for eighth place in a league that had swelled back to 18 teams. The Packers also finished the season roughly $2500 in debt.

During the offseason, Turnbull seized the opportunity to rally the community behind the Packers and to put the team on solid financial footing. In December, he convened a meeting of a group of men—later dubbed the "Hungry Five"—who led the charge to save the team. In addition to Turnbull and Lambeau, the group consisted of Dr. W. Webber Kelly, lawyer Gerald Clifford, and grocer Lee Johannes. At a

> **"Oh, how we hated to see a sub come in."**
> —*Jug Earp*

public meeting in spring 1923, the pentad urged a crowd of 400 to get behind the team financially. At the end of the event, the group took pledges to buy ownership shares in the team for $5. Purchasers of at least five shares were guaranteed a season ticket for 1923. Another $5000 was raised from a group of 100 leading Green Bay businessmen and deposited in the bank as a "rainy day" fund.

With the financial commitment of the team's fans secured, the Green Bay Football Corporation came into being on August 18, 1923. One thousand shares of stock in the nonprofit corporation were issued and a 15-member board of directors and five-person executive committee were appointed to run the organization. Directors were offered no compensation and were further instructed to purchase at least six season tickets each. The articles of incorporation specified that any earnings were to be directed to Green Bay's Sullivan Post of the American Legion. In effect, Green Bay and its football fans owned the franchise, an arrangement that, miraculously, still remains in place. This quirky ownership structure gave Green Bay the ability to keep its team, even after football had long abandoned Canton, Hammond, Rock Island, and the other Midwestern factory towns whose names graced the NFL standings in the league's early years.

THE PACKERS MOVE TO A BASEBALL PARK

Relieved of the stress of running the Packers' business operation, Curly Lambeau focused his attention back on the football field as the 1923 season dawned—but it was a different field than in previous seasons. Hagemeister Park had been selected as the site of a new high school and construction was already underway as fall approached. The team was forced to play its home games at Bellevue Park, a relatively small minor league baseball venue located adjacent to the Hagemeister Brewery—which had been renamed Bellevue Products Co. because of prohibition. The wooden bleachers in the stadium could accommodate crowds of 4000 or so, but the facility was ill-suited for football. It was clear that Green Bay needed to provide the Packers a new, permanent home if it really wanted to be an NFL city.

No matter where the team played, Curly was more committed than ever to winning. He pared the roster down to a solid core of 17 talented players, 14

The Packers were a rarity in that they played in their own football-specific stadium. For the first several decades of the league's existence, NFL teams often utilized professional baseball parks. This scene from the late 1920s shows the hallowed grounds of Yankee Stadium set up for football; for a brief time the venue hosted a professional football team also called the New York Yankees. New York's better-known football team, the Giants, played at the Polo Grounds, home of baseball's Giants.
Diamond Images/Getty Images

of whom saw the majority of the playing time. The rugged bunch repaid the citizens of Green Bay with a strong 7–2–1 record and a third-place finish in the NFL. The highlight of the 1923 home slate was the first visit to Green Bay by the Chicago Bears. More than 5000 fans crammed into Bellevue Park for the October 14 contest. A field goal by the Bears' Ed Sternaman proved to be the game's only points and Chicago left town with a 3–0 victory.

In 1924, Curly stuck with his strategy of a smaller roster and keeping the same core group of players on the field for most of the game. His most noteworthy new recruit was Verne Lewellen from the University of Nebraska. A three-sport star at Lincoln (Nebraska) High and an inductee in the state's hall of fame, Lewellen was also a triple threat on the football field. He could pass the ball, was arguably the era's leading punter, and was a formidable halfback who racked up 37 rushing touchdowns—fourth highest in team history—during his nine-year Packers career.

The 1924 season ended up being another solid one for the team, but it did not start out that way. The Packers were forced to go on the road for their first

two games and ended up losing both contests, against the Duluth Kelleys and Chicago Cardinals, by a field goal's margin. The team quickly righted the ship by going undefeated through a five-game homestand that included four shutout victories, but it lost a late-season game to the Bears 3–0. They finished the season with a 7–4 record—good for sixth in the league. Curly Lambeau was not satisfied, but the team had pressing issues beyond won-loss records to address in the off-season—in particular, moving to a new home.

CITY STADIUM, THE ENVY OF THE NFL

Packers supporters realized that the team was not going to remain competitive for long playing in a minor league baseball park—the team would need a football-dedicated facility to have any hopes of long-term financial security. The Packers Corporation executive board joined forces with the city of Green Bay and the community's school board to build a new stadium. The facility was located next to where the team got its start, adjacent to brand-new Green Bay East High School, which stood on the former site of Hagemeister Park. The stadium was a traditional football stadium for its time, with open wooden bleachers running on both sides of the field between the 30-yard lines. Initial seating capacity is listed in various sources as being between 5000 and 6000, though expansion projects eventually would result in a horseshoe-shaped layout, with a capacity of 25000.

The facility—christened with the pedestrian name of City Stadium—was recognized as one of the better venues in the NFL, especially because it had a high-quality playing surface specifically designed for football. That said, City Stadium initially lacked most of the amenities of a modern sports park. There were no locker rooms on-site. The Packers used the East High locker rooms and visiting teams often dressed at their hotel before games. Plus, there were no toilets for fans during the first decade of operation; male spectators often relieved themselves under the wooden stands.

The Packers played their first game in City Stadium on September 20, 1925, against the Hammond Pros; reports indicate that the facility was barely completed in time for the game. About 3000 fans enjoyed a 14–0 Packer victory. One week later, a full house cheered the team on to its first victory over the Chicago Bears, 14–10. A fourth-quarter touchdown pass from Charlie Mathys to Vern Lewellen, followed by a Curly Lambeau interception, sealed the victory. City Stadium seemed to provide the Packers a strong home-field advantage, and they rolled through their home schedule undefeated in the new park. Unfortunately, the results were not as positive on the road, and the Packers again ended up in the middle of the NFL standings, finishing ninth in what had grown to a 20-team league, with an 8–5 record.

Over the next three years, the Packers' popularity continued to grow among Green Bay residents and their increasing attendance left them in a solid financial position—stronger than many other NFL teams. The mid-1920s were a challenging time for the young league. Teams were still struggling to attract fans away from the much more popular college game, but late in the 1925 season, college football's biggest star jumped to the pros and promised to bring legions of fans with him. Harold "Red" Grange—the "Galloping Ghost"—had exhilarated fans as a running back for the University of Illinois, and when he signed with the Bears, the team went on an unprecedented exhibition tour to show him off. Playing 19 games across the country, the Bears and Grange attracted huge crowds and gave the NFL a huge shot of positive publicity.

For the 1926 season, Grange's manager, C.C. Pyle, demanded a five-figure salary and one-third

ownership of the Bears for his young star. When the team refused, and the NFL turned down an application for a Grange team franchise, Pyle started a rival organization, the American Football League. Grange was the star of the flagship New York Yankees, and eight other teams joined the league, including the NFL's Rock Island Independents. The AFL played out its 1926 season in front of sparse crowds and then promptly folded.

Meanwhile, the NFL had reacted to the new competition by allowing its own ranks to swell to 22 franchises. Two of the teams, the Los Angeles Buccaneers and the Louisville Colonels, were actually based out of Chicago and played an all-road-game schedule. The Packers ended this odd 1926 season in fifth place with an 8–3–3 record.

Major upheaval in the off-season saw a dramatic pairing in the ranks of pro football teams. The 1927 season dawned with a single league, the NFL, consisting of just 12 teams. One of the remaining franchises was the AFL New York Yankees. The Packers meanwhile—now one of the most stable franchises in an unstable league—showed marked improvement on the field. As the season progressed, the team's first championship seemed within its grasp. In the end, their hated rivals, the Bears, proved to be their undoing again, inflicting the only two losses in an otherwise stellar 7–2–1 season.

The success showcased Curly Lambeau's gift for personnel management; he had remade the Packers roster before the season with a number of shrewd signings. Two Packers of note who made their debuts during 1927 were Lavern "Lavvie" Dilweg and Joseph "Red" Dunn, both future inductees into the team's Hall of Fame. Dunn was an all-purpose back who had played for Marquette University, as well as one season each for the NFL's Milwaukee Badgers and Chicago Cardinals. He played five seasons for the Packers, passing for 31 touchdowns and serving as the team's on-field leader. Dilweg, a talented two-way end, was a former Marquette and Milwaukee Badger player who starred for the Packers over eight seasons. When Dilweg wasn't playing football, he was practicing law, and after retiring from the game, he was elected to the U.S. House of Representatives.

Despite the fact the team seemed to be on the verge of greatness, the 1928 season proved to be somewhat of a disappointment. The team failed to get a win in its first three games before reeling off four straight victories, including a 16–6 decision over the Bears. Another three-game winless streak late in the season doomed the Packers to a 6–4–3 mark and fourth place in the league. The season ended on a high

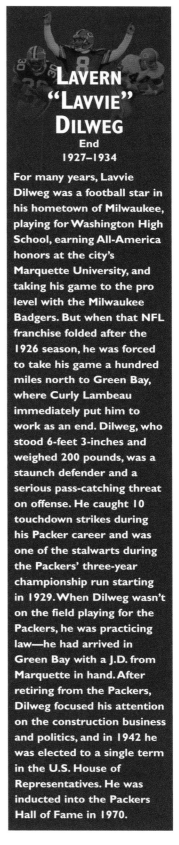

LAVERN "LAVVIE" DILWEG
End
1927–1934

For many years, Lavvie Dilweg was a football star in his hometown of Milwaukee, playing for Washington High School, earning All-America honors at the city's Marquette University, and taking his game to the pro level with the Milwaukee Badgers. But when that NFL franchise folded after the 1926 season, he was forced to take his game a hundred miles north to Green Bay, where Curly Lambeau immediately put him to work as an end. Dilweg, who stood 6-feet 3-inches and weighed 200 pounds, was a staunch defender and a serious pass-catching threat on offense. He caught 10 touchdown strikes during his Packer career and was one of the stalwarts during the Packers' three-year championship run starting in 1929. When Dilweg wasn't on the field playing for the Packers, he was practicing law—he had arrived in Green Bay with a J.D. from Marquette in hand. After retiring from the Packers, Dilweg focused his attention on the construction business and politics, and in 1942 he was elected to a single term in the U.S. House of Representatives. He was inducted into the Packers Hall of Fame in 1970.

point with a second win over the Bears, but it was clear to Curly Lambeau that if he wanted to pay back the citizens of Green Bay for their support by bringing home an NFL championship, he would have to inject some new talent into the team.

A TALENTED TRIO HELPS BRING HOME A CHAMPIONSHIP

During his years of leading the Packers, Curly Lambeau had developed into a polished salesman for his team, and in the months before the opening of the 1929 season, he put those skills to work as never before. The results of his efforts were the signings of three of the greatest players in pro football history: Robert "Cal" Hubbard, Johnny (Blood) McNally, and August "Mike" Michalske. This trio proved to be the final pieces in creating what proved to be the National Football League's first dominant team.

All three of these marquee players had prior NFL experience, but for one reason or another, proved a poor fit with their earlier teams. Cal Hubbard was a small-town kid from Missouri who had played college ball at Louisiana's Centenary College and Pennsylvania's Genava College. He played two strong seasons for the New York Giants but hated the big-city life and requested a trade to Green Bay after playing a game there in 1928. Playing for Curly Lambeau, Hubbard blossomed into the NFL's top lineman.

Mike Michalske had been an All-America fullback at Penn State and later for the AFL/NFL New York Yankees, but the team folded after 1928. Michalske landed in Green Bay where he became the prototype offensive guard of the era—strong, fast, and agile—leading interference on most running plays. He also developed a defensive style that was the precursor of today's blitzing linebacker. Because Michalske rarely missed a game or left the field during a contest, he earned the well-deserved nickname "Iron Mike."

New Richmond, Wisconsin, native John McNally was one of the most colorful and controversial characters in NFL history. He played for the Packers under the colorful *nom de plume* "Johnny Blood," adopted for playing semipro ball while trying to retain his college eligibility. (McNally chose the name after seeing a movie marquee advertising the Rudolph Valentino film *Blood and Sand*; his friend, Ralph Hanson, became "Ralph Sand.") McNally had already played for three previous NFL teams, but as a Packer, he became the top pass-catching halfback in the league.

> ## "I'm in the greatest town in the world and I'm glad to be in Green Bay."
> —*John (Johnny Blood) McNally, after winning the 1929 championship*

With the benefit of history, it is possible to see that Curly Lambeau had assembled one of the greatest rosters in NFL history. Ironically, the abundance of talent also meant that Curly's days as a player were over. In fact, he played part of just one game in 1929. But as a coach, Curly had reached his prime, and the Packers responded to his leadership by crushing the opposition week after week. Their defense was particularly fierce. Opponents scored a mere 22 points against the Packers all season. They trailed in a game only once, and would have finished 1929 with a perfect record if not for a scoreless tie against Frankford.

The season ended in an especially satisfying manner. The Packers traveled to Chicago for a December 8 showdown with the Bears knowing that a victory would clinch them their first championship. Green Bay responded by humbling their rivals 25–0, in the process limiting the Bears to a single first down. After staying in the Windy City overnight to celebrate, the team boarded an afternoon train for the return trip to Green Bay. On arriving at the station, the Packers were greeted by pandemonium: More than 20,000 fans had braved the cold to greet their hometown champions. During a celebratory banquet the following evening, each player received a $220 bonus—money raised through donations from Packer fans. Any doubts that little Green Bay truly loved and would support its football team disappeared on those December evenings. And as the NFL entered the 1930s, it was apparent to all that the heart of the league lay not in New York, Chicago, or any of its biggest cities, but in a frozen way post in the northeast corner of Wisconsin.

Pro Football Hall of Fame/WireImage.com

JOHN MCNALLY (JOHNNY BLOOD)

Halfback
1929–1933, 1935–1936

The NFL will likely never see another player quite like John "Johnny Blood" McNally—a man who embodied the term "free spirit," who loved the ladies and the night life, and who could quote Shakespeare, yet put fear into the hearts of defenders every time he stepped on the gridiron. McNally was an elusive open-field runner and one of the greatest pass-catching backs the game has ever seen. Playing under the Johnny Blood alias famously inspired by a movie marquee, McNally arrived in Green Bay in 1929 after bouncing around three earlier teams. He was a key contributor to the Packers' three-year championship run, and gladly took on the role of being the only player who would openly challenge Curly Lambeau. Despite his rebellion, the two got along quite well until Curly got fed up with his star's off-the-field behavior and, as McNally later recollected, "fired him" by selling his contract to the Pittsburgh Pirates. After a year, Curly allowed him to return to Green Bay, though their relationship was not the same during McNally's second, two-year stint with the Packers. McNally followed his own unique path throughout his life. After serving as player-coach in Pittsburgh for three seasons, he joined the Army Air Corps during World War II, returned to St. John's University to earn his college degree at the age of 42, wrote an economics textbook, and married in his late forties, starting a family that eventually included eight children. McNally was elected a charter member to both the Pro Football and Packer Halls of Fame.

THE 1930S:
GREEN BAY'S FIRST GLORY YEARS

2

Four Packers practice kicking in New York's DeWitt Clinton Park on November 8, 1934. Though unidentified in the photo, the players appear to be (from left) Hank Bruder, Clarke Hinkle, Arnie Herber, and Joe Laws. Three days later, Green Bay lost to the Giants at the Polo Grounds 17–3. *Bettmann/CORBIS*

As the 1930s started, the progress made by the Green Bay Packers in little more than a decade was remarkable to consider. What began in 1919 as a hastily thrown together amateur city team had evolved into the champions of the National Football League. Games once played on an empty lot were now played in front of thousands of fans in a stadium built exclusively for football. And a team that once consisted of a rag-tag group of factory workers moonlighting as football players now included several of the greatest talents in pro football history. Credit for this turnaround could be shared by many, including the football-crazy citizens of Green Bay who pledged their loyalty and their money to the team, and by civic leaders like A.B. Turnbull who risked their reputations on the team's success. But in the end, most of the credit for the Packers' success had to go to Curly Lambeau.

Lambeau is one of those characters that history regards with mixed feelings, but at this juncture of his career, on the heels of the Packers' first championship, he was one of the NFL's brightest lights—and deservedly so. In Green Bay, he was much revered, a hometown boy that every citizen could love. He was handsome and charismatic, a hard-working Catholic husband and father. Through his dogged determination, he not only brought pro football to the small city, he saved the franchise when it was on the verge of failing, *and* he turned the team into a winner. His star shone brightly within the NFL hierarchy as well. Green Bay had become a financially solid franchise in a league whose membership rolls still seemed to be fed by a revolving door. Joe Carr must have seen something in the young man when he transferred the team franchise to Lambeau in 1922, but it was doubtful he knew just how much impact his decision would have on the future of football.

In many ways, Curly Lambeau was a pioneer in establishing how football would be played, and how teams would be managed. Off the field, Curly was the prototype for the modern general manager. He was constantly assessing the talent available, both in the

college ranks and on other teams. On identifying players he wanted, he used his considerable salesmanship skills to recruit and sign them to the Packers' roster. And when it was time to negotiate contracts, he ruled with wile and an iron fist, convincing players that they weren't worth as much as they thought, and making them feel happy to sign for the amount he wanted to pay them. Though he had occasional rebels—not surprisingly, Johnny Blood held out for, and received, a richer contract one season—most players grudgingly accepted what Curly gave them then played their hearts out for him.

This ability to get the best out of players on the field was another of Curly Lambeau's greatest gifts and, again, his techniques created a template that some successful coaches still follow. Curly's philosophy was simple: He was in charge and the players had better do exactly what he wanted. His practices were notoriously regimented and rugged, and he demanded 100 percent from everybody. He was impatient, explosive, and loud. Years after their playing days were over, many former Packers admitted they did not like the man when they played for him, but they understood his methods. Curly's goal was to create a disciplined unit, one that could execute flawlessly during games, and on that point he succeeded admirably.

Curly's other major contribution to football was the forward pass. Obviously, Lambeau didn't invent the pass, but he was among the first coaches to see its potential, to develop an array of plays that employed passing, and to recruit players specifically for their talent in throwing and catching the ball. The Packers' offense in the 1920s and 1930s was pretty traditional—they employed the "Notre Dame Box" variation of the single wing, which Lambeau learned from Knute Rockne during his one year playing at the school—but the plays he ran from the formation helped revolutionize the game. Largely because of the success of the passing game started by Lambeau, the NFL changed its rules during the 1930s to encourage more passing. (It also adopted a slimmer, easier-to-pass ball, but the evolution of the ball's shape was largely a product of college football.) Many attribute the excitement of the NFL's pass-oriented offenses, and the subsequent stardom achieved by many of the game's greatest quarterbacks, to explain why the pro game eventually surpassed run-oriented college football in popularity.

THE RUN TO REPEAT

The 1930 season dawned in Green Bay with unbridled optimism. Though 10 players from the championship team were no longer on the roster, the core talent of

> **"Curly Lambeau was the founder, the creator, and the coach. But I never liked him. Not really respected him either, but he was paying me and I gave him a thousand percent every time I played football for him."**
> —*Clarke Hinkle*

the team—Dilweg, Dunn, Earp, Hubbard, Lewellen, McNally, and Michalske—returned intact. The rest of the league, now consisting of 11 teams, did not appear to have made up any ground on the Packers. The NFL was a far cry from its current makeup. In 1930, the Packers, Chicago Bears, and New York Giants were the league's only teams whose names would be recognizable to the modern fan. Prior to the season, there had been more turnover in NFL membership and two new franchises were added—the Newark Tornadoes and the Portsmouth Spartans (who eventually moved to Detroit and became the Lions)—but it was obvious that the Packers would be fighting it out with the Giants and Bears for first place.

Arriving at the start of the season was Arnie Herber, one of the greatest passers in NFL history. His story is a classic: A Green Bay native, he loved the Packers as a boy and sold programs at games so that he could watch the team play. He was a star basketball and football player in high school, but after short stints at two colleges, he was back in Green Bay at the age of 20, working as a handyman for the Packers. Curly Lambeau decided to give the kid a tryout, liked what he saw, and signed him to play for $75 per game. Herber ended up earning a starting job in the season opener against the Chicago Cardinals and tossed his first touchdown pass in the game—a 50-yard strike to Lavvie Dilweg that helped secure a 14-0 victory. Herber played 11 seasons for the Packers and threw another 64 touchdown passes—lofty numbers in an era still dominated by the run.

By November 9 the Packers were 8–0 and seemingly on their way to a second title as they entered a difficult stretch of seven straight roads games in a span of a little more than a month (scheduling was often inconsistent and illogical in the NFL's early years). After Green Bay dropped consecutive games to the Chicago Cardinals and New York, they found themselves tied for first with the Giants with four games to play.

With the championship on the line, Curly rallied his team and they responded with consecutive blowout victories over Frankford and Staten Island, while the Giants lost their next two games. The Packers season

MILT GANTENBEIN
End
1931–1940

Milton Edward "Milt" Gantenbein was born in tiny New Albin, Iowa, but grew up in La Crosse, Wisconsin, where he became a high school football star. Gantenbein took his talents to the University of Wisconsin, where he further excelled and caught Curly Lambeau's attention; Gantenbein signed on to play end with the Packers in 1931. He was not particularly big (6 feet, 193 pounds) or fast, but he was tough and a classic two-way player. On offense Gantenbein was a reliable receiver, spending several years as second fiddle to Don Hutson, but he nonetheless caught 77 passes for 1299 yards and 8 touchdowns. Gantenbein's most important contribution to the Packers was as a sturdy defensive end; he was a key member of the rugged units that yielded very few points throughout the 1930s. After retirement, Gantenbein went into coaching, including the head job at New York's Manhattan College.

> **"I was reckless, they said, on the football field. Reckless in a lot of things, I guess. I liked to have a good time back then."**
> —*John "Johnny Blood" McNally*

Below: In 1930 the Green Bay Packers won the second of three straight NFL Championships. This was arguably the most talented club of the league's early decades. The roster included several outstanding players, but the men who led the way were Cal Hubbard, John (Johnny Blood) McNally, and Mike Michalske—as well as legendary coach Curly Lambeau.
GreenBayAntiques.com/The Oneida Archive

finished with a trip to Portsmouth, Ohio. The Spartans shrugged off an earlier one-sided loss to the Packers and rewarded their fans with a 6–6 tie, but that was all Green Bay needed to earn its second championship. Because the NFL ignored ties in the standings, the Packers' 10–3–1 record and .769 winning percentage bested the Giants' 13–4 record and .765 winning percentage.

The Packers' return to Green Bay was a rerun of the previous year. The team's train pulled into the Green Bay station and was greeted by thousands of adoring fans. Motorcycle police and a marching band led the team on a parade through the streets of Green Bay, which was followed by a community reception to further honor the Packers, and the city's biggest star—Curly Lambeau.

In his brief remarks, Curly promised to try to keep bringing home championships, but this little bit of false humility was out of line with the reality of his situation: He had become one of the most famous football coaches in the country. In addition to the publicity

generated by the second championship, Lambeau was also enjoying a wave of positive press generated by George Calhoun, now publicity director for the Packers. Thanks to Calhoun, big-city newspapers were starting to provide coverage of the Packers and their charismatic coach.

On March 31, 1931, a tragedy unrelated to Green Bay probably helped Curly Lambeau's national profile as much as anything he had done on the field. On that day, Notre Dame coaching legend Knute Rockne was killed in a plane crash in Kansas. Rockne was America's greatest and most famous football coach, having led the Fighting Irish to six national championships. He was also the man who taught Curly Lambeau football, and despite the fact he had only played a single season at Notre Dame, Curly considered Rockne both a mentor and friend. Though he was devastated by Rockne's death, Lambeau was also helped by it. The American sporting press, looking for its next coaching legend, handed the mantle to Rockne's protégé, Curly Lambeau. Now it was up to Curly to live up to this honor—or burden.

LOWLIGHTS, HIGHLIGHTS, AND A THIRD CHAMPIONSHIP

The 1931 season was one of the strangest in Packers history, loaded with numerous highlights on the field but plagued by strange events off it. Lambeau had

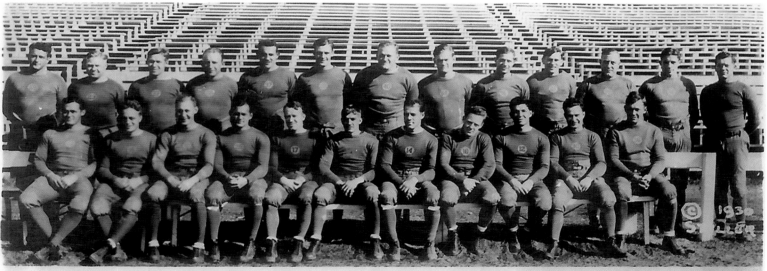

DARLING, WOODIN, MOLENDA, PERRY, NASH, DILWEG, HUBBARD, SLEIGHT, LEWELLEN, BLOOD, EARPE, MICHALSKE, LAMBEAU.
BOWDOIN, RADICK, ENGELMAN, McCRARY, DUNN, ZUIDMULDER, ZUVER, FITZGIBBONS, HERBER, O'DONNELL, LIDBERG.
GREEN BAY PACKERS 1930-PRO-FOOTBALL WORLD CHAMPIONS.
STILLER KODAK PHOTO.

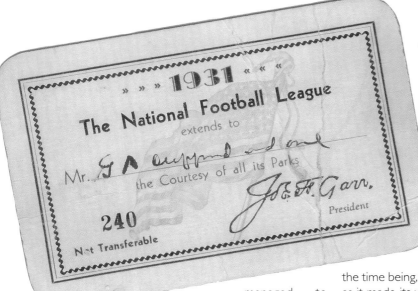

the league and played all its games on the road) that folded after the season was over. The following week, the Packers pounded the Brooklyn Dodgers 32–6 at City Stadium, but an incident in the stands cast a cloud over the team that lingered for more than two years. A drunken fan fell out of the stadium's wooden bleachers and was injured. The fan's injuries were not life threatening, but he filed a lawsuit against the team seeking $25,000 in damages. The team did not have that kind of cash, but it did have insurance, and for the time being, the issue was pushed to the back burner as it made its way through the legal system.

Left: **A rare National Football League courtesy pass, issued by the office of league president Joe Carr, which provided the bearer free access to any league game.** *GreenBayAntiques.com/The Oneida Archive*

managed to keep his stars happy and in the fold, plus he had gone out and recruited new talent, including two promising first-year players: Hank Bruder and Milt Gantenbein. Bruder had been a star at Northwestern University and he made an immediate impact as a back for the Packers. He went on to enjoy a productive 10-year year career for Green Bay. Gantenbein joined the Packers after starring at the University of Wisconsin and also stayed around for 10 seasons. Gantenbein was especially effective as a defensive end, but he also compiled respectable numbers as a receiver, too.

The Packers opened the 1931 season with a 26–0 drubbing of the NFL's newest team, the Cleveland Indians, a "road team" (meaning it was sponsored by

Another crisis—this one more immediately serious—erupted after the Packers had raised their record to 5–0. A formal complaint was filed with the NFL that claimed the Packers had broken the league rule of having more than 22 players under contract after the third game of the season; in fact, Curly had kept 27 players on his roster. For the second time in his tenure, NFL President Joe Carr threatened to make an example of the Packers by fining the team $500 and turning its two recent victories into forfeit losses. And for the second time, Curly Lambeau wriggled out of a tough situation—in the process managing to keep the victories—but he paid a price: To comply with league rules, Curly was forced to let go of long-time veterans Boob Darling and Whitey Woodin, along with

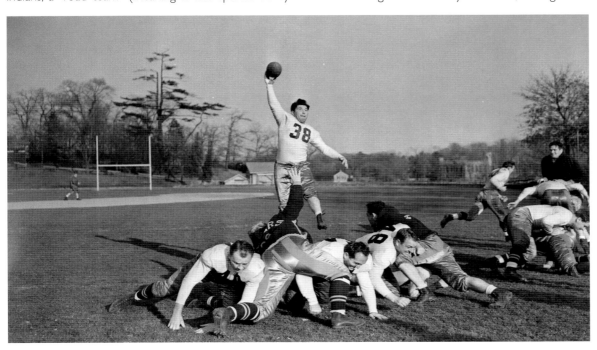

Arnie Herber, one of the Packers' three passing backs (along with Cecil Isbell and Bob Monett), unleashes a jump-throw in practice as the team prepares for its November 20, 1938, contest with the New York Giants. Green Bay lost the game 15–3, then came up short again three weeks later in a rematch with New York in the 1938 championship. *Bettmann/CORBIS*

promising youngsters Arnie Herber and Ken Radick. He also had to let tackle Claude Perry play for the Cardinals for the rest of the season.

Even this second off-the-field distraction of the year could not slow the Packers on the gridiron. By the time the gun sounded on their final game—a tight 7–6 loss to the Bears—they were in first place with a 12–2 record. But just when it appeared to be time for the team to enjoy a third straight championship celebration, yet another controversy emerged. The second-place Portsmouth Spartans, who had an 11–3 record, cried foul. During the season, the Packers had tentatively agreed to play a game in Portsmouth on December 13, then later backed out of their commitment, claming that league rules did not mandate playing games added to the schedule after the start of the season. Portsmouth demanded the game and a shot at the title, but Green Bay refused, and Joe Carr was called on to settle the dispute. Ironically, the man who only two months before had threatened to scuttle the Packers' season sided with

Green Bay and officially declared them the 1931 NFL champions.

A BIG-TIME COACH IN A SMALL-TIME CITY

The deepening Depression took a harsh toll on the National Football League, and as the 1932 season dawned, only eight franchises had survived. The Packers, whose finances for the time being remained solid, entered the season as optimistic as ever, despite the fact their success put more pressure on the team to win—anything less than another championship run would have been seen as a failure. But for Curly Lambeau, the third championship meant that his star shone ever more brightly on the national stage, and he clearly relished the attention. He appeared on the cover of national magazines. Hollywood stars wanted to spend time with him. He upgraded his wardrobe and soon his natty sideline attire prompted people to start calling him the best-dressed coach in the league.

With all this attention, the bigger question was whether Curly could keep his focus on football, and

Below: **The 1937 Packers scrimmage with intensity in a New York park in preparation for their November 21 clash with the Giants at the Polo Grounds. Hurdling a sprawling defender, future Hall of Famer Clarke Hinkle bursts through a wide hole in the line. The practice was to no avail as the Packers were shut out by New York 10–0.** *Bettmann/CORBIS*

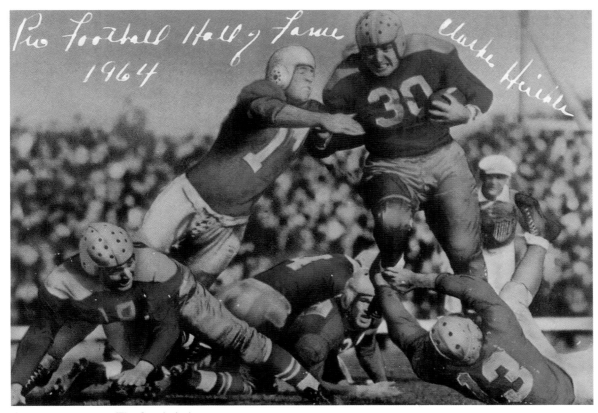

Pro Football Hall of Fame 1964

Clarke Hinkle

GreenBayAntiques.com/The Oneida Archive

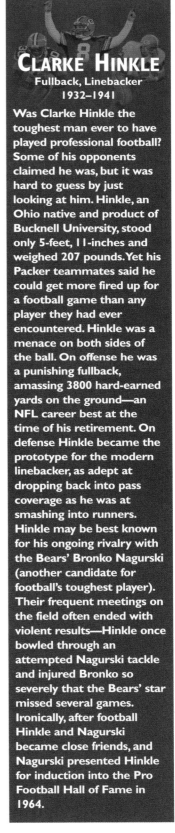

CLARKE HINKLE
Fullback, Linebacker
1932–1941

Was Clarke Hinkle the toughest man ever to have played professional football? Some of his opponents claimed he was, but it was hard to guess by just looking at him. Hinkle, an Ohio native and product of Bucknell University, stood only 5-feet, 11-inches and weighed 207 pounds. Yet his Packer teammates said he could get more fired up for a football game than any player they had ever encountered. Hinkle was a menace on both sides of the ball. On offense he was a punishing fullback, amassing 3800 hard-earned yards on the ground—an NFL career best at the time of his retirement. On defense Hinkle became the prototype for the modern linebacker, as adept at dropping back into pass coverage as he was at smashing into runners. Hinkle may be best known for his ongoing rivalry with the Bears' Bronko Nagurski (another candidate for football's toughest player). Their frequent meetings on the field often ended with violent results—Hinkle once bowled through an attempted Nagurski tackle and injured Bronko so severely that the Bears' star missed several games. Ironically, after football Hinkle and Nagurski became close friends, and Nagurski presented Hinkle for induction into the Pro Football Hall of Fame in 1964.

fans began to have their doubts. In particular, rumors of Curly's marital infidelity started circulating in Green Bay's small-town environment, in which few secrets could be kept. In later years, former Packers admitted that Curly's womanizing on road trips was legendary. Unmarried players often found themselves competing with their famous coach for the attention of attractive women—competition the players usually ended up losing.

Yet at this juncture, Curly Lambeau appeared to be just as focused on football as ever and driven to win another championship. His star-studded roster stayed remarkably stable during the off-season, and Curly even managed to upgrade the team with two key additions. Arnie Herber, forced off the field in 1931 thanks to Joe Carr's punishment for team roster violations, returned—and with a vengeance. Resuming his role as the Packers' leading passer, Herber threw nine touchdowns and was named to the NFL All-Pro team. In addition to Herber, Lambeau also brought in a rookie who was destined to make a huge mark in the NFL: fullback Clark Hinkle.

Hinkle's hard-nosed, up-the-gut running quickly became the perfect complement to the Packers' passing game. The Ohio native had played college ball at Bucknell, and he was an effective linebacker, kicker,

and punter as well. Hinkle was not a big man—only 5-feet 11-inches and about 200 pounds—but he was fearless, and he loved delivering punishment to his opponents. In particular, Hinkle loved mixing it up with Bears' star Bronco Nagurski, and their frequent on-field battles became the stuff of NFL legend. When Hinkle retired after the 1941 season, he was the NFL's career rushing leader with 3860 yards and he'd tallied 35 touchdowns—stats that easily earned him a 1964 induction into Canton.

Despite their new offensive firepower, points were harder to come by for the 1932 Packers, but fortunately their defense was as stout as ever, surrendering only 63 points for the season. After a scoreless tie against the Bears at City Stadium the second week of the season, the Packers rolled through the season in convincing fashion. The final game of the 1932 regular season found the 10–2–1 Packers playing the Bears at Wrigley Field with a fourth championship on the line. Green Bay's offense sputtered and the Bears emerged with a 9–0 victory. The Packers were not going to be champions—but who was?

Ironically, the champion was going to be one of two teams with only six wins and, together, an amazing 10 ties. At 10–3–1, the Packers were in third place behind Chicago at 6–1–6 and Portsmouth at 6–1–4, both tied

ARNIE HERBER
Back
1930–1940

Hollywood could not have scripted a story as compelling as Arnie Herber's. A schoolboy star in basketball and football at Green Bay West High School, Herber sold programs at City Stadium so he could watch his beloved Packers. He attended the University of Wisconsin and Denver's Regis College for a short time, but by the age of 20 was back in Green Bay working for the Packers as a handyman. Curly Lambeau gave the young Herber a tryout before the 1930 season and signed him to a contract. By 1932 he had earned a role as the Packers' primary pass-throwing back and he led the NFL in passing. His ability to throw the long ball with incredible accuracy changed the face of pro football, especially after the speedy Don Hutson became his primary target. Injuries and a struggle with his weight threatened to derail Herber's career, but he remained an important part of the Packers' offense, even after Curly brought in Bob Monett, then the talented Cecil Isbell to replace him. After Isbell finally established himself as the Packers' primary passer in 1940, Herber was cut by Lambeau—but that was not the end of his career. In 1944 Herber joined the war-ravaged Giants and he played two strong seasons for New York, leading them to the 1944 championship game—where they were beaten by the Packers. Herber's career numbers of 8000-plus yards passing and 81 touchdowns made him an easy selection for the Pro Football Hall of Fame in 1966.

Arnie Herber was pro football's first great passer. Shown here in 1936, he could heave a ball sixty yards with ease. Herber's story is especially remarkable considering that he was working as the Packers' handyman when Curly Lambeau gave him a tryout and decided to sign him on as a player.
Bettmann/CORBIS

> **"Contract negotiations with Curly were like a three-act play. You started out full of hope. Then Curly started to talk down your demands. At the end you felt like a bad guy trying to rob the Packers."**
> —*Charles "Buckets" Goldenberg*

for first thanks to the NFL practice of ignoring ties in figuring the standings. To break the tie, the NFL scheduled a playoff in Chicago, but heavy snow forced the game inside Chicago Stadium. The playing surface was dirt left over after a recent circus; the arena could only accommodate an 80-yard field without end zones. Chicago ended up winning the bizarre game 9–0, officially breaking the Packers' championship run.

FROM CHAMPIONSHIP TO RECEIVERSHIP

Thanks, in part, to some lessons learned in the oddball indoor playoff game, the National Football League made some of its most sweeping rule changes in the off-season—changes that made the sport look more like the modern game. Two of the revisions were largely meant to encourage passing. First, the league added hash marks to the field, a feature first employed on the cramped field in the 1932 indoor playoff—but with obvious advantages in any venue. With the ball always spotted near the center of the field (between the hash marks), offenses started using more rollout passes, an exciting innovation that led to more scoring.

The other change was what some called the "Nagurski Rule," thanks to a controversial touchdown pass the Bears' star threw against Portsmouth. Previously, passers had to be at least 5 yards behind the line of scrimmage before releasing the ball. Portsmouth protested that Bronko was much closer to the line when he let loose his touchdown throw to Red Grange during the playoff. NFL officials realized that allowing throws from anywhere behind the line of scrimmage would make pro football much more exciting and high scoring, and so they turned what was probably an officiating error into a permanent rule change.

One other significant alteration made by the NFL was to break the league into two five-team divisions. At the end of the season, the first-place teams in each division would meet in a championship game. The Packers joined the Western Division with the Bears, Chicago Cardinals, Cincinnati Reds, and Portsmouth Spartans. With only four teams to beat to reach the championship, and with new rules in place to encourage its pass-happy offense, the Packers team

appeared in perfect position to reclaim the NFL championship—but off-the-field events seemed to derail the season before it even started.

In July 1933, Willard Bent—the drunken fan who had fallen out of the City Stadium bleachers two seasons earlier—finally had his day in court and was awarded $5200 in damages. Since the accident, the Packers' insurance company had declared bankruptcy and was unable to pay the judgment. When it was revealed that the team had debts of more than $12,000 and no assets to pay them off, they were forced into receivership, a stunning turn of events for what had recently been seen as one of the NFL's leading franchises. But as with the team's earlier financial crisis, Green Bay citizens—especially one of the legendary "Hungry Five"—emerged to support the team.

In August 1933, a Brown County circuit court judge appointed Frank Jonet as receiver to manage the claims of all creditors. The Packers could not have asked for a better person in the position. As both a certified public accountant and an avid Packers fan and stockholder, Jonet had the wherewithal to sort out the financial situation—but he clearly would act with the team's best interest at heart. After Jonet's appointment, team president and "Hungry Five" member Lee Johannes personally lent the team $6000, which was used to pay off half the debt. Now the team's largest creditor was also its president. The Packers could play out the season and hopefully earn enough money at the gate to pull itself out of debt.

Unfortunately, the 1933 Packers seemed distracted by the turmoil off the field and could never quite get on track, failing to secure a win until the fourth game of the season. Other than a couple of mid-season routs, the offense struggled to score points, despite the presence of some of the greatest offensive players in NFL history. A three-game skid in November assured the team of its first losing season as an NFL franchise; the Packers ended up in third place in the Western Division with a 5–7–1 record.

Nobody seemed to take this fall from the top harder than Curly Lambeau, who became physically ill as the season went on. He visited a doctor in New York after the team lost to the Giants late in the season. Green Bay papers reported that he was suffering from an unspecified stomach ailment.

The one event of note in an otherwise forgettable season took place on October 1, 1933. In an attempt to broaden its fan base and generate more cash to pay off its debts, the Packers played a "home" game against the Giants in Milwaukee, Wisconsin's largest city. The Packers lost the game 10–7, but more than 12,000 spectators filled Borchardt Field, home of the minor

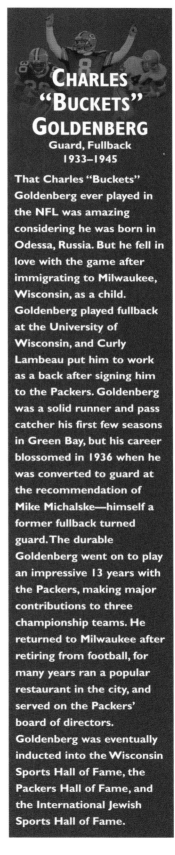

CHARLES "BUCKETS" GOLDENBERG
Guard, Fullback
1933–1945

That Charles "Buckets" Goldenberg ever played in the NFL was amazing considering he was born in Odessa, Russia. But he fell in love with the game after immigrating to Milwaukee, Wisconsin, as a child. Goldenberg played fullback at the University of Wisconsin, and Curly Lambeau put him to work as a back after signing him to the Packers. Goldenberg was a solid runner and pass catcher his first few seasons in Green Bay, but his career blossomed in 1936 when he was converted to guard at the recommendation of Mike Michalske—himself a former fullback turned guard. The durable Goldenberg went on to play an impressive 13 years with the Packers, making major contributions to three championship teams. He returned to Milwaukee after retiring from football, for many years ran a popular restaurant in the city, and served on the Packers' board of directors. Goldenberg was eventually inducted into the Wisconsin Sports Hall of Fame, the Packers Hall of Fame, and the International Jewish Sports Hall of Fame.

KEY PLAYS: DON HUTSON'S FIRST NFL PLAY

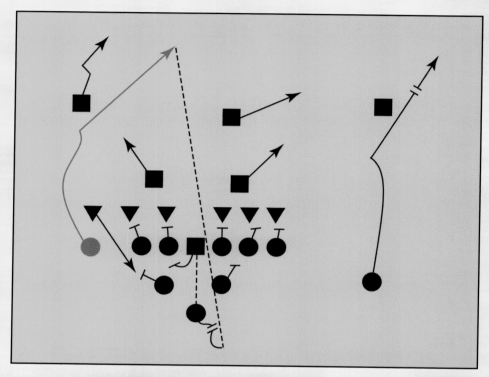

When Don Hutson joined the Packers, he forever changed the game of pro football—literally from his very first play. Playing the Bears in Green Bay on September 22, 1935, the Packers had the ball on their own 17. Hutson lined up at "flexed" left end (slightly split off the tackle). Playing the deep back in the single wing, Arnie Herber took the long snap from center and made a short drop to pass. John McNally, split wide on the right as a wingback, appeared to be the primary target; he ran at the defender before breaking to the right. Herber looked at McNally and faked a pass. Meanwhile, Hutson had broken casually off the line of scrimmage, running toward Chicago All-Pro defensive back Beattie Feathers. When Feathers bit on Herber's fake and paused, Hutson angled towards the center of the field, switched into high gear, and left Feathers in the dust. Herber hit Hutson in stride, heaving a bomb that traveled 66 yards in the air. The 83-yard touchdown was the game's only score. Hutson's speed and athleticism—especially his ability to run precise, multiple-fake pass routes—revealed the power and excitement of the passing game, which pro football soon embraced with fervor, much to the delight of fans.

When Don Hutson arrived in Green Bay, he showed the true potential of the passing game as practiced by a gifted, athletic receiver. This scene shows a relatively rare occurrence—Hutson dropping a pass during the 1938 championship game against the Giants—but he went on to catch 488 passes during his remarkable career.
Bettmann/CORBIS

"It was a great start for me, gave me a great deal of confidence. After that I didn't spend a lot of time thinking about other ways to make a living." —Don Hutson, commenting on the effect of catching an 83-yard touchdown pass on his first NFL play

league baseball Milwaukee Brewers. The field was ill suited for football and an angry Curly Lambeau said afterward that his team would never play there again. Yet the financial rewards and increased publicity from playing in a large city were undeniable. Despite Curly's opinions, it looked like Milwaukee might continue to play a role in the team's future.

GREEN BAY FANS SAVE THEIR TEAM

Changes abounded for the Packers during the 1933–1934 off-season. One of the most startling developments occurred off the field when Curly returned home from a West Coast scouting trip and told his wife, Marguerite, that he wanted a divorce. During his trips to California, Curly had met and fallen in love with blonde-haired, 25-year-old model, Susan Johnston, and he intended to marry her. Tongues wagged in Green Bay—had Curly "gone Hollywood?" This seeming betrayal of Midwestern values—coupled with the losing season—prompted Green Bay fans to begin openly questioning the coaching acumen of their hometown hero.

Despite the changes in his personal life, Curly Lambeau appeared impervious to the criticism and, as always, focused on his team. Partly by choice and partly because of developments beyond his control, Curly started remaking his roster. First, he became fed up with John McNally, suspending "Johnny Blood" when he showed up drunk for practice and shipping him off to Pittsburgh after the season. Then, Curly had to say goodbye to stalwart lineman, Cal Hubbard, who had accepted a coaching position at Texas A&M. The punishing nature of two-way football was starting to take its toll on other long-time Packers as well, but Lambeau continued to display his knack for locating and signing talented reinforcements.

As Curly Lambeau retooled the roster, club president Lee Johannes focused his attention on returning the Packers to solid financial standing and securing its future in the NFL. Calling a meeting with 25 of Green Bay's leading businessmen, Johannes asked them to lead a fund-raising campaign. The city's fans responded with $15,000, more than enough for the team to satisfy its debt. Player and lawyer Lavvie

Dilweg drew up the papers to reorganize Green Bay Packers, Inc., which stipulated issuing 600 shares of stock with no par value and, as before, instructing that any profits be donated to the local American Legion post.

The team showed some improvement in the 1934 season but continued to struggle when it came to scoring points. Clarke Hinkle proved a worthy replacement in the backfield for John McNally, and by season's end, he was the team leader in both rushing yards and passes caught. In addition, Arnie Herber continued to affirm his status as the league's leading passer. The Packers' two biggest problems were division rivals Chicago Bears and Detroit Lions; each raced to 10–0 records, leaving Green Bay in the dust. The Packers finished a respectable 7–6, again good for third place in the Western Division, but they looked outclassed by the Bears, who finished the regular season with an unblemished 13–0 record. In a remarkable turn of events, the Giants dominated the Bears in the league's first championship game, taking a 30–13 win on the ice-encrusted surface of New York's Polo Grounds. Several Giants switched to basketball

The letterhead used by the 1936 Packers featured a team picture and a note proclaiming "Three Times World's Champions." In fact, by the end of the season, the team would make it four championships. This rare document outlines the club's construction, maintenance, and insurance costs for Green Bay's City Stadium.
GreenBayAntiques.com/The Oneida Archive

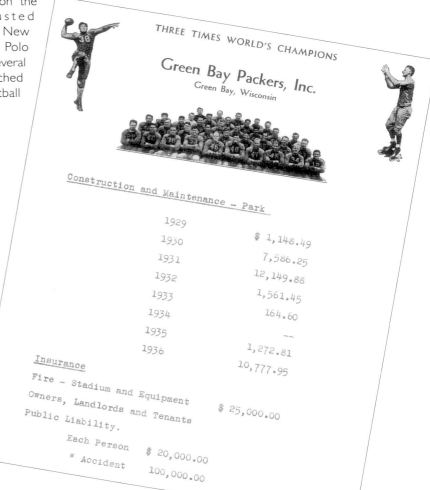

One of the "rewards" for NFL championship teams was an exhibition game before the start of the following season against the College All Stars. The September 1, 1937, contest did not offer much of a reward to the Packers, who lost 6–0. Packers' back George Sauer is shown trying to gain yards on a sweep around the right end during the first quarter of the game, which was played at Chicago's Soldier Field.
Bettmann/CORBIS

shoes at halftime to get better footing in what became known as the "Sneaker Game."

HUTSON ARRIVES AND FOOTBALL FOREVER CHANGES

Two interesting Curly Lambeau experiments marked the start of the 1935 season. First, Curly became one of the first coaches to experiment with the offsite training camp when he took the players to Rhinelander, Wisconsin, for a week of intense practice. Second, he decided to change uniforms, and for the first time, the Packers wore green and gold, abandoning the dark blue jerseys they had worn every season up to this point in time. Yet one development overshadowed everything else that happened during the 1934–1935 off-season: The Packers signed speedy receiver Don Hutson.

When Curly Lambeau watched the University of Alabama All-American embarrass Stanford defenders in the 1935 Rose Bowl, he knew he had found the perfect player to return the Packers to greatness. Unfortunately, Green Bay was not the only NFL team that wanted Hutson, and he ended up signing contracts with both the Packers and the Brooklyn Dodgers. Joe Carr was called on to settle the dispute and he ruled in the Packers' favor—apparently because their contract reached him via mail first. After this fortuitous development, Curly rewarded his new star with the richest paycheck in team history—$300 per game. To keep the amount secret, Lambeau each week mailed two $150 checks to Hutson accounts at two different Green Bay banks.

Once the 1935 season started, Green Bay took advantage of their new offensive weapon almost immediately. After sitting out the first game (a 7–6 loss to the Cardinals), Hutson stepped on the City Stadium turf for the first time in a Packers uniform early in the Week 2 tilt against the Bears. On his first play, Hutson

sprinted past the Bear defenders and Arnie Herber hit him in stride with a missile of a pass. The resulting 83-yard touchdown was the game's only score … and an NFL legend was born.

When football historians discuss the game's greatest players, Don Hutson's name invariably comes up—in part, because he probably had more impact on shaping the game into its current form than any other player, and also because no single player has dominated the league for so long a period. At 6-feet 1-inch, 185 pounds, and able to run a 9.7 in the 100-yard dash, Hutson became the prototype for wide receivers that the NFL still uses today. He had sure hands, was an elusive open-field runner, and ran remarkable pass patterns in which he would fake himself free of the double and triple coverage he invariably faced. When his career ended after 11 seasons, Hutson had accumulated eye-popping numbers for a receiver: 488 catches, 7991 yards, and 99 touchdowns. Even with the game's shift to the pass, he remains among the career leaders in many categories, and most consider his record of eight seasons leading the league in receiving as untouchable.

Despite their new offensive weapon—supplemented by a rejuvenated John McNally, recalled from his one-year exile in Pittsburgh—the 1935 Packers found themselves in a dogfight in the evenly matched Western Division. The team stayed in the title hunt until the last game of the season, but despite a 13–6 win over the Philadelphia Eagles, Green Bay ended up in second with an 8–4 record. Detroit won the division with a 7–3–2 mark and went on to knock off the Giants in the championship game.

The Packers failed to win the title, but Green Bay fans loved their competitiveness and wide-open offense, and healthy attendance boosted the team's bottom line. In addition, the Packers seemed to unearth a potential gold mine in Milwaukee, despite the fact that Curly Lambeau had vowed to never again play there. During the off-season, *Milwaukee Journal* reporter Oliver Kuechle helped broker a deal that led to the Packers agreeing to play two games each season at Milwaukee's State Fair Park. The facility was better equipped to handle football and had a capacity of 32,000, significantly more than City Stadium. October games at State Fair Park were well received by fans and Curly raised no objection, setting the stage for a long-term relationship between the Packers and Milwaukee.

BACK ON TOP

The Packers appeared to have all the weapons they needed for a championship in 1936, though the roster had undergone quite a makeover. Veterans who had been responsible for the 1929–1931 championship run started retiring, including Cal Hubbard, Mike Michalske, and Claude Perry. But Lambeau had been cultivating replacements and several former backups saw their stars shine in 1936—particularly guard Lon Evans and tackle Ernie Smith, who both earned spots on the NFL All-Pro team. The NFL had also instituted the college draft before the season, and Lambeau used the Packers' first pick to select Russ Letlow, a guard from the University of San Francisco. Letlow became a defensive-line standout and was eventually inducted into the Packers Hall of Fame.

After the Packers took the opener from the Chicago Cardinals, the Bears came to town on September 20 and hammered Green Bay 30–3. The prospects for a championship looked dim, but there was hope. John McNally had missed the first two games, staging what was the first contract holdout in team history. After the Bears game, the Packer executive committee told Curly to get McNally under contract. He complied, and with the distraction removed and one of their best players back on the field, the Packers' turnaround started immediately. Green Bay never lost another game en route to a 10–1–1 season.

Arnie Herber and Don Hutson were magnificent, leading the league in passing and receiving, respectively, but the rushing offense—led by Clark Hinkle, George Sauer, Bob Monett, and Milt Gantenbein—was just as effective, racking up nearly 1700 yards on the ground. The Packers won the Western Division comfortably and earned the right to play in their first championship

game. They met the Boston Redskins at New York's Polo Grounds (chosen over Boston because the Redskins had drawn such meager crowds during their home games). Three minutes into the game, Hutson caught a 42-yard touchdown pass from Herber, and the Packers never trailed en route to a 21–6 victory. More than 10,000 fans greeted the team at the Green Bay train station. Maybe the crowds weren't as large or as boisterous as those that gathered after the first couple of championships, but Green Bay was obviously pleased to be back on top of the NFL.

EXHIBITION BLUES AND ANOTHER CHAMPIONSHIP RUN

After their 1936 championship, the Packers embarked on a West Coast tour, a common practice for the NFL during this era. The exhibition games played were a good source of extra money for the team and players, so few people complained. Another exhibition that the champions played was the annual contest against the college all-stars before the start of the following regular season. The 1937 game turned out to be one that the Packers would rather have not played. They were humbled by the collegians 6–0 (the first loss suffered by the NFL in the game) and Arnie Herber suffered an injury that hindered him for the rest of the year.

With additional seating in City Stadium (an expansion of roughly 6,000) promising new attendance records, the Packers promptly dropped their first two games of 1937. Without Herber to pass the ball, the offense—limited primarily to a ground game—struggled to put points on the scoreboard. When Herber came back for the third game, the team embarked on a seven-game winning streak to pull itself back into contention. Back-to-back losses on the road

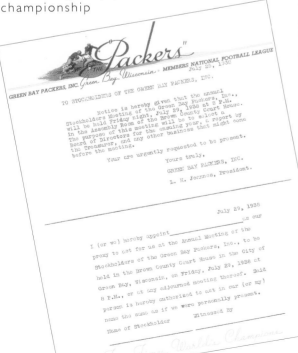

This letter from Packers President Lee Johannes went out to stockholders—largely consisting of Green Bay citizens—inviting them to attend the team's 1938 annual meeting. The Packers' long history of public ownership is unique among NFL teams and is responsible for the survival of the team in its small Midwestern home city.
GreenBayAntiques.com/The Oneida Archive

DON HUTSON
End
1935–1945

"The Alabama Antelope" was the NFL's first dominant pass receiver—and dominate he did, leading the league in catches for an amazing eight of his 11 seasons with the Packers. Hutson, a native of Pine Bluff, Arkansas, was built like a modern receiver: 6-feet, 1-inch and 185 pounds. He was blazing fast and had great hands, but the key to his success may have been his brilliant route running, which was often punctuated by multiple fakes to shed the double- and triple-coverage he often drew. Hutson caught passes thrown to him by Arnie Herber and Bob Monett, but it was probably when Cecil Isbell became the Packers' primary passer that Hutson became especially dangerous. The two men worked at the same factory during the off-season and practiced in the parking lot during lunchtime. Their efforts led them to perfect a number of timing patterns, where Isbell would throw to a spot, knowing Hutson would be there to catch the ball—the first time this now-standard technique was regularly used in the NFL. Hutson was NFL MVP in 1941 and 1942, and retired in 1945 after accumulating what were then staggering career numbers: 488 catches for 7991 yards and 99 touchdowns. He served as a Packer assistant coach for four seasons before leaving Green Bay for Racine, Wisconsin, where he owned and ran a Chevy and Cadillac dealership for more than three decades. The Packers honored Hutson in 1994 by naming their indoor practice facility after him.

One of the reasons the 1937 College All Stars were able to defeat the defending champion Packers was TCU star Sammy Baugh, shown here eluding a Green Bay defender on a punt return during the September 1 contest. "Slingin' Sammy" threw the pass leading to the game's only score, then went on to a stellar sixteen-year career as a quarterback with the Washington Redskins.
Bettmann/CORBIS

against the Giants and Redskins (now playing in Washington) left the Packers with a 7–4 record and in second place behind the Bears. Chicago finished the regular season with the league's best record but lost an exciting championship game to the Redskins, led by sensational rookie quarterback Sammy Baugh, 28–21.

With Arnie Herber in apparent decline, Curly Lambeau thought his top priority during the off-season was finding another passer to help feed the ball to Don Hutson. For Hutson to achieve his potential, he would need the help of an exceptional passer—and that's what Curly hoped he was getting when he selected Cecil Isbell of Purdue University with his first pick of the December 1937 draft. His instincts turned out to be correct. Isbell made his mark immediately in 1938, but he shared time as primary passer with Herber and Bob Monett in the Packers' offense for his first three seasons. When Isbell finally became the primary passer, he broke out for two of the most prolific passing seasons in NFL history—then amazingly called it quits as a player and became a college coach.

Playing in front of ever-larger crowds (thanks to yet another City Stadium expansion, this time to a capacity of nearly 25,000), the entertaining Packers put together a strong 1938 season despite a disappointing 2–0 loss to the Bears in their second game. A late-season run of five straight wins helped propel the Packers to yet another division title and championship playoff, this time against the Giants. More than 48,000 fans enjoyed a hard-fought game at the Polo Grounds. The Packers kept it close despite the fact that Don Hutson was injured and largely ineffective, but two blocked punts proved their undoing and they dropped a 23–17 heartbreaker. The game was marred by a bizarre incident: Curly Lambeau took a wrong turn on his way to the locker room at halftime, walked out a door, and found himself locked out of the stadium. It took him several minutes to talk his way back into the Polo Grounds, but he missed most of halftime and an opportunity to talk to his team.

Fortunately, the 1939 Packers found themselves with an opportunity to shake off the memories of their

"Isbell was the best, with Sid Luckman of the Bears a close second and Sammy Baugh of the Redskins a long third....Isbell was a master at any range. He could throw soft passes, bullet passes, or long passes."
—Curly Lambeau, on the best passers of all time

championship near miss—and their famous coach's embarrassing loss of direction during the season's biggest game. Defense was not this team's forte: The 1939 Packers yielded 153 points, at that time the highest total in team history. Fortunately, the offense was as potent as ever, featuring Don Hutson, who led the league in receiving; Arnie Herber and Cecil Isbell, a fearsome passing duo; and a potent running game utilizing a host of backs (led by Isbell and Clark Hinkle) who together accumulated more than 1500 yards on the ground.

The key to the season may have been the addition of rookie Larry Craig, a sixth-round pick out of South Carolina. Coach Lambeau put Craig in Don Hutson's defensive end slot and moved his star receiver to the less-demanding position of safety. Some speculate the move may have added years to Hutson's career and provided him the edge he needed to continue confounding defensive backs.

Thanks to the Bears and Lions, 1939 offered no cakewalk through the Western Division. After losing to Chicago 30–27 on November 5, the 5–2 Packers were in second place behind Detroit. They closed the season with a string of four impressive road victories—the last one a 12–7 over the Lions—and wrapped up their second consecutive Western Division title. Waiting for them in the championship game were the New York Giants. It was supposed to be a home game for the Packers, but the league insisted that the game be played in Milwaukee's State Fair Park because of the venue's larger capacity. Though the decision was unpopular with Green Bay city leaders, it was a good one financially. The game drew 32,279 fans (paying $4.40 each for the best seats) and the Packers achieved the biggest gate in their history.

On the field, the game was not even a contest. The Giants held Don Hutson in check, but not Milt Gantenbein and Joe Laws, who each caught touchdown passes. Meanwhile, the Packers defense, which had been suspect during the season, proved stifling. The only thing more punishing was the cold and windy weather. In the end, the Packers left Milwaukee with a 27–0 victory. More importantly, they were NFL champions for an unprecedented sixth time, ending the 1930s right where they started—as the undisputed best team in the league.

Below: The Packers ended the 1930s the way they started the decade: as champions. On December 10, 1939, more than 32,000 fans jammed Milwaukee's State Fair Park to watch Green Bay whitewash the Giants 27–0. This scene from the game's fourth quarter shows the Packers' tenacious defense wrapping up New York back Tuffy Heemans after a short gain. *Bettmann/CORBIS*

Ticket stub. *GreenBayAntiques.com/ The Oneida Archive*

RESERVED
SEC. C ROW 25 SEAT 36
DEC. 10, 1939
EST. PRICE — — $1.50
FED. TAX — — .15
TOTAL — $1.65
WORLD'S PROFESSIONAL CHAMPIONSHIP

CHAPTER 3

THE 1940S: FROM THE HIGHEST HIGHS TO THE LOWEST LOWS

Opposite: **Thirty thousand fans watch Packers halfback Roy McKay kick off to the Cardinals during the second half of the two clubs' November 10, 1946, game at Chicago's Comiskey Park, home of baseball's White Sox. Green Bay went on to win the contest 19–7 en route to a 6–5 season record and a third place tie with the Cardinals in the NFL's Western Division.** *Bettmann/CORBIS*

The Green Bay Packers left the 1930s the same way they entered the decade—as champions, but the world in which they played had changed dramatically. Though the United States had persevered and emerged from the long-term economic doldrums following the 1929 stock market crash, other challenges lay ahead. The Nazi blitzkrieg during the fall of 1939 had left Europe engulfed in war. It seemed only a matter of time before the United States was dragged into the conflict, and sports became secondary to much more important matters.

Despite this looming world crisis, the Packers could still enjoy the benefits of being on top of the NFL, though the league was a very different entity from the one that existed only 10 years earlier. Thanks to rule changes that encouraged more offense (especially passing) and differentiated pro ball from the popular college game, and to the emergence of several exciting stars—including the Packers own Don Hutson—the NFL was attracting more fans than ever before. In fact, during 1939, the league enjoyed single-season game attendance in excess of one million for the first time.

Part of the reason for this success is that the NFL had emerged from the Depression as a big-city-oriented operation. There may have been fewer teams, but gone were the Portsmouths and Providences that had populated the league in its initial seasons. The larger cities had the potential for much bigger fan bases, better coverage from the press, higher revenues from ticket sales, and the ability to weather future economic downturns. The lone remaining exception to the NFL's new big-city profile was the Green Bay Packers.

Everyone recognized that the Packers were an anomaly. They had nearly succumbed to their own financial crisis during the Depression, but with two league championships and ever-increasing attendance in the interim, the receivership of 1933 seemed a distant memory. Thanks to the league's most enthusiastic fan base, and to the continuing football genius of Curly Lambeau, Green Bay had played itself back to the top of the heap. But the future still was not secure. Besides being a small city, Green Bay was a far-flung outpost on the northwest corner of what was still an eastern league. Consider the fact that the Cleveland Rams also played in the league's Western Division. Players from eastern teams saw games in Chicago as requiring a long road trip—and Green Bay was a change of trains and a journey of several hours north of the Windy City.

Another problem that the Packers would face during the 1940s was what to do about City Stadium. At one time envied because of its excellent playing surface designed especially for football, the facility was starting to draw jeers from the rest of the league. Though repeated expansions had left City Stadium with a U-shaped surround of stands and a respectable capacity of around 25,000, the facility still did not live up to the league's other big-city venues. A growing problem was the fact that visiting teams were still forced to dress at the East High locker rooms (or in their hotel) on game days. During renovations, the Packers had added a locker room for themselves (as well as much-needed restrooms for

> **"I hadn't been up long when I saw Lambeau tell players like Herber, Gantenbein, and Bruder they were done. I vowed I'd quit before they came around to tell me."**
> —*Cecil Isbell, explaining his early retirement*

spectators), but had failed to provide dressing facilities for visiting teams.

In the midst of this atmosphere, the Packers themselves seemed to start hearing the siren call of the big city, much to the chagrin of their loyal small-town supporters. The team seemed very pleased with its two-games-per-year agreement to play in Milwaukee. Though State Fair Park was not a great facility, it was larger than City Stadium and the 1939 championship game proved that Milwaukee offered the potential to generate significant revenues for the

team. Plus, playing in Milwaukee earned expanded press coverage for the Packers, the NFL liked the team having a big-city foothold, and—most importantly—Curly Lambeau was pleased with the arrangement.

And what about Curly Lambeau at the beginning of 1940? In the midst of his continuing success as a coach, the previous year had not been a good one for him personally. His father had passed away at the relatively young age of 63, and his second marriage was collapsing. Curly was said to be on the prowl again for female companionship. And while Green Bay citizens may have gossiped about their gifted coach and disapproved of his personal life, the greatest fear of many fans was undoubtedly that their star would leave them for greener pastures. Yet despite his infatuation with fame, fortune, and beautiful women, Curly's heart would continue to remain true to the two constants in his life: Green Bay and the game of football. He wouldn't give up either without a fight—which, as the 1940s progressed, seemed destined to happen.

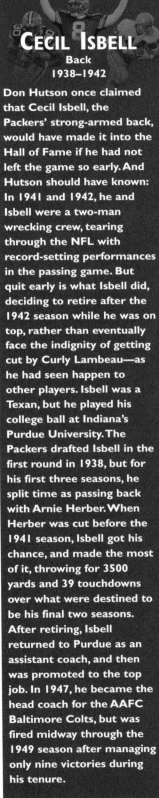

CECIL ISBELL
Back
1938–1942

Don Hutson once claimed that Cecil Isbell, the Packers' strong-armed back, would have made it into the Hall of Fame if he had not left the game so early. And Hutson should have known: In 1941 and 1942, he and Isbell were a two-man wrecking crew, tearing through the NFL with record-setting performances in the passing game. But quit early is what Isbell did, deciding to retire after the 1942 season while he was on top, rather than eventually face the indignity of getting cut by Curly Lambeau—as he had seen happen to other players. Isbell was a Texan, but he played his college ball at Indiana's Purdue University. The Packers drafted Isbell in the first round in 1938, but for his first three seasons, he split time as passing back with Arnie Herber. When Herber was cut before the 1941 season, Isbell got his chance, and made the most of it, throwing for 3500 yards and 39 touchdowns over what were destined to be his final two seasons. After retiring, Isbell returned to Purdue as an assistant coach, and then was promoted to the top job. In 1947, he became the head coach for the AAFC Baltimore Colts, but was fired midway through the 1949 season after managing only nine victories during his tenure.

STRUGGLES IN THE WAKE OF A CHAMPIONSHIP

The 1940 Green Bay Packers were a mystery. They returned most of their talented players from the 1939 championship campaign, putting on an offensive clinic against a talented college all-star team in beating them 45–28 in front of a huge crowd at Chicago's Soldier Field. Years later, Lambeau called it his most satisfying coaching victory, in part because he felt it validated his opinion that pro football had finally become superior to college ball. No wonder he was so optimistic heading into the season—yet the team could not deliver on its promise.

The regular season started out eerily like the 1936 championship campaign: The Packers enjoyed an opening-week victory, only to suffer a blowout loss at home to the Bears. Unfortunately, there was no nine-game winning streak after this loss to the Bears. Instead, the Packers yo-yoed through 1940, following big wins with disappointing losses.

The reasons for the team's struggles were not obvious. On offense, Cecil Isbell emerged as the primary passer, still sharing duties with Arnie Herber, but together the two men were very productive. Don Hutson remained their favorite target. Clark Hinkle led a potent rushing attack, and on the other side of the ball, the Packers established a team record by holding their opponents to 1040 yards on the ground. Yet, they could not win the games they needed to win, dropping both contests to the Bears and finishing second to their Chicago rivals with a 6–4–1 record.

The Bears would go on to rout the Giants 73–0 in the most lopsided championship game in league history, but the season would be better remembered for a couple of developments that would begin to usher the league into the modern era. First, Mutual Broadcasting System paid $2500 for the rights to broadcast the championship game live to a network of 120 radio stations. The fee was small change compared to today's multi-billion dollar television contracts, but with people across the country listening to Red Barber's play-by-play, the NFL had every reason to think of itself as a national phenomenon.

Another development that promised to help spread the reach of the NFL involved the Packers. When Curly Lambeau arranged for the Packers to board two planes in Chicago and fly to New York for their November 17, 1940, game with the Giants, Green Bay became the first pro football team to use the burgeoning world of airline transportation. Ironically, bad weather grounded the flight after a refueling stop in Cleveland, and the team was forced to catch a train for the rest of the journey, but that's the way the 1940 season went for the team.

Nonetheless, the event started a change in the way the league viewed itself. California was booming and also a hotbed of college football. Though a long train ride from the league's eastern nucleus, the West Coast was a manageable plane ride away. Not surprisingly, the NFL started looking west.

THE PACKERS SAY GOODBYE TO HERBER

In 1941 the NFL took further steps to professionalize itself and raise the league's profile. Dipping into the elite levels of college football, the league hired Elmer Layden—Notre Dame coach and athletic director and one of Knute Rockne's famed "Four Horsemen"—to become the first NFL commissioner. The position replaced the league president, which had been held on an interim basis by Carl Storck since the 1939 death of Joe Carr. Layden moved the league headquarters from Columbus, Ohio, to Chicago.

With the 1941 season approaching, Curly Lambeau did not see the need to make many major changes to the roster—with one exception, and the circumstances behind the move were questionable. With the emergence of Cecil Isbell, Arnie Herber's role with the team seemed to be diminishing and just prior to the season he was released. While there may have been good football reasons for the move, David Zimmerman's book *Curly Lambeau: The Man Behind the Mystique* suggests that Herber was let go because he and his wife had taken in Curly's ex-wife, Susan, who was pregnant with what the coach thought was another man's baby. No matter the real reason for the roster move, it was a tough end to a stellar career.

The draft had become the professional franchises' primary means of adding new talent, and though in 1941 the event stretched for 22 rounds, the process ended up being hit and miss for most teams. Curly had found some gems through the draft, but he had also picked some clinkers; 1941 was no exception. The Packers' top two picks never played a game for the team. Yet buried in the sixth round was a player who would leave his mark on Green Bay for years to come.

Tony Canadeo was only 5 feet, 11 inches tall and weighed 195 pounds, but he could do it all—run, throw, and catch the ball. He was a fine punter and a feared kick returner. He was a fleet-footed and elusive halfback. He was a hard-hitting defensive back. He starred for the Packers over the course of 11 seasons (he took 1945 off to serve in the military) and piled up impressive career numbers. After retiring, Canadeo joined Ray Scott as color commentator on Packer broadcasts, and later served on the team's executive committee.

The 1941 Packers were probably the best Green

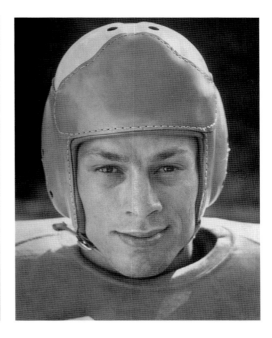

Bay team to not win a championship. As usual, the Chicago Bears were the primary barrier to the Packers' title hopes. The Bears' offense, led by star quarterback Sid Luckman, was probably the league's best—with the possible exception of the Packers. Cecil Isbell and Don Hutson put up eye-popping numbers in the passing game, and the Packers backfield by committee (still led by durable Clarke Hinkle) ground out 1550 yards and 13 touchdowns on the ground.

After opening 1941 with two wins, the Packers met the Bears in week three and came up on the short end of a 25–17 decision. A November 2 rematch at Wrigley Field ended as a Packers' 16–14 victory. Both teams won their remaining games, finished with identical 10–1 records, and faced a December 14 playoff to determine the division champion. One week before that game, the Japanese attacked Pearl Harbor and America was thrust into the war that it somehow managed to stay out of for more than two years. Though the Bears defeated the Packers 33–14 in the playoff, and easily won another championship over the Giants, 37–9, even diehard fans were focused on things other than football. The next few years promised to be challenging ones for the NFL.

ISBELL AND HUTSON SHINE DURING WARTIME

Getting fans to focus on games during the war was the least of the NFL's problems; finding enough warm bodies to fill out team rosters was a bigger issue. By the start of the 1942 season, roughly 100 NFL players were serving in the armed forces. Fifteen Packers from

the 1941 team joined the armed forces, including star running back Clarke Hinkle. In addition, most of the Packers' draft class had been called up for the war. Only 18th-round pick Bob Ingalls, a center from Michigan, made it to the 1942 Packers roster. The war ended up having a long-term effect on the team and the league, with many of its young, talented players lost for good, including 10 of the Packers who departed in 1942. Some drifted away from the game or were physically unable to play again. Others lost their lives on battlefields around the world, including one former Packer, guard Howard "Smiley" Johnson, who was killed on Iwo Jima.

Despite the hardships brought on by the war, the NFL was a business that needed to keep playing games to generate money. Plus, the games were good entertainment for workers committed to the war effort as well as for servicemen putting their lives on the line around the world. Nonetheless, it is safe to say that the quality of entertainment offered by the NFL in 1942 was not up to the standards of previous seasons.

The Packers were fortunate in that many of their offensive weapons remained intact. In the backfield, Tony Canadeo and an unexpected find, rookie fullback Ted Fritsch, led the way. Fritsch was a multi-sport talent: After graduating from little Stevens Point (Wisconsin) State College, he went on to play both professional basketball and baseball, in addition to starring with the Packers.

And then there were Cecil Isbell and Don Hutson, who turned the 1942 season into a year-long passing clinic. Both men shattered existing NFL season records. Hutson caught 74 passes for 1211

1940s-Style Headgear: As these photos attest (showing, from left, Walter Teninga of the University of Michigan, Bobby Layne of the Chicago Bears, and Charles Justice of the University of North Carolina) football helmets were not yet standardized in the 1940s, though it was during this decade that the NFL first required their use. Most remained undecorated, they lacked facemasks, and because many were still made of leather, they provided questionable protection. The Los Angeles Rams were the first pro team to paint their helmets, in 1948. Technology improvements in the 1950s resulted in the use of rigid polymer materials and the addition of facemasks.
All three: Time Life Pictures/Getty Images

On October 27, 1943, Packers coach Curly Lambeau poses with his two top passers—single-wing backs Tony Canadeo (3) and Irv Comp (51)—and leading receiver Don Hutson. With World War II raging, Green Bay was lucky to retain talented players like these (though Canadeo would soon get the call up), but it was not enough to carry the team to the championship game: The Bears narrowly edged the 7–2–1 Packers for the Western Division title.
Bettmann/CORBIS

yards and 17 touchdowns. Isbell completed 146 passes in 268 attempts for 2021 yards and 24 touchdowns. As a result of their firepower, the Packers put 300 points on the board in 11 games—but they needed the scoring, because the porous defense gave up 215 points.

The season opened with a 44–28 loss to the Bears, who seemed unaffected by the fact that coach George Halas had joined the Navy. Chicago went on to dominate opponents en route to a rare undefeated regular season and a third straight trip to the championship game. The Packers, meanwhile, rebounded nicely to win six straight games, and they finished the season in second place behind the Bears with a creditable 8–2–1 record. Chicago, seemingly invincible during the regular season, dropped the title game to the Washington Redskins 14–6.

> **"If [Isbell] had stayed around the NFL, I believe that he would have become the game's most successful passer and his name would be all over the record books."**
> **—Don Hutson, on what would have happened if Cecil Isbell hadn't retired early**

THE WAR EXACTS A TOUGH TOLL ON FOOTBALL

During the off-season, the war continued to exact a harsh toll on the NFL. Cleveland Rams owner Dan Reeves, serving in the armed forces and unable to

devote time to his team, surprised the NFL by asking for a one-year suspension of operations. The league assented and the Ram players were dispersed to other franchises. Frustrated by their inability to find enough talented players, the two Pennsylvania franchises, the Pittsburgh Steelers and Philadelphia Eagles, merged for the 1943 season, becoming the Phil-Pitt Steagles. The resulting NFL consisted of just two four-team divisions, so the league shortened the schedule to only 10 games.

The league made two other significant changes in 1943. First, it moved the annual draft from December to April, the schedule it has followed ever since. Today, the draft has evolved into one of the biggest NFL events of the year, followed by legions of diehard fans looking for a shot of football during the long off-season. The other change was to allow free substitutions for the first time. This change was meant to help make the games easier on the remaining players, many of whom were older or in less-than-stellar physical shape, but the new rule had much broader effects. Free substitution eventually led to the development of separate offensive and defensive platoons and the end of two-way football.

The Packers lost more players to the armed forces and in August, with the season a little more than one month away, Curly Lambeau received an unanticipated two-barreled blast of bad news: Both Don Hutson and Cecil Isbell announced their retirements. Hutson was distracted by the war (his brother was killed in action shortly before the season started) and a growing interest in business management. Isbell claimed he wanted to leave on his own terms, when he was still at his peak, and preferred to quit before Curly forced him to retire. In the end, Hutson changed his mind, but Isbell departed for an assistant coaching position at Purdue.

Many of the names on the 1943 roster are unfamiliar to Packer fans, but the largely unknown group still had a coaching legend telling them how to play football. With Cecil Isbell gone, Tony Canadeo became the team's primary offensive threat (in addition to Don Hutson); he finished the season as the team leader in both passing and rushing. Also making a significant contribution on both offense and defense was back Irv Comp, a future inductee into the team's Hall of Fame.

The Packers tied the Bears in the season opener, won their next two games, then were crushed in Milwaukee by the defending champion Redskins. They rebounded nicely and were still in the hunt for the division title going into a November 7 rematch with the Bears. Chicago won a 21–7 mudfest at Wrigley Field and never looked back en route to another championship. At 7–2–1, the Packers had finished what many might call

a successful season, but four straight second-place finishes to the Chicago Bears were not sitting well with Green Bay fans—or Curly Lambeau. It was time to shake up the status quo in the Western Division.

LAMBEAU LEADS THE PACKERS BACK TO THE TOP

The war dragged on in 1944 and continued to take players away from the NFL. Only 12 of the 330 players drafted actually played for their teams, and more veterans were called up for military duty. The league was increasingly forced to turn to retired players to fill roster spots—Arnie Herber was signed by the Giants. Despite the dearth of available talent, the league actually grew by two teams. The Cleveland Rams returned to action, and to maintain balance, the league granted an expansion franchise to the Boston Yanks. Philadelphia became an independent team again, but the Steelers decided to pair up with the Chicago Cardinals for 1944.

The Packers were not immune to player personnel issues. The biggest loss came when the Army called up Tony Canadeo and stationed him at Fort Bliss in Texas. In the fall, Canadeo was granted leave when his wife gave birth to their first child. During his time at home, Canadeo played in three mid-season games before the Army called him back and eventually sent him over to Europe. With Canadeo unavailable, Irv Comp assumed the passing duties and fed the ball to Don Hutson, who had threatened to retire again but came back for another season of leading the league in receiving.

The best development as far as the Packers were concerned was that the Bears' roster seemed to be raided more aggressively by the armed forces than other teams, and for the first time in years they looked beatable. The Packers did just that during the second week of the season, inflicting a 42–28 drubbing on Chicago at City Stadium, but they lost a November 5 rematch 21–0. Despite the loss, the Packers remained in control of the Western Division and advanced to the championship with an 8–2 record.

In the title game, Green Bay met the New York Giants, led by the revitalized Arnie Herber. Only a month earlier, the Giants had drubbed the Packers 24–0 in their poorest performance of the season. Curly focused on the championship game as never before, running his team through a week of tough practices in Charlottesville, Virginia, to get them ready for the Giants. His preparation delivered the performance he wanted, and the Packers beat the Giants 14–7 in front of 46,016 fans at the Polo Grounds. After the game, the league awarded each Packer $1449 as his share of the gate (compare that to the $68,000 that each Steeler received after winning

Don Hutson set the standard for the modern wide receiver during his eleven years with the Packers. He was tall, fast, and extremely athletic, able to shed defenders with multiple-fake moves and then make spectacular circus catches, as he shows in this demonstration during a 1944 practice. He led the NFL in receptions eight seasons, and in scoring five seasons.
Bettmann/CORBIS

Opposite: Ticket stub for the Packers 1944 NFL championship game against the Giants in New York.
GreenBayAntiques.com/The Oneida Archive

"My right leg isn't quite sure what my left leg is going to do."
—Tony Canadeo

the 2006 Super Bowl), but the money was probably secondary to the thrill of playing pro ball for several men who might not have even made the team under normal circumstances.

THE WAR ENDS BUT THE PACKERS' TROUBLES BEGIN

Though Green Bay fans could not have known it at the time, the 1944 championship was the high-water mark before the start of a long Packers drought. As with everything else in the team's history, the beginning of the end can be traced to Curly Lambeau. In early 1945, no problems were apparent, and in fact, the executive committee rewarded Lambeau by extending his contract through the 1949 season. With this latest taste of success, something may have changed inside the head of Curly Lambeau—maybe he lost his drive to win, maybe his ego finally started to get the better of his common sense. Whatever the reason, 1945 marked the start of a distinct change in his relationship with the Packers and the city of Green Bay—and a decline in the performance of his teams.

As in earlier years, Curly Lambeau's personal life had an impact on his football life. During the off-season, Curly began a relationship with wealthy California socialite, Grace Garland. She was four years older than the 45-year-old Lambeau, owned four different homes on the West Coast, and counted several Hollywood stars among her circle of friends. The couple was married in August 1945, and for the first time, it became apparent that Green Bay was going to be Lambeau's home only during the football season.

With the war finally drawing to a close, a few players started returning from their service commitments, but it was going to be a while before the NFL approached its previous talent level. The war had required the efforts of 638 NFL players, 21 of whom had lost their lives in the conflict. With more players available, Pittsburgh and the Chicago Cardinals ended their association, but the league returned to its 10-team lineup when Brooklyn, winless in 1944, merged itself into the Boston Yanks.

Before the season, Curly Lambeau solved what had become an annual problem when he convinced Don Hutson to come back for one final season, this time as a player-coach. Even at the

age of 32, Hutson was still the team's most potent offensive weapon, as well as the best receiver in the league. Other pieces of the offense, including Irv Comp and Ted Fritsch, were also in place for what should have been a strong run at back-to-back championships.

The season began with tremendous promise, including a victory over the Bears (who were struggling with George Halas still in the Navy) and a 57–21 rout of the Lions in which the Packers set a single-game record for points scored. Yet the Packers could not maintain this momentum and stumbled their way to a 6–4 record, only good enough for third place behind the Rams and Lions. Hutson led the league in receiving again, but he tired as the season progressed and was not much of a factor in the team's final games. As expected, Hutson officially announced his retirement at the end of the season, as did long-time Packers Buckets Goldenberg and Joe Laws. Curly Lambeau had been masterful at rejuvenating his team's talent base, but it would take a miracle to replace one of the greatest players in league history—and Lambeau appeared to be running out of miracles.

A RIVAL CHALLENGES THE NFL

The year 1946 will go down as one of the most significant in National Football League history. Renewed optimism with the end of the war and the return of players to the field was quickly tempered when a new rival league, the All-American Football Conference, started playing in 1946. Few fans today know much about the AAFC, which survived only four years, but it had a lasting effect on the NFL. The AAFC spawned three of the NFL's most-successful franchises: the San Francisco 49ers, the Baltimore (now Indianapolis) Colts, and the Cleveland Browns. It also influenced pro

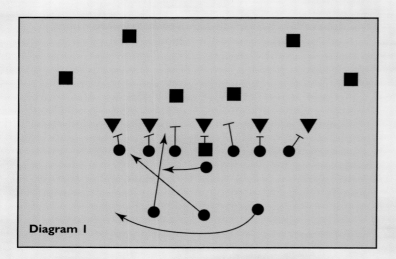

Diagram 1

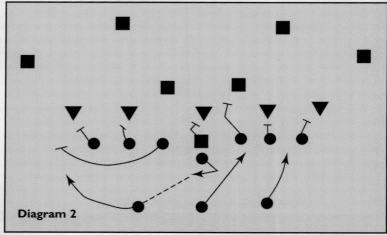

Diagram 2

KEY PLAYS:

RUNNING THE MODERN T FORMATION

When Curly Lambeau abandoned the single wing in favor of the Modern T for his offensive formation in 1947, it was a huge change for the coach—but necessary, because other teams, especially the Bears, were eclipsing the Packers with new offenses. The key to the Modern T was that it put a Packer quarterback directly under center for the first time. While much has been made of how this helped encourage passing, the new formation probably had a greater impact on the running game because it injected two important elements: speed and misdirection. The most basic play out of the Modern T was the dive (Diagram 1). The quarterback (Jack Jacobs for the 1947 Packers) would take the snap, turn, and hand the ball to a halfback (usually Tony Canadeo) charging toward the line. The runner was often through the line before the defense could react; linemen only had to hold their blocks momentarily. Further throwing defenses off balance were fakes and counters. For example, Jacobs might fake the handoff to Canadeo and hand the ball to fullback Ted Fritsch, who followed on the halfback's heels and ran off tackle. For a counter, Jacobs would take the snap, turn, and fake the dive to the right halfback, then pivot and

execute a running play to the left. In the example shown (Diagram 2), Jacobs would fake the dive, pivot, and toss a counter pitch to Canadeo, and the "Gray Ghost" would run a sweep around the left end.

The Packers rushed for more than 2,100 yards after embracing the Modern T formation in 1947; Tony Canadeo (shown here eluding two defenders during a 1941 game) led the way. The "Gray Ghost of Gonzaga" was the Packers' unquestioned offensive leader throughout the 1940s.
Vic Stein/WireImage.com

football in other important ways, including introducing the use of zone defenses and encouraging the participation of African-Americans, who had largely been shut out by the NFL.

The birth of the AAFC forced the NFL into making a geographically significant decision: to allow the Cleveland Rams, fresh off the 1945 NFL championship, to relocate to Los Angeles after the AAFC put teams in both Cleveland and L.A. The NFL did not think the Ohio city could support two pro teams, and it did not want to concede California to this new rival, so it solved two problems with one decision. Despite this franchise-related chess game, the NFL could not stop the AAFC from signing players, both veterans and college draftees, and the rival league became a talent drain nearly as significant as the just-ended war.

In Green Bay, the Packers managed to stave off AAFC attempts to lure away key veterans, but the 49ers signed their first-round draft pick, Marquette's Johnny Strzykalski. In addition, Green Bay's vaunted passing game was crippled thanks to Don Hutson's departure. As a result, in 1946 the team could muster only 841 yards and four touchdowns through the air. With Tony Canadeo back home from Europe, the Packers turned to the running game as never before, but teams knew what to expect when they played the Packers. While most teams were employing new offensive strategies, Curly still relied on the old-fashioned single-wing formation. For the first time in its history, Green Bay gave up more points than it scored—not a formula for football success.

The season opened ominously with a 30–7 drubbing at the hands of the Bears in front of a capacity crowd at City Stadium. Despite an early run of three straight wins, the Packers never scored more than 20 points in a game all season and ended up in third place with a 6–5 record. The resurgent Bears, with George Halas back at the helm, won both the division and the NFL championship. While most of Curly's off-season attention should have been committed to finding the players to keep pace with the Bears, it instead seemed to be increasingly focused on a lodge located 15 miles outside of Green Bay.

THE ROCKWOOD LODGE SAGA BEGINS

Curly Lambeau envisioned Rockwood Lodge as a unique amenity that would improve the Packers; it ended up driving a wedge between Lambeau and members of the Packers executive committee. The beautiful stone lodge, which had 40 rooms and sat on 55 acres northeast of Green Bay, had once been a retreat for the Norbertine Order. Lambeau convinced the executive committee to spend $25,000 to buy the place. His vision was to turn it into the NFL's first

By the time that Don Hutson retired after the 1945 season he had rewritten the record book for NFL receivers. Hutson returned to the Packers' sideline in 1946 as an assistant coach, directing the backs and ends. *Getty Images*

Champions again! The Packers celebrate in the Polo Grounds' locker room after defeating the New York Giants 14–7 to win the 1944 National Football League title. Getting hoisted to shoulder level are two heroes of the game, fullback Ted Fritsch (64) who scored both Green Bay touchdowns, and coach Curly Lambeau, who led his team to the championship over an opponent that had trounced the Packers only a few weeks earlier during the regular season. *Bettmann/CORBIS*

dedicated team headquarters and training center. The Packers invested $8000 in renovations to the main building in addition to constructing six prefab houses intended to house married players and their families throughout the season.

Lambeau's stated intention may have been to provide housing for his ballplayers, but it was his underlying hope that Rockwood would allow him to exert more control over his team. It was also probable that he was trying to physically distance himself from the prying eyes of both the executive committee and the citizens of Green Bay. Curly and Grace redecorated one of the Rockwood houses to serve as their Green Bay home and presented the bill to the team to pay—which set off a firestorm of protest

within the club's finance committee.

While some of the players appreciated the inexpensive housing, many resented Curly's control over their lives thanks to the new arrangement. Plus, the facility was located far enough from Green Bay that they felt isolated from the community and entertainment sources. A more pressing problem experienced at Rockwood was a physical one. The practice field was laid out on thin soil underlain with rock. Players complained about shin splints and nagging leg injuries—to such an extent that the team was soon being bussed back to Green Bay for practice. In retrospect, with most modern NFL teams maintaining dedicated headquarters and practice facilities, Curly's Rockwood experiment looks downright visionary. But

> **"We had to do it. I think the Packers and the Steelers were the last two teams to go to the T-formation ... Although I like Curly as a coach and a person, I think he fell behind in pro football."**
> **—Dick Wildung, Packer lineman, on the 1947 switch to the T-formation**

at the time, the place became a lightning rod for everybody who had a gripe with Curly Lambeau—and in 1947 that group counted some surprising new members.

Throughout 1947, Curly made decisions unrelated to football that made enemies out of many former supporters. In March, he replaced long-time public relations director George Calhoun—the man whose street-corner conversation with Lambeau helped launch the team in 1919—with George Strickler. Sadly, Curly never personally informed Calhoun of the decision; Calhoun discovered his firing while reading a wire-service report on Strickler's hiring. Later that year, Lambeau replaced Dr. W. W. Kelly, one of the "Hungry Five" and influential member of the executive committee, as team physician, a move that shocked many people. Another member of the Hungry Five ended his association with the team in July 1947 when team president Lee Johannes resigned after 18 years in the position. He was exhausted by his increasing conflict with Lambeau.

The board of directors replaced Johannes with Emil Fischer, who most viewed as being even more hostile towards Lambeau. Fischer's first moves were to weaken Lambeau's power by increasing membership of the executive committee and board of directors, and by creating a variety of subcommittees that took over responsibilities previously handled by Lambeau—and with whom the coach/general manager would have to consult before making just about every decision regarding the team apart from which plays to call during the game. Not surprisingly, Lambeau was furious, and as the 1947 season approached, the coach was practically at war with the business leaders that ran the Packer corporation.

Despite these off-field distractions, Curly Lambeau seemed surprisingly focused on winning football games in 1947. And to kick-start the team's anemic offense, Lambeau finally abandoned the old-fashioned single wing for the T formation. Compared to today's multiple-set, misdirection offenses, even the modernized 1940s version of the T seems simplistic and archaic, yet this was a significant change for

Lambeau. The Notre Dame Box and single wing long used by the Packers employed long snaps and runners who doubled as passers. The Modern T employed the direct center-to-quarterback "handoff" snap, enabling quick-hitting dives, counter plays, and play-action passing. The quarterback became the focal point of the offense and needed to be more than just a good passer. He had to be smart, sure-handed, and unflappable, the coach on the field.

For his first quarterback in this new system, Lambeau turned to "Indian" Jack Jacobs, obtained in a trade with the Redskins. The Native American Jacobs was a tremendous athlete who had started his career in 1942 with the Rams. He put up some impressive numbers as the Packers' first true quarterback, passing for 1615 yards and 16 touchdowns. In fact, Curly's embrace of the T seemed to be just the medicine for the Packers' ailing offense and they piled up the points in 1947—274 in total, nearly double the previous season's output. On the ground, Tony Canadeo led the way, but a whole host of backs contributed to more than 2100 yards of rushing. Green Bay started the season in promising fashion, with back-to-back wins over the Bears and Rams.

Despite their offensive ability, this was a young and relatively inexperienced Packers team and they struggled to win close games. A particularly trying four-game stretch at midseason saw Green Bay go 0–3–1 despite the fact that their opponents outscored them by a combined *five* points. The Packers finished the season with a respectable 6–5–1 record, but it could easily have been much better—they had been tantalizingly close to yet another division title. Unfortunately, Curly Lambeau's escalating dispute with the executive committee threatened to undermine the team's efforts to make it back to the top of the NFL.

THE WORST SEASON IN TEAM HISTORY
Even as Curly Lambeau was taking steps to bring his offense up to modern standards, other football coaches were already introducing philosophies that easily eclipsed the T formation. The leading offensive innovator was actually working in the All-American Football Conference: Paul Brown, coach, part owner, and namesake of the Cleveland Browns. Coach Brown's offensive genius forever changed pro football. He used multiple formations that for the first time split the ends, put two halfbacks in flanker positions, and sometimes left the quarterback in the backfield with only a fullback behind him. Instead of having one receiver run a precision timing route (a Don Hutson innovation), Brown sent two or three receivers down the field simultaneously, offering the quarterback multiple targets. And for the first time, Brown

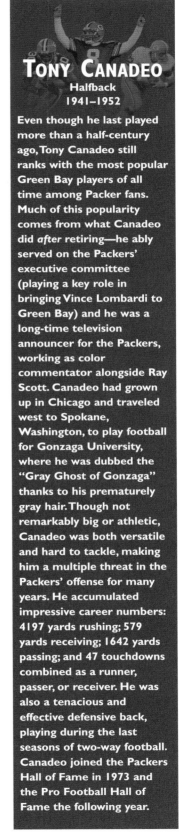

TONY CANADEO
Halfback
1941–1952

Even though he last played more than a half-century ago, Tony Canadeo still ranks with the most popular Green Bay players of all time among Packer fans. Much of this popularity comes from what Canadeo did *after* retiring—he ably served on the Packers' executive committee (playing a key role in bringing Vince Lombardi to Green Bay) and he was a long-time television announcer for the Packers, working as color commentator alongside Ray Scott. Canadeo had grown up in Chicago and traveled west to Spokane, Washington, to play football for Gonzaga University, where he was dubbed the "Gray Ghost of Gonzaga" thanks to his prematurely gray hair. Though not remarkably big or athletic, Canadeo was both versatile and hard to tackle, making him a multiple threat in the Packers' offense for many years. He accumulated impressive career numbers: 4197 yards rushing; 579 yards receiving; 1642 yards passing; and 47 touchdowns combined as a runner, passer, or receiver. He was also a tenacious and effective defensive back, playing during the last seasons of two-way football. Canadeo joined the Packers Hall of Fame in 1973 and the Pro Football Hall of Fame the following year.

During the last game of the 1947 season, the Packers came face to face with the league's top running back—and a harbinger for the future. Steve Van Buren, shown here being tackled by Green Bay's Bruce Smith during the Eagles' 28–14 victory, scored three times and racked up 96 yards on the ground en route to setting a new NFL single-season rushing record with 1,008 yards. The Packers finished the season 6–5–1, but it would be their last record above .500 until 1959. *Bettmann/CORBIS*

employed an offense that moved steadily down the field by completing short passes, rather than using runs for short gains and passes for longer ones.

The Browns were the cream of the AAFC. They had the best quarterback in Otto Graham, two of the best receivers in Mac Speedie and Dante Lavelli, and one of the best running backs in Marion Motley. Over the four-year history of the AAFC, the Browns racked up a regular season record of 47–4–3, and they won all four of the league's championships. But they were

one of few bright spots for the rival league. Despite the fact that, on average, AAFC games actually drew larger crowds than NFL games, the long-term prospects for the AAFC were bleak. Merger talks started—and failed—in late 1948—but it looked likely that at least some of the AAFC teams would soon join the NFL.

In Green Bay at the start of the 1948 season, there was a growing contingent that realized—or feared— the end of the Curly Lambeau era was also near. Despite its new offense and decent record the previous season, the team's overall talent was relatively weak. Only a handful of players remained from the 1944 championship squad and Curly had done a poor job replacing them. The Packers had been hit hard by the AAFC, which had signed many of the team's draft choices, but Lambeau seemed to have no backup plan to offset this lost inflow of talent—other than signing players cut by other teams.

The way Lambeau handled player salaries also undermined the 1948 season. Stung by the AAFC consistently outbidding him, Lambeau was determined to sign his first-round draft choice, Wisconsin's Earl "Jug" Girard. Lambeau got his man, but he had to pay him $10,000 per year—$2,000 more than Tony Canadeo was making. Canadeo and other veterans resented the rich contract, and before the season, he demanded more money. Lambeau stonewalled the halfback and threatened to trade

him. Canadeo gave in, but the dispute hurt team morale—especially when it became clear that the young Girard was not going to make much of a contribution his rookie season.

Lambeau made another stupid salary-related move once the season started. The Packers won two of their first three games, then played poorly in losing to the defending NFL champion Cardinals 17–7. Furious, Curly fined everyone on the team half a game's pay, citing "indifferent play" and hoping that hitting the players in their wallets would motivate them. The ploy worked and the Packers knocked off the Rams the following week 16–0. The players, assuming that Lambeau would reward their spirited performance by paying back the fine from the previous week, were stunned when Curly kept the money. The coach lost his players' respect and never won it back. The team

Packers defensive back Herman Rohrig, a rookie from Nebraska, is swarmed by Chicago Cardinals as he attempts to return a fumble he has just recovered. This action is from the second quarter of the Packers 19–7 victory over the Cardinals on November 10, 1946.
Bettmann/CORBIS

> **"We didn't have much [talent] besides Canadeo....The team was pretty much done and gone with. Nobody said anything about it, but that was the general feeling."**
> **—Earl "Jug" Girard, on the Packers in 1948 and 1949**

lost all its remaining games and finished with a 3–9 record, worst in team history.

Lambeau vowed that the next season would be better, but the executive committee was starting to wonder if that was possible. On top of that, the team's poor play was keeping fans away and the team was again struggling financially. It was starting to look like the Packers' bottom line would be the most challenging opponent facing Curly Lambeau in 1949.

THE SAD FINAL CHAPTER FOR A BRILLIANT COACH

Contrary to Curly Lambeau's optimistic public announcement, 1949 was not better—in fact, it was one of the worst seasons in team history. Though the team's final record was not the worst of all time (the 1958 Packers earned that unfortunate distinction), poor play, combined with constant strife off the field, made 1949 a year that most Green Bay football fans would rather forget. Lambeau's power struggle with the executive committee became more heated than ever, and there was increasing feeling that despite all the good he had done, it might be time to bid Curly farewell. A deadline was looming: Lambeau's contract expired on January 1, 1950. Fans in Green Bay debated amongst themselves whether it should be renewed.

Over the off-season, not much had been done to upgrade the Packers' roster. Lambeau signed his first-round draft pick, quarterback Stan Heath, but Heath became a backup to Jug Girard. Fortunately, Tony Canadeo was still around, playing his heart out. Canadeo would rush for more than 1000 yards in 1949, the season's primary offensive highlight for a team that could score only 114 points. As bad as the offense was, the defense was worse. Packer opponents ran through or passed over them at will, racking up an incredible 329 points.

Curly Lambeau's coaching could not be blamed for the team's poor game performance, because after a season-opening loss to the Bears, Lambeau handed his coaching duties over to three assistants, Bob Snyder, Charley Brock, and Tom Stidham. Lambeau claimed that he was going to focus his time on being general manager, but most thought he was simply trying to

save himself the pain of coaching a losing team. The move was a surprise to both the players and the executive committee, which lost even more confidence in Lambeau.

With their three-headed coaching staff (plus Lambeau as a behind-the-scenes "advisor"), the Packers stumbled to a 2–10 record and last place in the Western Division. With the ugly football on the field, fans stayed away from Packer games (only 5483 showed up for the November 20 game in Milwaukee) and the team's already weak finances went into a tailspin. Curly Lambeau had become a challenge, but dealing with him paled in comparison to the money problems faced by the team. By November, the Packers were $90,000 in debt, and the company needed a quick infusion of $50,000 if it wanted to stay afloat.

Further complicating this dire situation was the impending collapse of the AAFC and a possible merger with the NFL. Some observers thought that NFL commissioner Bert Bell might use a merger to eliminate one or two of the weakest NFL franchises—which now included the Green Bay Packers. Unless the team could prove its long-term financial viability to the league, the NFL might finally have a good reason to shed its remaining small-city franchise.

As with previous financial crises, the team turned to the citizens of Green Bay, embarking on a drive to raise $50,000. The centerpiece of this effort was a Thanksgiving Day intrasquad exhibition game that brought back several stars from the past, including John McNally, Don Hutson, Arnie Herber, and Lavvie Dilweg. Despite a heavy snowstorm, a large crowd was treated to the Blue team, led by Jug Girard, defeating the Gold team, quarterbacked by Stan Heath, 35–31. But on this day, the score was not important. Instead, the event was a celebration of Green Bay football, and of the Packers' special relationship with their fans—who had again come to the team's rescue. Thanks to the event, Green Bay raised cash and pledges in excess of $50,000 and averted its short-term financial crisis.

But as the 1940s drew to a close, there were still many questions to be answered. Would there be a place for them in the new NFL? If yes, what could the team do to secure its long-term financial security? And—most importantly in the eyes of many Green Bay fans—what was Curly Lambeau's future with the team? Answers to all these questions would be coming, and sooner than most people expected.

TED FRITSCH
Fullback
1942–1950

You occasionally hear about two-sport stars among pro athletes, but Ted Fritsch was a true rarity—he played professionally in *three* different sports. Though he achieved his greatest success in football, Fritsch also played pro baseball, reaching the Triple A level with the Toledo Mud Hens, and pro basketball with the Oshkosh All-Stars of the National Basketball League, a predecessor of the NBA. That Fritsch achieved such success was unlikely considering that he was a product of tiny Stevens Point State College (now the University of Wisconsin-Stevens Point). Not surprisingly, Fritsch's athleticism allowed him to do it all for the Packers: his career numbers included 10 interceptions, a 38.6-yard punting average, 170 points scored as a kicker, and a 26.6-yard kick-return average. But Fritsch was best known as a tough fullback and the perfect up-the-middle complement to halfback Tony Canadeo. In that role, Fritsch rushed for 2200 yards and 31 touchdowns. After retiring from the Packers, Fritsch followed a second career as a teacher and coach at Green Bay Premontre (now Notre Dame) High School.

CHAPTER 4

THE 1950S:
ONE COACHING LEGEND DEPARTS, ANOTHER ARRIVES

Snow is a fact of life for Green Bay football, and it has often been the team's ally. Such was the case on November 25, 1950, when Tony Canadeo (3) shrugged off the cold weather on this run while leading the Packers to a 25–21 win over the 49ers.
Vernon Biever/WireImage.com

As 1950 dawned in northeastern Wisconsin, there were many unanswered questions about the future of the Packers. Not only was the team sitting on the league's doorstep, they were in debt, the only coach the team had ever known was no longer under contract and his status was unclear, and the NFL was undergoing dramatic change that threatened to dislodge the team from the league. Despite the fact that Green Bay had rallied behind its team yet again with $50,000 worth of support, many long-time fans wondered if the city had witnessed its final pro football game.

Some of the uncertainty about the 1950s pro football landscape had been resolved on December 9, 1949, when NFL commissioner Bert Bell announced the merger of three All-American Football Conference teams into the elder league. For a time, the new entity was referred to as the "National-American Football League," but that mouthful was eventually scrapped in favor of retaining "the NFL." The three AAFC interlopers could not have been more different. The Cleveland Browns were the dominant team in the rival league, and with their talented roster and innovative offensive philosophy, they threatened to make a mockery of the stodgy NFL. The San Francisco 49ers finished second in the AAFC's last season and gave the NFL another coveted franchise on the West Coast. The addition of the Baltimore Colts was puzzling because they were the AAFC's worst team. Nonetheless, they were championed by Washington Redskins' owner George Preston Marshall, who saw the Colts as the perfect rival for his team—a short, inexpensive road trip away.

With the new pro football league potentially consisting of 13 teams—an unwieldy number for scheduling—rumors circulated that the league was considering paring down to a more manageable dozen teams. In fact, Green Bay was at the center of the debate. With the Packers' shaky finances, their status as the remaining small-city franchise, and the uncertainty surrounding Curly Lambeau, there were league owners who advocated eliminating the franchise. A final decision looked to be a couple of months away, and in the meantime, the team's board of directors needed to resolve things with its legendary coach.

> **"We're not taking a chance on Ronzani, he's taking a chance on us. Hell, he doesn't even know if he is going to get paid."**
> —*Packers executive committee member Lee Johannes*

A FIRE AND A RESIGNATION

Despite its dispute with Lambeau, the board had, in fact, taken steps to keep him around as head coach. At the end of a heated meeting on November 30, 1949, the board voted overwhelmingly to extend his contract by two years. This fact soon became public knowledge, but by late January 1950, Curly had still not signed. Conflicting accounts suggest that the contract was either never presented, or it was presented and Curly rejected it. Regardless of what transpired, Curly Lambeau appeared to be on his way out of Green Bay.

On January 25, 1950, a stunning event seemed to prophesy Lambeau's fate with the team. Rockwood

Lodge—still the Packers training facility, and still a source of controversy—caught fire and burned to the ground. Faulty wiring was cited as the cause. In an ironic twist, the facility in its demise offered the team a much-needed infusion of cash in the form of a $75,000 insurance settlement.

Five days after the fire, the development that many Packer fans had feared—and even five years before would have been unthinkable—finally came to fruition: Curly Lambeau submitted his resignation to Packer president Emil Fisher. Citing a "dangerous disunity of purpose within the corporation," Lambeau walked away from the team that had been the focus of his life for more than 30 years, and said goodbye to the city and fans who had long adored him.

In making his departure from Green Bay, Curly Lambeau was not taking leave of football. The coaching legend had already accepted the position of vice president and head coach with the Chicago Cardinals. The Cardinals had always been the Windy City's number two team, but they had enjoyed a couple of strong seasons after World War II, including the 1947

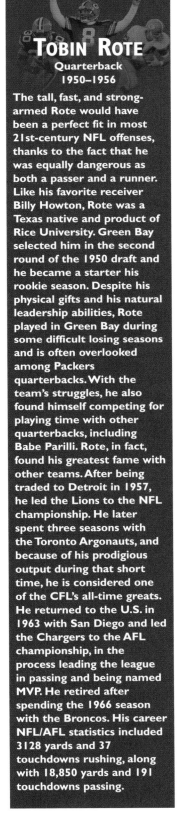

TOBIN ROTE
Quarterback
1950–1956

The tall, fast, and strong-armed Rote would have been a perfect fit in most 21st-century NFL offenses, thanks to the fact that he was equally dangerous as both a passer and a runner. Like his favorite receiver Billy Howton, Rote was a Texas native and product of Rice University. Green Bay selected him in the second round of the 1950 draft and he became a starter his rookie season. Despite his physical gifts and his natural leadership abilities, Rote played in Green Bay during some difficult losing seasons and is often overlooked among Packers quarterbacks. With the team's struggles, he also found himself competing for playing time with other quarterbacks, including Babe Parilli. Rote, in fact, found his greatest fame with other teams. After being traded to Detroit in 1957, he led the Lions to the NFL championship. He later spent three seasons with the Toronto Argonauts, and because of his prodigious output during that short time, he is considered one of the CFL's all-time greats. He returned to the U.S. in 1963 with San Diego and led the Chargers to the AFL championship, in the process leading the league in passing and being named MVP. He retired after spending the 1966 season with the Broncos. His career NFL/AFL statistics included 3128 yards and 37 touchdowns rushing, along with 18,850 yards and 191 touchdowns passing.

The Packers' athletic quarterback Tobin Rote stiff-arms would-be Cleveland tackler Chuck Noll (the future Steelers coach) during the Browns' 41–10 rout of Green Bay on October 23, 1955.
Bettmann/CORBIS

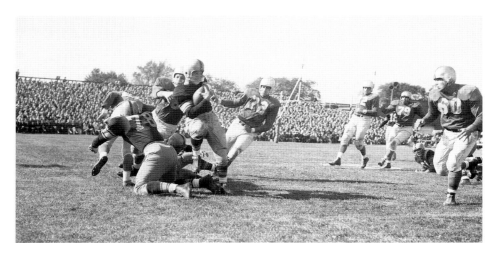

A Green Bay crowd of more than 22,000 watches the Lions bring down Packers halfback Breezy Reid after a six-yard gain during the second quarter of the 1955 season opener between the two teams. The Packers won 20–17, en route to a 6–6 record.
Bettmann/CORBIS

another shot as a head coach with the Redskins but was fired after two largely forgettable seasons. In the 1950s, it seemed that football truly had passed by Curly Lambeau.

ANOTHER STOCK SALE AND A NEW COACH

Back in Green Bay, the team leadership had to act quickly and decisively to convince the NFL hierarchy that the Packers deserved to stay in the league. The two major issues needing to be addressed were getting the franchise's financial house in order and finding a new coach for the team. On the financial front, the Packers moved forward on an idea approved at the November 30, 1949, board meeting: to sell more stock in the team. This would be the third time in team history that the Packers had resorted to a stock sale to raise money. That the public would get behind the maneuver was amazing. Many of the people being asked to pony up had lived through the 1929 market crash and had a natural skepticism of stocks. Furthermore, it was common knowledge that the stock issued would offer little monetary value to investors.

NFL championship. They appeared to be on the verge of falling back into oblivion and hoped that Lambeau could revitalize the franchise. In fact, Lambeau's tenure turned out to be a disaster. After a mediocre first season, the bottom fell out in 1951, and Lambeau—seemingly repeating history—started fighting with Cardinal ownership before finally quitting late in the season. Still living off his past glory, Lambeau earned

Forget monetary value: Fans wanted to keep the Packers in Green Bay, plus they wanted a sense of

Packers rookie running back Veryl Switzer breaks into the open field for a 33-yard gain during the first quarter of a November 7, 1954, contest against the Bears at Wrigley Field. Chicago stopped a last-minute Green Bay drive to hold on for a 28–23 victory.
Bettmann/CORBIS

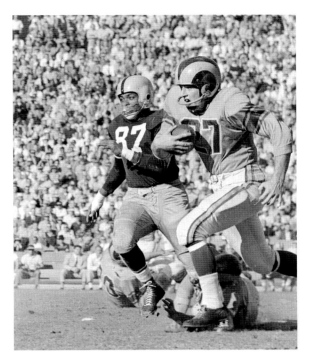

During the 1950s, the Packers finished every season with a road trip to play the NFL's two California teams. They rarely won these games and a December 1955 visit to the L.A. Coliseum proved typical for the decade. When the Rams' Ron Waller raced past Green Bay defensive end Nate Borden for a 55-yard first-quarter touchdown, L.A. was off and running en route to a 31–17 victory. *Bettmann/CORBIS*

ownership in their beloved team. Not surprisingly, the stock sale—at $25 per share—was a success, and the team raised $118,000. The significance of the public investment in the club became more apparent when word got out that in November 1949 Curly Lambeau had approached the Packers board on behalf of four investors who had pledged $200,000 to the team if it was converted to a for-profit corporation. The board, enticed by the money but realizing it would open the door to a future sale of the team to a private entity (that might take the franchise elsewhere), turned down the offer. The board's "no" vote, which in effect was a vote of confidence for public, not-for-profit ownership, was vindicated by the latest stock sale.

The other issue to settle was finding a head coach, and the Packers wasted no time, offering the job (along with the general manager position) to Gene Ronzani less than a week after Lambeau's resignation. The man given the unenviable task of following a legend nonetheless seemed to have all the credentials to succeed. Ronzani was a native of Iron Mountain,

Michigan, located not far north of Green Bay, and he had strong Wisconsin ties, thanks to a brilliant athletic career at Milwaukee's Marquette University, where he was a star in track, basketball, and football. After college, Ronzani signed with the Chicago Bears. He played halfback for the Bears from 1933 to 1938, then joined the team's coaching staff. He was serving as an assistant to George Halas when the Packers offered him their head-coaching job.

With these two critical issues settled, the Packers awaited a March 1950 league meeting to learn their fate. In the end, the support of commissioner Bert Bell and team owners, including—ironically—George Halas, assured the team's future in the league. The memorable meeting established the framework for the new 13-team league, and big changes were in store for pro football. While reasserting itself as "The National Football League," the organization embraced a taste of the AAFC by throwing out divisions and instead breaking itself into National and American "conferences." The Packers became part of the seven-team National Conference. In addition, one old NFL team, the New York Bulldogs was renamed the New York Yanks. That franchise and the New York Giants were given the right to split the players from the AAFC New York Yankees. The rest of the AAFC players were dispersed via a draft. Each team was given 10 draft choices, except for the hapless Colts, who received 15 picks.

Only one important rule change resulted from the meeting, but it forever and dramatically altered the way football was played: Free substitution was again readopted after having been eliminated after World War II. This time, rather than giving a break to aging players, the NFL made the move with one important goal in mind—to open the door to two-platoon football. With the amazing advances in offensive strategy in the postwar years, it was evident that football now demanded separate offensive and defensive units. The league correctly predicted that this would promote greater specialization and more exciting football. The 1950s promised to be a great decade for the NFL.

A POOR START TO THE RONZANI ERA

Gene Ronzani had little respect for the roster built by Curly Lambeau, and he gutted it as the 1950 season approached. His aggressive rebuilding was not a surprise: Curly had not left much talent behind, and to make matters worse, quarterbacks Jack Jacobs and Stan Heath had departed for the Canadian Football League. (Jacobs became a CFL superstar, passing for more than 11,000 yards and 104 touchdowns in five seasons with the Winnipeg Blue Bombers.) Ronzani

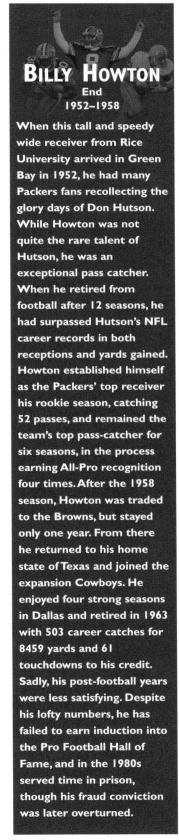

BILLY HOWTON
End
1952–1958

When this tall and speedy wide receiver from Rice University arrived in Green Bay in 1952, he had many Packers fans recollecting the glory days of Don Hutson. While Howton was not quite the rare talent of Hutson, he was an exceptional pass catcher. When he retired from football after 12 seasons, he had surpassed Hutson's NFL career records in both receptions and yards gained. Howton established himself as the Packers' top receiver his rookie season, catching 52 passes, and remained the team's top pass-catcher for six seasons, in the process earning All-Pro recognition four times. After the 1958 season, Howton was traded to the Browns, but stayed only one year. From there he returned to his home state of Texas and joined the expansion Cowboys. He enjoyed four strong seasons in Dallas and retired in 1963 with 503 career catches for 8459 yards and 61 touchdowns to his credit. Sadly, his post-football years were less satisfying. Despite his lofty numbers, he has failed to earn induction into the Pro Football Hall of Fame, and in the 1980s served time in prison, though his fraud conviction was later overturned.

Above: **The Packers' Len Szafaryn gives it his all trying to block a San Francisco punt, but ends up missing the ball and landing on his head. The team fared better during this December 4, 1955, contest at Kezar Stadium, beating the 49ers 28–7 and earning a rare Green Bay victory on the West Coast.**
Bettmann/CORBIS

Above right: **Bob Mann—shown making a spectacular one-handed grab for a touchdown—was the first African-American to play for the Packers. He was one of the team's top receivers from 1951 to 1953. After football, the University of Michigan graduate went on to a long and successful career as a lawyer.**
Pro Football Hall of Fame/WireImage.com

turned to the AAFC dispersal draft and the college draft to rebuild the team, and he had some success with his picks.

Halfback Billy Grimes of the Los Angeles Dons was the Packers' top prize in the AAFC draft, and he went on to lead the team in rushing in 1950. The college draft yielded one player of note: quarterback Tobin Rote of Rice University. The lanky Texan was as effective running the ball as he was passing, and he was a natural leader. Though he had strong years with the Packers, Rote's greatest success came with other teams when he lead the Lions to the 1957 NFL championship and the San Diego Chargers to the 1963 American Football League title, while also being named AFL most valuable player.

The Gene Ronzani era began on a sour note when the Detroit Lions humiliated the Packers 45–7 in the 1950 season opener. The highlight of the day was the Packers' new green-and-gold uniforms, which replaced the traditional blue-and-gold colors that the team had worn for all but two years of play. The Lions exposed Green Bay's porous defense: The 1950 team yielded nearly 34 points per game, easily the highest per-game average in Packer history. The Packers won their next two games and were tied for first place, but that was the high point of the season. They won only once more en route to a 3–9 record and a fifth-place finish. The

league title went to the newcomer Cleveland Browns, who found play in the NFL tougher than the AAFC, but still prevailed over the Rams 30–28 in one of the most exciting championship games ever played.

In 1951 Gene Ronzani looked to his passing game to turn around Packer fortunes. In Tobin Rote, he thought he had the quarterback to get the job done, though he also obtained Bobby Thomason from the Rams as a second option. The team's breakout receiver turned out to be a player added to the roster late in 1950. Bob Mann was a fine athlete and a quiet, unassuming man, but he was both an unlikely star and a source of great controversy in Green Bay—because he was the first African-American to play for the Packers. Mann had starred at the University of Michigan and led the Detroit Lions in receiving in 1949. With the 1951 Packers, Mann caught 50 passes, including eight for touchdowns. After his career was cut short by a knee injury, Mann earned his law degree and enjoyed a successful 30-year career as a Detroit attorney.

Ronzani continued his roster makeover, but the escalating Korean War created new problems for the NFL. Though the impacts on league talent were not as significant as those experienced during World War II, many players were called up for active duty and many college players were forced to delay their pro careers. The Packers lost five veterans to the war effort, and

Ronzani altered his draft strategy and tried to avoid picking players likely headed to the military. As a result, 1951's crop of rookies was pretty weak.

The Packers made a decent start in the 1951 season, standing at 3–2 after five weeks. The passing attack was particularly effective, with Rote and Thomason combining for 2846 yards and 29 touchdowns. But the emphasis on the pass was countered by a downturn in the Packers' running game, and the defense was only marginally improved over the previous season, yielding 375 points. Yes, the Packers were better in Year 2 of the Ronzani era—but not much better. A seven-game losing streak to end the season dropped them to a second straight 3–9 record. The Packer faithful had saved their team, but they seemed to be a long way from earning a reward for their loyalty.

THE PACKERS SHOW IMPROVEMENT

Even with its rival vanquished and the popularity of pro football growing dramatically, the National Football League in 1952 remained an ever-changing landscape populated by teams with tenuous futures. One franchise—the Baltimore Colts—had died after the 1950 season, leaving the league with 12 teams. In 1952, the New York Yanks, after losing an eight-year battle as the Big Apple's Number Two team, were sold and the franchise moved to Dallas. The aptly re-named Texans became the Lone Star State's first pro football team, but the move proved a disaster. Crowds were sparse at Dallas home games and by midseason the Texans had become a full-time road team headquartered in

Hershey, Pennsylvania. The franchise folded after the season—the last time an NFL team went out of business.

Also changing the NFL was an influx of talent via the college draft. Historians look back on the 1952 draft as one of the best in league history. It introduced a memorable batch of new stars to the league, including future Hall of Famers Frank Gifford, Hugh McElhenny, Gino Marchetti, and Bill George. The draft was also a good one for the Packers, providing the best injection of impact players that the team had seen in years. Five of the players picked by Green Bay in 1952 eventually went on to become Pro Bowlers: Vito "Babe" Parilli, Bill Howton, Bobby Dillon, Joel David Hanner, and Deral Teteak. All made significant contributions to the Packers in their rookie season.

In making Babe Parilli his first-round pick, Gene Ronzani suggested that he still did not have complete confidence in Tobin Rote. Parilli had been a star quarterback at Kentucky, where he played for Bear Bryant. Billy Howton was a speedy receiver from Rice University who to some fans represented the second coming of Don Hutson. Of course, Howton was not quite as gifted as Hutson, but starting in 1952, he led the team in receiving for six seasons. Hanner, Dillon, and Teteak became defensive stalwarts. Linebacker Teteak was undersized at 5-feet, 10-inches and 210 pounds, but he was a fierce hitter who spent six productive seasons in Green Bay. Safety Bobby Dillon was blind in one eye, but he had no trouble finding the football while playing in pass coverage. He grabbed 52 interceptions during eight stellar seasons as a Packer. "Hawg" Hanner (so nicknamed by his teammates as a

Above: **Packers kicker (and fullback) Fred Cone attempts a field goal from the hold of Tobin Rote during Green Bay's October 23, 1955, game at Cleveland. The Browns** manhandled the Packers 41–10 and went on to win the NFL championship, their third of the decade. *Bettmann/CORBIS*

BOBBY DILLON
Safety
1952–1959

Defensive back Bobby Dillon was a terror to opposing quarterbacks and receivers during the 1950s, and he still ranks as Green Bay's career leader in interceptions with 52—despite the fact he was blind in one eye. Dillon was born in Temple, Texas, and played his college ball for the Texas Longhorns, earning All-American status. The Packers selected him in the third round of the 1952 draft, in the middle of a gifted run of four picks that included Babe Parilli, Billy Howton and Dave Hanner. The tenacious Dillon was in the starting lineup his rookie season, often assigned to cover the opponent's top receiver. The following year he led the league in interceptions (9) and was named All-Pro despite missing the last two games with a knee injury. Earlier in the 1953 contest in which he was hurt, Dillon had punished Detroit—and tied a single-game NFL record—with four interceptions. When he retired in 1959 after nine seasons, Dillon had led the team in interceptions for seven of those years and been named All-Pro seven times.

tribute to his Arkansas Razorback roots) was a fixture at defensive tackle for 13 seasons. In all, Hanner was part of the Packers organization for 44 years, staying on as an assistant coach and scout after his playing days.

Thanks to this talented crop of rookies, the Packers were much more competitive in 1952. They lost to the Bears in the season opener but rebounded for a particularly satisfying victory over Curly Lambeau's Redskins. After a fourth-quarter collapse and loss to the Rams (who scored 24 points in the final 12 minutes), the young team responded with a four-game winning streak. Green Bay found itself in playoff contention with three games left on the schedule, but three convincing losses left the team at 6–6 and in fourth place in the National Conference. Still, progress had been made. With its crop of young stars, Green Bay fans had reason to be optimistic about the upcoming 1953 season.

A NEW STADIUM...IN MILWAUKEE

The Packers' 1953 season opened with a landmark event: The debut of professional football in brand-new Milwaukee County Stadium. The Packers for many years had played their Milwaukee games at State Fair Park, then in 1952 moved to tiny Marquette Stadium, which could only hold 15,000 fans.

Though the Packers welcomed the move to County Stadium, the facility was not built with football in mind. Milwaukee wanted to be part of Major League Baseball and the publicly financed stadium was built to lure prospective teams. The plan worked. Just three weeks before the start of the 1953 baseball season, the Boston Braves relocated to the Beer City. Milwaukee loved its Braves, rewarding the team with record-setting attendance for three years running. And the team returned the favor, winning the 1957 World Series. Then as quickly as the love affair had blossomed, the relationship between team and fans chilled. The Braves lost, fans stayed away, and in 1966 the franchise relocated to Atlanta. Such is the impermanent world of professional sports.

The Packers (who ended up playing in County Stadium a lot longer than the Braves) were rewarded with an increase in Milwaukee attendance. Initially, the stadium could hold only 36,000 fans, but it had an eventual football capacity of just over 55,000. Though it was a vast improvement over previous Milwaukee facilities, County Stadium was not particularly accommodating to football. The gridiron was wedged tightly into the expanse from the third base line to right field, sitting at odd angles relative to the stands. The infield dirt ran through one corner of the football field and the right-field warning track dominated one

end zone. Oddly, both teams' benches were located on the same side of the field, occupying what in the summer were left and center fields.

The Cleveland Browns, fresh off a 17–7 loss to Detroit in the 1952 championship game, were the Packers' opponent in their County Stadium debut. The Browns gave Green Bay a glimpse of how the season would progress by pummeling the Packers 27–0. The result stunned many fans, who had no reason to think that the 1953 Packers would not at least equal the previous season's performance.

Part of the Packers' optimism was fueled by what looked to be another decent crop of draftees, highlighted by three future Pro Bowlers. Roger Zatkoff played defensive line at Michigan but excelled as a linebacker in four years with the Packers. Bill Forester, a third round pick from SMU, was also a defensive lineman whose career blossomed when switched to linebacker in 1957. The third member of the trio was a future Pro Football Hall of Famer. Center Jim Ringo was one of the NFL's all-time most durable players, at one stretch starting 182 straight games. He played 11 seasons with the Packers and then was traded to the Philadelphia Eagles, for whom he played through 1967.

As the 1953 season progressed, it became evident that things had gone terribly wrong with the Packers. The defense took a big step backward, giving up yards and points generously, and the offense floundered, particularly through the air. Neither Tobin Rote or Babe Parilli was effective at quarterback, and the team couldn't put points on the board, scoring but 200 during the season. The Packers won two games, but both were over the resurrected Baltimore Colts, actually a new team created from the ruins of the Dallas Texans.

The end came for Gene Ronzani with two games remaining on the schedule. After the Lions humbled the Packers 34–15 on Thanksgiving Day, the executive committee demanded and received Ronzani's resignation. Assistant coaches Ray "Scooter" McLean and Hugh Devore were tabbed to run the team. The Packers finished with back-to-back blowout losses on the West Coast at the hands of the 49ers and Rams. The Gene Ronzani era had lasted four years (only 27 years short of Curly Lambeau's tenure), and his primary success seemed to be proving true the old saying about it being tough to replace a legend.

BLACKBOURN TAKES THE REINS

Leadership roles in the NFL have evolved throughout the league's history, though the evolution has not always been linear—or logical, for that matter. In the early days, teams were often run by one person who did almost everything: play, coach, recruit and sign players, set up schedules, manage business affairs, and so on. The prototypes for this role included George Halas and Curly Lambeau. But as the league matured, the labor required to run a team grew exponentially. To stay competitive, some teams decided to break business management apart from coaching by creating standalone general manager positions.

The Packers' executive committee was wrestling with this issue as it considered its next coach. Gene Ronzani had held the dual titles of general manager and coach and failed. Thinking that it was time to separate the two jobs, the committee hired former Packer star Verne Lewellen as the team's first general manager and filled its coaching vacancy with Marquette University head coach Lisle Blackbourn.

Blackbourn had been a star at Lawrence University in Appleton, Wisconsin (a short drive from Green Bay), but he never played pro ball. Instead, he went into coaching and became a legend in the prep ranks, leading Milwaukee Washington High School to an amazing 22-year record of 141–30–6. After serving as a college assistant for a few years, Blackbourn was named the head man at Marquette. His teams compiled an unspectacular four-year record of 18–17–4.

Blackbourn was a curious choice for the position. Though his Wisconsin roots were a strong selling point, his lack of pro experience put him at a sharp disadvantage. One explanation for choosing Blackbourn may have been that the executive committee wanted to avoid hiring a coach with strong ties to another pro team. Gene Ronzani's long history

> **"It just wouldn't have been appropriate if we hadn't won."**
> **—Billy Howton, after the Packers beat the Bears in the first game at the new City Stadium**

with the Bears had actually undermined his relationship with veteran Packers who had little respect for their Chicago rivals.

Despite his weak pro-game credentials, Lisle Blackbourn was considered a fair judge of football talent and, in fact, stayed on with the Packers as a scout after his coaching days. Blackbourn drafted some of the men who blossomed into stars under future coach Vince Lombardi, but his first and most important draft yielded few reinforcements. The only notable addition was fifth-round pick Max McGee, who was a leading receiver for the Packers over the course of 12 seasons. McGee became one of the most popular Packers of all time, especially after his star performance off the bench led the team to victory in the first Super Bowl, and because he became a longtime Packers radio broadcaster.

Though he hit with his pick of Max McGee (who caught nine touchdowns in his rookie campaign), Blackbourn missed with a much-ballyhooed trade that sent Babe Parilli and a high draft pick to Cleveland for four promising players, none of whom made a contribution. With the trade, Tobin Rote became the

Packers defensive back Doyle Nix fights off a blocker as he pursues 49ers running back Hugh McElhenny (a future Hall of Famer) during Green Bay's December 4, 1955, game in San Francisco. The stiff Packers defense limited the 49ers to a single first quarter touchdown en route to a 28–7 victory.
Bettmann/CORBIS

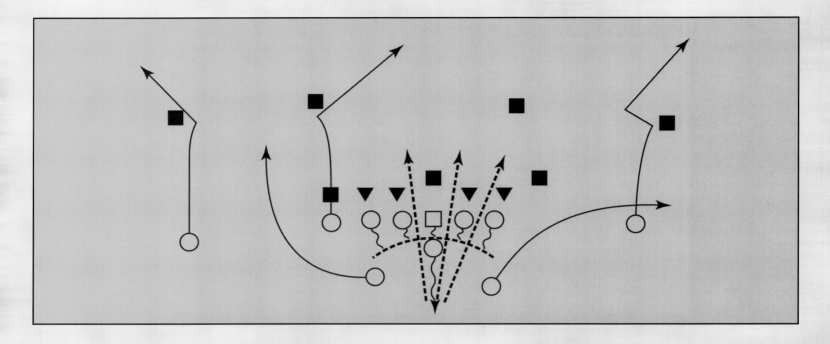

KEY PLAYS:

TOBIN ROTE AND THE QUARTERBACK DRAW

During the 1950s, the gutsy play of Tobin Rote was a notable bright spot during an otherwise bleak period of Green Bay football. Rote looked a lot like a 21st-century quarterback. He was big (6-feet, 3-inches and 211 pounds) and just as dangerous running the ball as he was passing. The Packers took advantage of this fact by making effective use of the quarterback draw. Bart Starr (who, during his rookie season, was Rote's backup) described Rote as the best he ever saw at running the play. The key to the quarterback draw's success was first selling the pass. The Packer offense lined up in a pass formation and on the snap, Rote backpedaled as if he was going to throw. The linemen pass-

blocked and the ends and backs took off on a variety of pass routes. Sending out the multiple receivers accomplished two goals: To further convince the opposition that a pass was coming; and to pull the defensive backfield away from the line of scrimmage and the center of the field (note that most of the "receivers" are running outside routes). When Rote finished his drop, he had a split second to read the field. If the defense was still "cheating" for a run, he would often fake a pass. But if there was an opening, Rote would immediately tuck the ball and take off running. As the diagram shows, Rote had an option to choose whatever route out of the pocket offered him the most daylight.

primary quarterback and responded with a gritty season that included 14 touchdowns passing and eight touchdowns rushing. The defense was also improved, yielding only 251 points, but the 1954 Packers were usually overmatched. Still, they played hard and remained competitive for most of the year. After reaching a mark of 4–4, the team stumbled through the end of the season (including their annual road trip to California) to finish 4–8. The Packers had improved over the previous season—but not much, and the club

was facing more challenges unrelated to performance on the field.

THE PUSH TO REPLACE CITY STADIUM

When City Stadium opened in 1925, it was the envy of the league. By 1955, it was the laughingstock of the NFL. Its decrepit wooden bleachers and inadequate toilet and locker room facilities were only part of the problem. It was also small, which only emphasized the fact that the Packers were a small-town team. Though

NFL stadiums in the 1950s were a far cry from the luxurious facilities teams occupy today (and many teams were sharing stadiums built primarily for baseball), several had the capacity to hold impressive crowds. In fact, both Los Angeles and Cleveland played in stadiums that could accommodate more than 70,000 fans.

The opening of Milwaukee County Stadium only exacerbated Green Bay's problems with City Stadium. Now the Packers were playing two or three of their six home games in a legitimate major league facility. Opposing teams preferred playing in Milwaukee; the stadium was better, the trip was easier, and the city was a fun place to visit. The league started taking notice of the disparity between the two Packer venues. The question became clear to NFL leadership—why was this team still located in Green Bay?

The NFL and its owners approached the team in 1955 with an ultimatum: Build a new stadium, or the league would force the franchise to relocate to Milwaukee. For the executive committee, dominated by Green Bay businessmen, moving the franchise was not an option. They also realized the team did not have the funds to build a new stadium. That meant the Packers would once again have to ask the people of Green Bay to empty their pockets to help the team. And considering the Packers' performance in recent years, this was not the best time to ask the city to bail out what had become a truly mediocre team.

The 1955 Packers did not offer any indication they would be giving fans a lot to cheer about. The team did

"The [1958] Packers underwhelmed ten opponents, overwhelmed one, and whelmed one."
—Sportswriter Red Smith describing Green Bay's 1–10–1 season

not appear to improve itself—in fact, it appeared to have taken a big step backward when it was learned that rookie receiving sensation Max McGee would be lost for two seasons while he fulfilled his military obligation as an Air Force pilot. The draft yielded a group of largely forgettable picks. Fortunately, several veterans stepped up their games and made the season interesting. Again, Tobin Rote led the way on offense, using both his arm and his legs to account for 22 touchdowns. Billy Howton remained the Packers' leading receiver, but second-year end Gary Knafelc had a breakout season, catching a team-high eight touchdowns. Third-year halfback Howie Ferguson rushed for 859 yards, the best performance by a Packer back since Tony Canadeo's 1000-yard season in 1949.

The Packers thrilled City Stadium fans the first two weeks of the season with a last-minute victory over Detroit—thanks to a Rote-to-Knafelc touchdown pass—followed by a 24–3 humbling of the Bears. After that, the Packers' season was a roller-coaster ride that included a three-game losing streak followed by another pair of wins. Green Bay finally won a game played in California (a 28–7 victory over the 49ers),

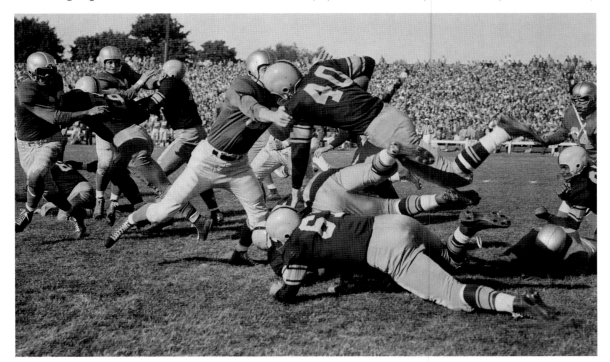

Green Bay's Joe Johnson returns a third quarter punt during the 1955 season opener at City Stadium against the defending conference champs, the Detroit Lions. When Tobin Rote's touchdown pass to Gary Knafelc secured a last-minute upset victory, Packers fans stormed the field in celebration.
Bettmann/CORBIS

A review of the 1956 draft list reveals the real highlights of the year for the Packers were several new players who were bound for greatness. The picks included tackle Forrest Gregg, tackle Bob Skoronski, end Hank Gremminger, and little-known Alabama quartback Bart Starr in the 17th round. All four men would play key roles for championship teams and end up in the Packers Hall of Fame. In addition, Gregg and Starr would both be inducted at Canton and serve as Packer head coaches.

As the Packers struggled to return to greatness, the NFL was enjoying unparalleled success. A prime factor in the game's rise was the spread of television. In 1956, CBS started broadcasting regular-season games to selected parts of the country. Another reason for the growth was exciting and competitive play. For the first time since they joined the NFL in 1950, Cleveland missed out on the championship game when the 1956 contest featured two old-time NFL mainstays, the Giants and the Bears, with the Giants prevailing 47–7. New York's dominating offense was directed by a highly regarded assistant coach, Vince Lombardi. The Brooklyn native was itching for his first head-coaching opportunity … but that was still a few years away.

CHRISTENING A SHRINE TO PRO FOOTBALL

The 1957 season began on a tremendous high note for the Packers. On September 29, the team christened Green Bay's new City Stadium with all the pomp and circumstance appropriate for such an important event. There was a Saturday night fireworks display, a pre-game parade, and appearances by a host of visiting dignitaries, including Miss America, James Arness (Marshall Dillon on television's *Gunsmoke*), and Vice-President Richard Nixon. The packed house (short of capacity thanks to 18 reported no-shows) was entertained by a hard-fought 21–17 victory over the Bears. Unfortunately, the season went downhill from there.

This was something of a new-look Packers team, as Blackbourn had reshaped the roster with three major trades and the college draft. Tobin Rote, who had talked about retirement, was sent to the Lions, while Babe Parilli was retrieved from the Browns. In the end, young Bart Starr emerged as the primary quarterback. Former Lion Don McIlhenny became the leading rusher, but a promising rookie from Notre Dame, Paul Hornung, looked to be the team's back of the future. Hornung had been the Heisman Trophy winner and the first overall pick in the draft. Receiver Ron Kramer was the Packers' other significant addition from the draft.

Above: **When Vince Lombardi arrived in Green Bay before the 1959 season, the Packers were immediately transformed. Unlike his nice-guy predecessor Scooter McClean, Lombardi was fiery and determined to win—as this image of the coach sharing his opinions with a referee during a 1959 game reveals.**
Robert Riger/Getty Images

Far right: **Images of Vince Lombardi patrolling the sidelines in his trademark hat, tie, and overcoat have become an essential part of Packers history. Shown during November 1959 in his first season with the Packers, the coach wears his traditional serious "game face"—smiles were only seen after big victories, many of which were on tap in the years ahead.**
Robert Riger/Getty Images

but the best they could muster was a 6–6 record, good for third place in the Western Conference. Nonetheless, the performance was enough to create a sense of guarded optimism.

In 1956, the Packers' leadership effectively rode this small wave of optimism in presenting their plans for a new stadium to the citizens of Green Bay. They made it clear that without a replacement for City Stadium, the NFL was going to take away pro football. The message was effective and on April 3 Green Bay citizens responded by passing a bond-issue referendum to finance a new stadium. More than 70 percent of voters supported the measure (and an increase in their taxes). The new facility would cost just under a million dollars, hold 32,150 fans, and open in time for the 1957 season. The only thing needed to give the story an especially happy ending was a winning football team. That detail ended up being the most difficult part of the plan to fulfill.

Despite the hint of promise showed the previous year, 1956 turned out to be a forgettable season for Lisle Blackbourn's Packers. Tobin Rote and Billy Howton did their part, leading the league in passing and receiving, respectively, but the defense rarely stopped the opposition in yielding more than 28 points per game. The Packers lost all their games at City Stadium in its final year en route to a 4–8 record and a fifth-place finish.

"We're not just going to start with a clean slate. We're going to throw the old slate away."
—Vince Lombardi

After its opening victory, the Packers could never get back on track and ended up posting a disappointing 3–9 record. The team was back on the bottom of the conference looking up at the other five teams. Even the once-lowly Colts had been making steady improvement and finished with a winning record. The Packers executive committee had seen enough of Lisle Blackbourn, even though he had another year remaining on his contract. He was fired in January 1958. For Blackbourn's replacement, the executive committee turned to a trusted insider and one of the most popular men in Green Bay, long-time assistant coach Ray "Scooter" McLean.

Scooter McLean had enjoyed a solid eight-year pro career as a backup halfback for the Bears and then became the head coach at Lewis College before hiring on as an assistant with the Packers. Players loved McLean. He was low-key and considered "one of the guys." These were fine attributes for an assistant, but not for a head coach. Despite their decision, the

executive committee might have had some concerns—they only offered McLean a one-year contract.

Even with its gleaming new stadium, Green Bay had become the joke of the league, a place to which players on other clubs were threatened with banishment if they broke team rules or underperformed on the field. David Maraniss, in his wonderful Vince Lombardi biography *When Pride Still Mattered*, noted that at this time Green Bay was jokingly referred to as "the salt mines of Siberia" by other teams in the league.

In his single season as head coach, Scooter McLean did nothing to change this reputation—in fact, his tenure only reinforced the belief among NFL owners that Green Bay was the worst franchise in the league. There were few highlights in 1958 as the hapless Packers stumbled their way through the worst season in team history to finish with a 1–10–1 record. Fans were up in arms over the disgusting performance and relatively new team president Dominic Olejniczak was hung in effigy in downtown Green Bay. Not surprisingly, he forced McLean to resign. Worse than the ire of the fans were new rumblings from the NFL that the Packers needed to get their house in order. The team needed a proven winner to turn them around and save the franchise. Enter Vince Lombardi.

JOEL DAVID "DAVE" HANNER

Defensive Tackle
1952–1964

A product of the Packers' gifted 1952 draft (he was picked in the fifth round), Dave Hanner enjoyed a stellar career as a Packers player, followed by a long stint as an assistant coach and several years as a scout for the team. Hanner served in some capacity with the Packers for an amazing 44 years, a tenure that few people can match. Hanner played college ball for the Arkansas Razorbacks—the source of his "Hawg" nickname—and was an All-Pro defensive tackle by his second season. At 6-feet, 2-inches, and weighing somewhere in excess of 270 pounds, Hanner was one of the biggest players of his time. Despite his personal success, the 1950s were a tough time to play for the woeful Packers—until Vince Lombardi arrived in 1959. After just two days of the new coach's first training camp, Hanner lost 18 pounds and had to be hospitalized with sunstroke. The stiff regimen was worth it—Hanner slimmed down to 250 pounds and went on to play some of the best football of his life. He and Henry Jordan were arguably the best tackle tandem in the league and played key roles on Green Bay's 1961 and 1962 championship teams. Lombardi invited Hanner onto the coaching staff after he retired in 1964. Hanner later served as the Packers' defensive coordinator in the 1970s.

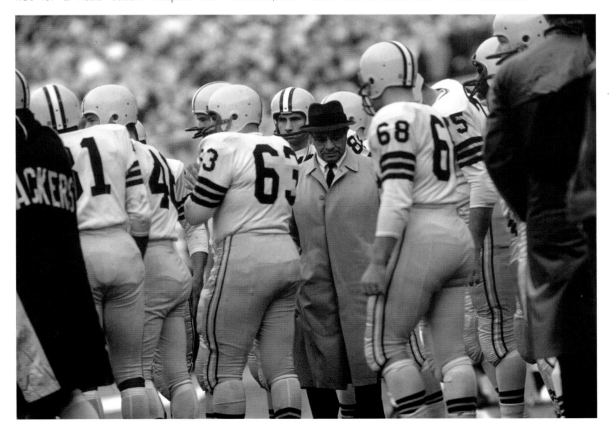

"WHO THE HELL IS VINCE LOMBARDI?"

When Vince Lombardi took over as Packers coach in 1959 he traded for the Giants' veteran defensive back Emlen Tunnell, who had played in New York while Lombardi was an assistant. Tunnell proved an invaluable leader for the young Packers. In 1967 Tunnell became the first African-American elected to the Pro Football Hall of Fame.
Bettmann/CORBIS

In February 1959, 45-year-old Vincent Thomas Lombardi became the man to whom the Packers' board handed the future of Green Bay's pro football franchise. But outside of the New York City area, he was little known—one Packer board member famously asked "Who the hell is Vince Lombardi?" when the Giants assistant was suggested for consideration for the Green Bay job. Despite limited head-coaching experience, Lombardi had been a winner during every stop in his football career. As a lineman at Fordham University, he had been one of the school's celebrated "Seven Blocks of Granite." As a high school coach, he turned Englewood, New Jersey's St. Cecilia into a prep powerhouse. At the United States Military Academy, he was offensive line coach for the legendary Red Blaik. And as offensive coordinator in New York, he had helped direct the Giants to the NFL championship.

The marriage between the New Yorker and the small Wisconsin city seemed an odd one, but there were several factors that helped make the arrangement work. The devoutly Catholic Lombardi felt very much at home in heavily Catholic Green Bay and that fact contributed to his quick acceptance by fans. There was also money—the job offered Lombardi a big raise and Green Bay's low cost of living allowed him a very comfortable life. Most importantly, the job promised the power and autonomy that Lombardi craved. The Packers' board and executive committee represented an odd management structure, and the team had the look of a rudderless, sinking ship. Out of desperation, Lombardi was offered the titles of general manager and coach and promised control of the team. Shortly after his hiring, Lombardi told the executive committee, "I want it understood that I am in complete command around here." Things had changed in Green Bay.

The Packer players sensed that change from the first day of training camp. Yes, Lombardi was loud and relentless in his verbal assault on his new team, but everyone sensed—for the first time in years—purpose behind the coach's words. Lombardi's drive was the missing ingredient for what, despite its terrible record, looked to be one of the most talented squads in the league. The previous year's draft, for example, included guard Jerry Kramer, fullback Jim Taylor, and linebacker Ray Nitschke, the latter pair future Pro Football Hall of Famers. The credit for the teams' assemblage of talent went to the Packers' brilliant scout, Jack Vainisi, who had created an effective information-gathering network for assessing college players.

Despite the talent base, Lombardi remade the roster by waiving and trading aging stars and replacing them with talent from other teams. Guard Fred "Fuzzy" Thurston, defensive tackle Henry Jordan, and defensive back Emlen Tunnell were notable additions. With the players he wanted assembled, Lombardi introduced a relatively simple offensive scheme and focused the Packers on discipline and execution.

The Green Bay team that took the field at City Stadium for the 1959 opener was not the same one that had embarrassed fans in 1958. The Packers stunned the Bears 9–7, and followed up with two more wins, over the Lions and 49ers. Yet, this was still not a championship-caliber team and the Packers stumbled to five straight losses. Toward the end of that run, Lombardi reinstalled Bart Starr as his starting quarterback, replacing veteran Lamar McHan, who had been obtained from Chicago. That move, along with

"I feared Lombardi more than any defensive end or linebacker I ever played against. I only had to deal with those guys once or twice a year. I saw Lombardi every day."
—*Gary Knafelc*

the fact that many of the team's young players began to understand and embrace their roles with confidence, ignited a five-game winning streak to close out the season. The Packers' 7–5 record was only good enough for a tie for third place, but it was the team's first winning campaign since 1947. Vince Lombardi was awarded Coach of the Year honors for his performance, but 7–5 was not good enough in his mind. Thanks to Lombardi's drive, and his players' growing confidence, it appeared the 1960s might be a special decade for the Packers—very special, indeed.

Bart Starr is considered by some the greatest quarterback of all time, but he struggled to earn the Packers' starting job during his first years with the team. It was not until midway through the 1960 season that Lombardi made Starr his starter—one of his best decisions as Green Bay coach.
Bettmann/CORBIS

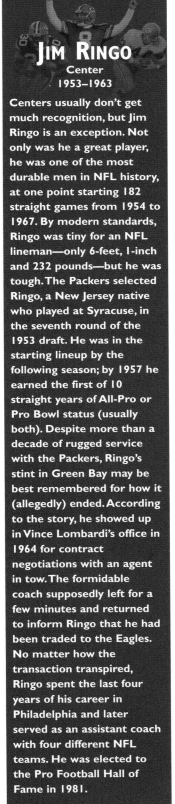

JIM RINGO
Center
1953–1963

Centers usually don't get much recognition, but Jim Ringo is an exception. Not only was he a great player, he was one of the most durable men in NFL history, at one point starting 182 straight games from 1954 to 1967. By modern standards, Ringo was tiny for an NFL lineman—only 6-feet, 1-inch and 232 pounds—but he was tough. The Packers selected Ringo, a New Jersey native who played at Syracuse, in the seventh round of the 1953 draft. He was in the starting lineup by the following season; by 1957 he earned the first of 10 straight years of All-Pro or Pro Bowl status (usually both). Despite more than a decade of rugged service with the Packers, Ringo's stint in Green Bay may be best remembered for how it (allegedly) ended. According to the story, he showed up in Vince Lombardi's office in 1964 for contract negotiations with an agent in tow. The formidable coach supposedly left for a few minutes and returned to inform Ringo that he had been traded to the Eagles. No matter how the transaction transpired, Ringo spent the last four years of his career in Philadelphia and later served as an assistant coach with four different NFL teams. He was elected to the Pro Football Hall of Fame in 1981.

THE 1960S: LOMBARDI CREATES THE NFL'S GREATEST DYNASTY

The 1960s were a watershed decade for professional football. Starting with a flourish in 1960, the sport enjoyed unprecedented growth by adding more teams, attracting more fans, and taking in more money than ever before. For the first time, people were starting to whisper that pro football had become America's number one sport, more popular than college football and, yes, even major league baseball. And in the midst of all this growth, one pro football team emerged as the best—of the decade, and maybe of all time: the Lombardi-era Green Bay Packers.

While the Packers had garnered some attention in 1959 for their first winning season in years, and for Vince Lombardi's coach-of-the-year honors, few in the National Football League leadership were paying much attention to the Packers. Thanks to Green Bay's new stadium and the team's new coach, the Packers had returned to the fold of successful franchises. The league had bigger issues to confront, including naming a new commissioner.

The estimable Bert Bell had been a forceful leader for 15 years, but on October 11, 1959, he died of a massive heart attack while in the stands at Franklin Field watching his beloved Philadelphia Eagles. Bell's death set off a scramble to name his replacement, but league owners reached an impasse. Marshall Leahy, Paul Brown and even Vince Lombardi were among the early candidates, but an angry Dominic Olejniczak blocked the league from hiring his star coach. In the end, the owners chose a "compromise" candidate: 33-year-old Pete Rozelle, the general manager of the Los Angeles Rams. Rozelle ended up being a brilliant choice, and is given much of the credit for the league's eventual rise to prominence.

There was a sense of urgency behind Rozelle's hiring because the NFL was facing yet another challenge from a rival league and this one seemed better organized and financed than previous ventures. The American Football League was the brainchild of young Texas multimillionaire Lamar Hunt. After getting

The Lombardi-era Packers employed a simple but devastating running game, highlighted by the team's famed sweep, in which the guards (here Fuzzy Thurston, number 63) would pull and lead the way for the halfback, in this case Paul Hornung.
Robert Riger/Getty Images

"You've got to like hitting people. If you're not willing to hit people, you don't belong on the field."
—Ray Nitschke

repeatedly rebuffed by Bert Bell in his attempts to gain an expansion team for his hometown of Dallas, Hunt recruited frustrated wannabe pro football team owners from other cities and quietly organized his own league. It is easy to argue that the birth of the AFL was a product of the conservative nature of the NFL, which had refused to expand beyond 12 teams despite spectacular growth in popularity in the 1950s. Many cities wanted teams, and there were many more players who wanted to play pro football than could be accommodated on the 36-man NFL rosters.

Bert Bell before his death appeared to be encouraging Hunt in his efforts, though at the same time he and George Halas were also quietly outmaneuvering the new league. To stifle the AFL in

A 49ers' pass threads its way through the outstretched arms of three Packers defenders during Green Bay's 41–14 rout of San Francisco at City Stadium on October 23, 1960.
Time & Life Pictures/Getty Images

two of its target cities, Bell awarded an expansion franchise in Lamar Hunt's backyard. The Dallas Cowboys were scheduled to start playing in the NFL in 1960. Meanwhile, Halas quietly worked to lure away the AFL's team in Minneapolis-St. Paul by promising that it could join the NFL in 1961 as the Minnesota Vikings. Undeterred, Hunt and the AFL owners moved forward with their plans to begin play in 1960 with eight teams: the Boston Patriots; Buffalo Bills; Dallas Texans; Denver Broncos; Houston Oilers; Los Angeles Chargers; New York Titans; and Oakland Raiders.

As Bert Bell had predicted, the primary conflict between the two leagues was over signing the top college players, which quickly came to fruition in the form of a lawsuit between Houston and the Rams over coveted running back Billy Cannon. The Oilers won the lawsuit, and the long-term effect was rising salaries for most newly drafted players. Television dollars also played a crucial role in the early success of the AFL, especially a unique agreement to share TV revenues equally among all the teams. The five-year, $8.5 million deal that the AFL signed with ABC proved a boon for both sides. The league received a much-needed revenue stream and ABC had an excuse to launch its sports division, which by the 1970s would be the best in American TV. With both leagues having everything they needed for success in place, it was time to play some football.

THE PUSH FOR A CHAMPIONSHIP

In Green Bay, Vince Lombardi was not satisfied with the previous year's winning record—he wanted nothing less than an NFL championship. His aspirations were not out of line, thanks to Lombardi and the efforts of Jack Vainisi; the Packers had assembled a truly exceptional roster. Prior to the 1960 season, two brilliant Lombardi personnel moves brought a pair of future Pro Football Hall of Famers to the team. Willie Davis was languishing in Cleveland as a backup offensive lineman; playing for Lombardi he became one of history's greatest defensive ends. Willie Wood had been a star quarterback for USC, but went undrafted. Lombardi signed him as a free agent, converted him to safety, and he enjoyed a brilliant career with the Packers.

The Packers were probably even more loaded with talent on offense, especially in the backfield. Lombardi utilized Paul Hornung's great gifts to the fullest. He was a threat to run or catch—or even pass—the ball, plus he was the Packers' kicker. In those various roles, he scored an NFL record 176 points during the 1960 season. Meanwhile, fullback Jim Taylor became the team workhorse and leading rusher. In 1960 he trailed only the Browns' incomparable Jim Brown in yards

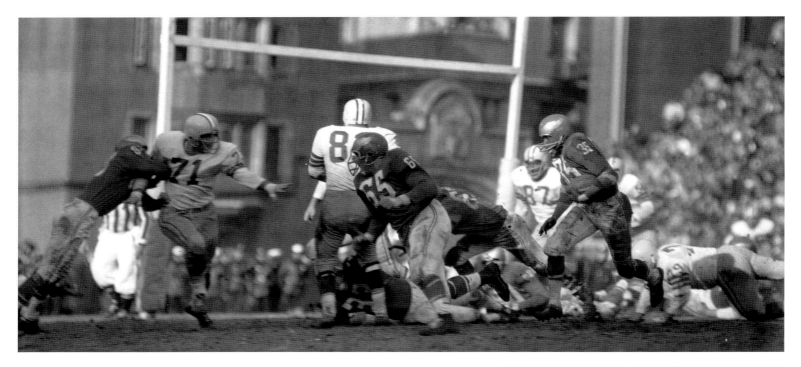

Above: **Oh how close!** Vince Lombardi took the Packers to the NFL championship in only his second season as head coach, but they lost the 1960 title game 17–13 to Philadelphia. Here the Green Bay defense tries to contain ball carrier Fred Dean, but the Eagles' running back scored a fourth-quarter touchdown that provided the winning margin.
Patrick Simione/Corbis

Right: Jim Taylor, shown bursting through an opening during a 1961 game against the Vikings, was the Packers' workhorse running the ball, as well as being one of football's all-time great fullbacks. Starting in 1960, Taylor rushed for more than 1,000 yards for an amazing five straight seasons.
Robert Riger/Getty Images

gained, with 1101. Despite these great gifts, Lombardi still had one huge question mark: Who would be his quarterback? Remarkably, Bart Starr—who some argue is pro football's all-time greatest quarterback—still had not secured his starting position, even though he was beginning his fifth season with the Packers.

Starr entered the 1960 season with high hopes and started the opening game against the Bears, but he played poorly and the team lost a heartbreaker, 17–14. To shake things up, Lombardi benched Starr in favor of Lamar McHan and the team responded with three straight wins. The next week, against the Steelers, McHan was not getting the job done and Starr returned, leading the Packers on a game-winning 66-yard drive in the fourth quarter. Even though Starr struggled off and on for the next few weeks, Lombardi stuck with him. As the season progressed, Starr settled down and assumed his role as team leader with increasing confidence. Lombardi had found his quarterback.

Three days after a Thanksgiving loss to the Lions, talented and popular Packer business manager and talent scout Jack Vainisi died of a heart attack at the age of 33. The team, sitting at 5–4 and with hopes of a championship fading, dedicated the next game to Vainisi's memory and came away with 41–13 rout of the Bears. When Green Bay closed out the season with back-to-back wins at San Francisco and Los Angeles, they earned their first trip to the championship in 16 years. The formidable Philadelphia Eagles awaited them in the title game.

Paul Hornung was a great runner, but he could do it all—catch passes, kick field goals, even pass the ball. From 1959–1961 he led the league in scoring, in 1960 amassing an NFL record 176 points.
Pictorial Parade/Getty Images

The Eagles were led by two stars, quarterback Norm Van Brocklin and center/linebacker Chuck Bednarik, pro football's last two-way player. More than 67,000 Philadelphia fans watched Van Brocklin (who retired after the game) lead his team to a come-from-behind 17–13 victory over the Packers, in which Bednarik tackled Jim Taylor on the last play of the game, just a few yards short of a touchdown. The Packers were left tantalizingly short of a championship, but their future looked bright. Pro football, too,

Bart Starr hands off to Jim Taylor during the Packers' 1960 NFL championship contest against the Eagles. More than 67,000 Philadelphia fans watched the home team take the title with a 17–13 decision.
Wally McNamee/CORBIS

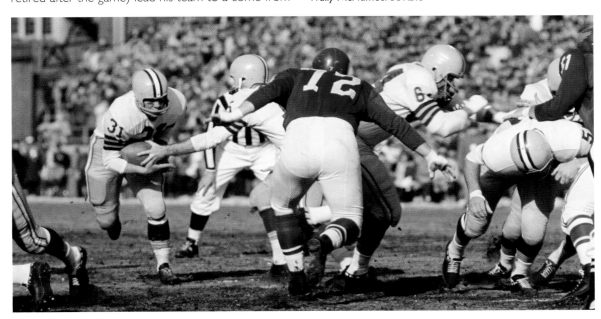

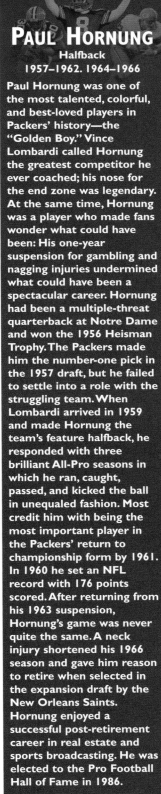

PAUL HORNUNG
Halfback
1957–1962. 1964–1966

Paul Hornung was one of the most talented, colorful, and best-loved players in Packers' history—the "Golden Boy." Vince Lombardi called Hornung the greatest competitor he ever coached; his nose for the end zone was legendary. At the same time, Hornung was a player who made fans wonder what could have been: His one-year suspension for gambling and nagging injuries undermined what could have been a spectacular career. Hornung had been a multiple-threat quarterback at Notre Dame and won the 1956 Heisman Trophy. The Packers made him the number-one pick in the 1957 draft, but he failed to settle into a role with the struggling team. When Lombardi arrived in 1959 and made Hornung the team's feature halfback, he responded with three brilliant All-Pro seasons in which he ran, caught, passed, and kicked the ball in unequaled fashion. Most credit him with being the most important player in the Packers' return to championship form by 1961. In 1960 he set an NFL record with 176 points scored. After returning from his 1963 suspension, Hornung's game was never quite the same. A neck injury shortened his 1966 season and gave him reason to retire when selected in the expansion draft by the New Orleans Saints. Hornung enjoyed a successful post-retirement career in real estate and sports broadcasting. He was elected to the Pro Football Hall of Fame in 1986.

appeared to have a bright future, despite the competition between the two leagues. In all, roughly 4 million spectators attended pro football games in 1960, and countless more watched games on television. The sport had truly arrived.

LOMBARDI BATTLES THE MILITARY

Many experts pointed to the Green Bays Packers before the 1961 season and declared them the likely champion. The Eagles and Giants both looked strong, but the two teams would start the season with new head coaches. Meanwhile, Green Bay appeared to have the best coach in the league. Accordingly, Vince Lombardi was rewarded with a generous new five-year contract. Lombardi was pleased with this development and the direction his team was going, but privately he was scared—of not winning during the upcoming season. The pressure to win was enormous, and he responded by pushing his team harder than ever in training camp.

The roster continued to improve; talented cornerback Herb Adderley and defensive tackle Ron Kostelnik arrived via the draft. Future stars emerged, in particular, Willie Wood, who replaced the retired Emlen Tunnell at free safety, and Ron Kramer, an outstanding blocker who became the starting tight end. And Bart Starr finally entered a season with a firm lock on quarterback. He would respond with an outstanding year, passing for 2418 yards and 16 touchdowns.

Despite these seeming certainties in training camp, uncertainty on the world stage played havoc with the

> **"Jim Brown will give you that leg and then take it away from you. Jim Taylor will give it to you and then ram it through your chest!"**
> —*Vince Lombardi, comparing the styles of the NFL's two leading running backs in the 1960s*

Packers during the season. Three of the team's stars—Boyd Dowler, Ray Nitschke, and Paul Hornung—were military reservists who were called to active duty as a result of tension in Europe caused by the construction of the Berlin Wall. Lombardi, with connections at the Pentagon, thanks to his years coaching at West Point, worked furiously to keep the players—especially Paul Hornung—on the field. Ultimately, Lombardi failed in his attempts to sway the military bureaucracy and the trio had to report for duty October 18. They rarely practiced with the team after that, but used weekend passes to play. Dowler did not miss a game, and Hornung and Nitschke played in all but two contests.

The season started on the wrong foot with a 17–13 loss to Detroit, likely the Packers' toughest competition in the Western Conference, but Green Bay turned things around and won nine of its next 10 games. The Packers clinched a spot in its second consecutive NFL championship game with a come-from-behind 20–17 win over the Giants with two

During Green Bay's 1962 championship campaign, opponents like the Bears seemed powerless to stop the Packers' running game. Here another sweep develops—Starr hands off to Taylor while guards Kramer (64) and Thurston (63) pull to lead the way. Green Bay prevailed 38–7 in this November 4 contest in Chicago.
George Silk/Time Life Pictures/Getty Images

weeks left in the regular season. They split their final games and finished 11–3. A rematch with the Giants for the NFL title, on December 31 at City Stadium, awaited the Packers.

Championship game day dawned clear and cold, with crews clearing a layer of snow off the tarp that protected the field. The highs were expected to only be in the teens for the afternoon game; nonetheless, a bundled-up full house of more than 39,000 turned out for the game. Another 55 million fans were expected to watch the game on television, a record audience delivered by CBS as a result of the NFL's exclusive $9.3 million two-year contract with the network.

Remarkably, all three of the military Packers were not only present for the game—they spent all week practicing with the team. Hornung was at the game only because his commander at Fort Riley, Kansas, had received a personal phone call from a particularly powerful friend and admirer of Vince Lombardi—President John F. Kennedy—who instructed that the halfback would be given a week's leave. Other Packers were banged up as the game approached. Star guard Jerry Kramer was out with a broken ankle, and both Bart Starr and Jim Taylor were hobbled with injuries. The Giants would be inspired to avenge their earlier loss, and to beat their former assistant coach.

In the end, the game was not a contest. The Packers jumped out to a 24–0 halftime lead and cruised to an easy 37–0 victory. Hoisted to his players' shoulders, a beaming Lombardi left the field with the championship he had worked so hard to earn. And more importantly, the Packers had routed a big-city rival to return the small burg to the pinnacle of pro football. Green Bay had a new hero in Vince Lombardi.

"THE WORLD'S GREATEST FOOTBALL COACH"

Repeating as NFL champion was a much more difficult proposition for the 1962 Packers than that faced by Green Bay's previous repeat team in 1930. The league had a more equal distribution of talent and resources among its 14 teams and had become a big, prosperous business. On the whole, the franchises were on solid financial footing, thanks in part to the $664,000 each club earned as part of the league's shared television revenues. Not even competition for the top college players from the AFL seemed to hurt the NFL. Court victories gave the senior league the leverage to sign many of its top picks. Nonetheless, the AFL soldiered on, playing quality football in front of growing crowds. The new league threatened to become a permanent part of the pro football landscape.

Packers' guard Fuzzy Thurston knocks Vikings' linebacker Cliff Livinston on his rear end, clearing the way for a Paul Hornung touchdown from the 7 yard line during Green Bay's 1962 season opening 34–7 victory over Minnesota at City Stadium. *Bettmann/CORBIS*

The 1962 Packers were fully equipped for the challenge of repeating. Football historians point to the team as one of the most talented and best-coached squads ever to grace a professional gridiron. While the Packers' offensive talents—Starr (who led the league in passing), Hornung (back from the service), and Taylor (who led the league in rushing)—jump readily to mind, it was the 1962 defense that keyed the team's success. With the Ray Nitschke manning the center of the field, and with other future Hall of Famers playing in front of (Henry Jordan and Willie Davis) and behind (Willie Wood and Herb Adderley) the feared linebacker, the Packers dominated their opponents, holding them to an average of only 10 points per game. Meanwhile, the offense was scoring nearly 30 points per game, a sure recipe for success.

Green Bay steamrolled through its schedule and reached a Thanksgiving Day tilt with Detroit undefeated. The 9–2 Lions pinned the only loss of the season on the Packers, 26–14, and for a time made the Western Conference race interesting. The Packers bounced back with three straight wins to finish 13–1 and book a return engagement in the 1962 NFL championship game with the Giants, but this time at New York's Yankees Stadium.

In the run-up to the big game, *Time* magazine ran an article that described Vince Lombardi as "the world's greatest football coach." The press coverage was

Above: **Despite a slow start to his career, Bart Starr developed into probably the best game-managing quarterback the NFL has ever seen. He was cool under fire, made great split-second decisions, and kept mistakes to a minimum.**
Getty Images

Right: **The key to the Packers' dominance in the 1960s was their defense, probably the greatest pro football has ever seen. Here Green Bay's pass rush collapses the Bears pocket during a November 1962 rout of Chicago in the Windy City.**
Time & Life Pictures/Getty Images

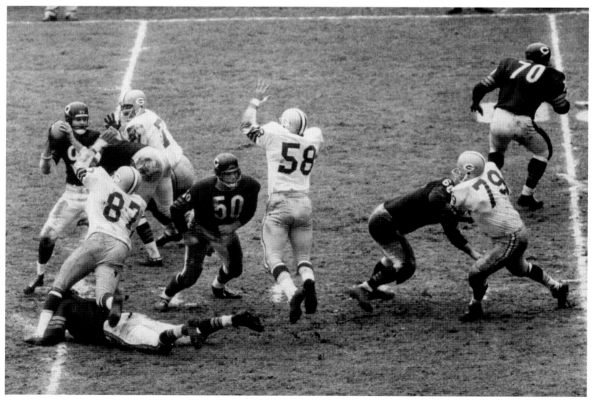

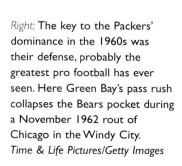

Most of his players acknowledged that Vince Lombardi's greatness was most evident not *during* games but *before* them. The former teacher was a master of preparation, instructing, drilling, and motivating his team in advance of every game.

Robert Riger/Getty Images

remarkable for the NFL, which rarely garnered much attention from the mainstream media. The inspiring Packers, along with the hard work of New York-based commissioner Pete Rozelle, were combining to raise the profile of pro football in America.

The New York game-day weather was more like what might be seen in Green Bay—windy and temperatures in the high teens—and the field was in poor shape. As with the previous season, the Packers entered the game banged up after the long regular season. Hornung, in particular, was so slowed by injuries that he had to forego his kicking duties. Guard Jerry Kramer took over and delivered three

"My life story is football. I have lived it, loved it, played it, sweated with it, laughed at it, cried with it, and rejoiced in it for as long as I can remember."
—Bart Starr

field goals, the winning margin in a blood-and-guts 16–7 Packer victory that probably reminded aging observers of old-time football. For the second time in their history, the Packers were two-time defending champions—and an opportunity to duplicate the 1929–1931 three-year title run awaited them the following season.

THE GOLDEN BOY FALLS FROM GRACE

The off-season delivered a stunning blow to the sky-high Packers: In April 1963, Paul Hornung, along with the Lions' defensive line star Alex Karras, was suspended for the upcoming season for gambling on football. Before making his announcement, Pete Rozelle invited Vince Lombardi to his office and presented him with the overwhelming evidence against Hornung. The commissioner understood that Lombardi and Hornung enjoyed a special relationship,

After two straight championships, the Bears stunned the 1963 Packers (shown during a 30–7 win over the St. Louis Cardinals) by taking the division and league titles, despite the fact that Green Bay racked up an impressive 11–2–1 record.

Robert Riger/Getty Images

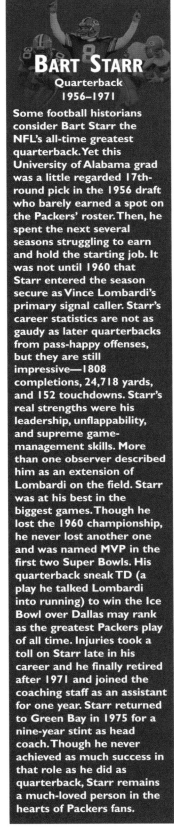

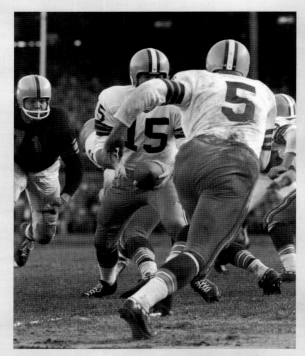

KEY PLAYS: THE LOMBARDI SWEEP AND THE PASSING GAME IT CREATED

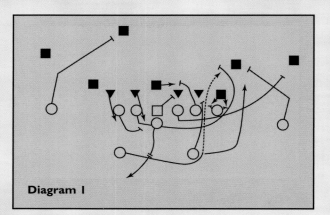

Diagram 1

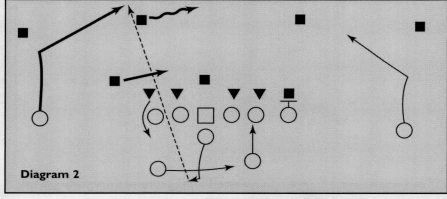

Diagram 2

One of the most storied plays in Packers history—and NFL history—has come to be known simply as the "Lombardi Sweep," or the "Packers Sweep." The play was classic power football, not that far removed from a single-wing play that might have come out of Curly Lambeau's playbook, but it was further refined by the inclusion of option blocking and option running principles championed by Lombardi's mentor, Army coach Red Blaik. In the NFL, Lombardi felt that a simple power offense was the perfect antidote to increasingly complex defenses—and he was right.

The Lombardi Sweep was elegant in its simplicity. The play, as illustrated in Diagram 1, shows quarterback Bart Starr taking the snap and making a deep handoff to halfback Paul Hornung. Guards Jerry Kramer and Fuzzy Thurston pulled to lead the play to the right. In line with

Lombardi's "Run to Daylight" philosophy, Hornung had the option of following fullback Jim Taylor's block off the right tackle or running farther outside—utilizing whichever path was more open.

The Packers' offensive success in the Lombardi era largely revolved around exploiting the threat of the sweep. As defenses adjusted to covering the sweep, the Packers would fake it and run other plays. In particular, Lombardi liked to use the sweep to set up play-action passes as shown in Diagram 2. This play would have been particularly effective to call if the safety and linebacker on the left had started cheating to the right, expecting a sweep to that side. Starr would fake the sweep handoff to Hornung (as shown in the photos above) and hit left end Boyd Dowler running a simple down-and-in pattern into the area vacated by the safety.

in some ways more like father and son than coach and player. While heartbroken, Lombardi could not disagree with the punishment Rozelle recommended. Both men were united in their desire to keep the game free from the influence from gambling—even small-scale betting like Hornung's that had no impact on the outcome of any contest. For true believers like Rozelle and Lombardi, protecting the sanctity of football always came first.

Even with the loss of Hornung, the 1963 Packers still had all the elements they needed for yet another championship run. Fullback Jim Taylor delivered his third straight thousand-yard season and the tandem of Tom Moore and Elijah Pitts ably combined to replace Hornung at halfback. The already-formidable defense was further bolstered by a pair of talented rookies, linebacker Dave Robinson and end Lionel Aldridge. Yet, as the season unfolded, it appeared the main roadblock to the Packers' third-straight championship would not be the team, or its play, but rather their archrival Chicago Bears.

The 1963 Bears were still coached by their founder and owner, 68-year-old George Halas. "Papa Bear," as he was affectionately known, had outlasted just about

everybody else with whom he had founded the NFL. He had also retired from coaching three times in his career, only to come back and enjoy more success. His 1963 team was a great one. Assistant George Allen installed a new zone defense that stymied opponents, holding them to only 10 points per game. On offense, the Bears were led by an intense young tight end named Mike Ditka.

Above: **Green Bay's Jim Taylor has the ball and is trying to elude the Colts' All-Pro defensive end Gino Marchetti (89) during an October 1964 game in Baltimore. Green Bay lost the game 24–21 and ended up finishing second to the Colts in the Western Conference.**
Diamond Images/Getty Images

Below: **The Packers' future Hall of Fame defensive end Willie Davis tries to fight his way through double-team blockers during a 1965 game against the San Francisco 49ers.**
Robert Riger/Getty Images

Above: **Four of the most powerful men in the NFL are all smiles during a break in the 1965 league meetings. From left, Vince Lombardi; Tex Schramm (Dallas Cowboys** **general manager); Pete Rozelle (NFL commissioner); and Wellington Mara (New York Giants vice president).**
Bettmann/CORBIS

Halfback Donny Anderson, shown picking up yards during a 1966 game against the Rams, was drafted in the first round out of Texas Tech in 1965. Fullback Jim Grabowski was Green Bay's number one pick the following year. The young backs were nicknamed "The Gold Dust Twins" thanks to their hefty contracts, but never quite lived up to the lofty standards set by their predecessors Hornung and Taylor.

Focus on Sport/Getty Images

The Packers and Bears opened the 1963 season at City Stadium, and Green Bay managed only one field goal against the Bears' new defense; they lost 10–3. When the two teams met at Wrigley Field in November, it wasn't nearly that close. Bart Starr was missing (he sat out four midseason games with a broken hand), and the Packers dropped a 26–7 decision. The two losses were the only ones suffered by the Packers in an otherwise-outstanding 11–2–1 campaign. The seemingly unbeatable Bears only finished a half game better at 11–1–2, but it was enough of a margin to propel them to the conference title and a 14–10 championship victory over the New York Giants. The Packers had not really slipped, but at least one team had caught up. How would they respond to this challenge?

Through the mists of time, the Vince Lombardi-coached Packer teams of the 1960s are often remembered as being practically unbeatable and the perennial league champion. The Packers of the era *were* good—arguably some of the greatest pro teams of all time—but they did not win the championship every year, and they were not always unbeatable. Along those lines, many fans seem content to forget the 1964 season.

The amazing Bears of 1963 nose-dived the season after their championship, leaving the door open for the Packers to re-take the Western Conference. There was a lot of optimism in Green Bay, especially because Paul Hornung had been reinstated by the league. The Golden Boy returned, but he was not as effective as before his suspension. His kicking, in particular, suffered. Hornung made only 12 field goals in 38 attempts; his 26 missed kicks remain an NFL record.

In the past, Lombardi might have handed kicking duties over to Jerry Kramer, but the All-Pro guard missed

much of the season with an abdominal abscess. Surgeons removed three large wooden splinters, embedded in Kramer since a childhood farming accident, which caused the problem. That one of pro football's toughest linemen could be sidelined by some pieces of wood was amazing, and a terribly unfortunate break.

Other than the loss of Kramer, the Packers still had many of the league's most talented players on the roster—which left Green Bay fans mystified when the team struggled to a 3–4 record to open the season. The defense was as stout as ever, but the team could not overcome silly mistakes (including missed field goals and turnovers at critical times) and dropped a number of close games. Particularly frustrating was a 24–23 home loss to the Minnesota Vikings. The emerging rivals were only in their fourth season, but they had developed into a serious contender.

The Packers rebounded in the second half of the season, thanks primarily to their reliable offensive weapons, Bart Starr and Jim Taylor. Starr led the league in passing and threw only four interceptions all season, while Taylor again rushed for more than 1000 yards. The late-season run left the Packers tied for second with the Vikings at 8–5–1, but they were nowhere close to the conference champion Colts at 12–2. Green Bay edged out Minnesota in the head-to-head total-score tiebreaker and earned a spot in the Playoff Bowl, the NFL's season-ending game that pitted the runners-up in each conference, but the Packers

There was nothing subtle about Jim Taylor—his running style was all about straight-ahead power and punishing would-be tacklers, the perfect on-field application of Vince Lombardi's offensive philosophy.
Robert Riger/Getty Images

Old-school football: This September 1965 mudfest in Cleveland represents classic gridiron action the way it was meant to be played. While the Browns' Vince Costello has Jim Taylor wrapped up on this play, the fullback would later catch a short touchdown pass from Bart Starr to earn a hard-fought 21–20 win for the Packers.
Art Rickerby/Time & Life Pictures/Getty Images

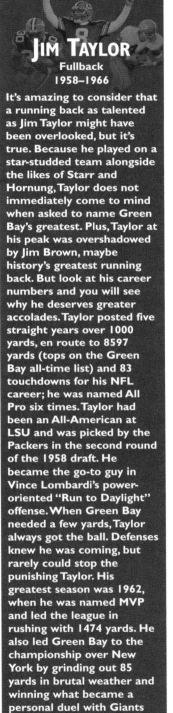

JIM TAYLOR
Fullback
1958–1966

It's amazing to consider that a running back as talented as Jim Taylor might have been overlooked, but it's true. Because he played on a star-studded team alongside the likes of Starr and Hornung, Taylor does not immediately come to mind when asked to name Green Bay's greatest. Plus, Taylor at his peak was overshadowed by Jim Brown, maybe history's greatest running back. But look at his career numbers and you will see why he deserves greater accolades. Taylor posted five straight years over 1000 yards, en route to 8597 yards (tops on the Green Bay all-time list) and 83 touchdowns for his NFL career; he was named All Pro six times. Taylor had been an All-American at LSU and was picked by the Packers in the second round of the 1958 draft. He became the go-to guy in Vince Lombardi's power-oriented "Run to Daylight" offense. When Green Bay needed a few yards, Taylor always got the ball. Defenses knew he was coming, but rarely could stop the punishing Taylor. His greatest season was 1962, when he was named MVP and led the league in rushing with 1474 yards. He also led Green Bay to the championship over New York by grinding out 85 yards in brutal weather and winning what became a personal duel with Giants linebacker Sam Huff. Taylor spent his last season, 1967, with the expansion New Orleans Saints. He was elected to the Pro Football Hall of Fame in 1976.

Green Bay was under tremendous pressure to show the NFL's dominance and win the first Super Bowl over the AFL Kansas City Chiefs. The stress of the game is evident in this sideline view of, from left, Taylor, Hornung, Starr, and Lombardi. Despite their concern, the Packers easily won the January 15, 1967, championship game, 35–10.
Bettmann/CORBIS

negotiated with CBS delivered $18.8 million for exclusive one-season TV rights, plus another $2 million for televising the championship game.

On the marketing front, two creative ventures helped the NFL greatly increase the profile of pro football in daily life. In 1962 Rozelle granted the rights to filming and producing the highlight program for the league championship game to a little-known production company headed by Ed Sabol. It was a huge risk, but everyone agreed the resulting half-hour production was the best football film anyone had ever seen. In 1965 Rozelle hired Sabol and made his company a full-time, league-wide venture—NFL Films Inc. Sabol's *NFL Game of the Week* became must-watch television for all serious fans, and his films of the era's biggest games still get regular screening on ESPN and the NFL Network. Another Rozelle stroke of genius was his 1963 founding of National Football League Properties, Inc., which ensured that high-quality, officially licensed gear—hats, shirts, bobble-head dolls, and much more—was available for all 14 teams. Today we take for granted the fans who proudly wear their favorite team's logo and colors, but it's easy to appreciate Rozelle's genius when you think of those people as millions of walking billboards for the NFL and its franchises.

Parallel to the success of the NFL in 1965 was the resiliency of the American Football League, which had proven itself a worthy competitor to the older league, and in 1964 had signed its own five-year, $36-million television contract with NBC. The AFL had remained an eight-team league despite the financial struggles of three franchises—Oakland, Denver, and especially New York. After an ownership change, the Titans became the Jets, moved to Shea Stadium, and started to offer the Giants some serious competition for fans.

dropped a 24–17 contest to the St. Louis Cardinals. It was a fitting end to what would be a very forgettable season in the midst of the Packers' most dominant era.

PRO FOOTBALL BECOMES AMERICA'S GAME

To say that pro football was growing in popularity in the middle of the 1960s was a gross understatement—the game was becoming one of the most important elements of American popular culture. Two factors drove this unprecedented growth—television and creative marketing—both emphasized by NFL commissioner Pete Rozelle, who was beginning to look like a genius. The 1965 television contract that Rozelle

A time to celebrate: Packers players carry Vince Lombardi off the field after Green Bay has won the league title and the opportunity to play in the first NFL-AFL championship game by beating the Dallas Cowboys 34–27, on January 1, 1967.
Bettmann/CORBIS

Meanwhile, Lamar Hunt grew tired of losing money in competition with the Cowboys and moved the Texans to Kansas City, where they became the Chiefs. The strength of the sport became apparent in 1965 when both leagues decided to expand by one franchise, starting with the 1966 season. The NFL was adding the Atlanta Falcons and the AFL the Miami Dolphins.

The primary field of conflict between the two leagues remained competition for draft choices. The 1965 draft has gone in the record books as one of the all-time best, and the NFL signed most of the big-name players—including Dick Butkus, Bob Hayes, and Gale Sayers—but the AFL signed the most coveted player. The Jets gave Alabama quarterback "Broadway" Joe Namath an unprecedented $400,000. The wisdom of their investment would be realized in a couple of years, but from the start, Namath became one of pro football's most flamboyant stars, further pushing the sport into the mainstream of American culture. Meanwhile, the old-school NFL owners were shocked at how much it was starting to cost them to pay players, and they wondered how long they could sustain this battle with the AFL before franchises started going belly up under the financial strain.

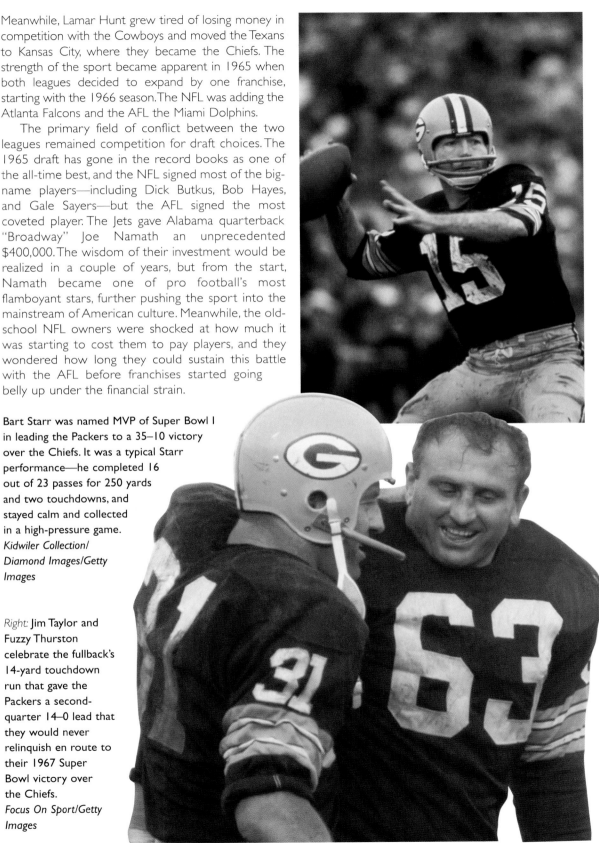

Bart Starr was named MVP of Super Bowl I in leading the Packers to a 35–10 victory over the Chiefs. It was a typical Starr performance—he completed 16 out of 23 passes for 250 yards and two touchdowns, and stayed calm and collected in a high-pressure game. *Kidwiler Collection/ Diamond Images/Getty Images*

Right: Jim Taylor and Fuzzy Thurston celebrate the fullback's 14-yard touchdown run that gave the Packers a second-quarter 14–0 lead that they would never relinquish en route to their 1967 Super Bowl victory over the Chiefs. *Focus On Sport/Getty Images*

HERB ADDERLEY
Cornerback
1961–1969

Herb Adderley had been a running back in college and after the Packers selected him in the first round of the 1961 draft, Vince Lombardi was convinced the former Michigan State star should stay on offense, possibly as a receiver. Adderley had other ideas: He wanted to play in the defensive secondary. Lombardi resisted and later admitted that his stubbornness nearly cost the team maybe the greatest cornerback in its history. When starter Hank Gremminger was injured, Adderley received his opportunity late in his rookie season, and he never gave up the left cornerback spot until Green Bay traded him to Dallas before the 1970 campaign. Adderley intercepted 39 passes with the Packers, including a memorable pick in Super Bowl II against Oakland that he returned 60 yards for a touchdown. He was also a superb kickoff return man, averaging 25 yards per return and scoring two touchdowns. In all, Adderley played on amazing six championship teams—five with the Packers and one with the Cowboys. He retired after the 1972 season and was elected to the Pro Football Hall of Fame in 1980.

Vince Lombardi celebrates Green Bay's fourth-quarter touchdown in Super Bowl I that locked up a 35–10 win over the Chiefs. Before the game, the coach was not so relaxed; observers recall him so nervous that he was visibly shaking.
Bettmann/CORBIS

People close to Vince during this time recall that he was sometimes paranoid and overly sensitive to what he perceived as slights to his status. The June 1965 death of Curly Lambeau provided a flashpoint for Lombardi's sensitivities. As a tribute to the Packers' founder and longtime coach, City Stadium was renamed Lambeau Field. Privately, Lombardi seethed at the move. He was bothered by Lambeau's reputation as a womanizer and was jealous of having Green Bay's spotlight directed on some other coach.

But even with distractions like this, Lombardi had little trouble focusing his attention on coaching his team, and in 1965 he delivered what may have been his finest performance. The roster was largely unchanged from the under-achieving 1964 squad (with the exception of new kicker Don Chandler), and some Packer stars appeared to be on the decline, most notably Jim Taylor and Paul Hornung. As a result, Green Bay's running game delivered its most anemic numbers in years (1488 yards and 14 touchdowns). Fortunately, the defense remained outstanding and, most importantly, the team possessed a will to win games that it could not afford to lose.

After opening the season with six straight wins, the Packers sputtered and found themselves 8–3 and in second place behind the resurgent Colts. After losing to the Rams, Lombardi accused the Packers, gathered for a meeting, of not caring whether they won. Star tackle and future Packer coach Forrest Gregg flew into

CITY STADIUM BECOMES LAMBEAU FIELD

Back in Green Bay, 1965 was shaping up to be a critical year for Vince Lombardi. He was sick of losing (to him, two seasons with no championship was "losing") and he had made a commitment to stay in Green Bay despite being approached by other teams (including the Jets). He was obsessed with winning the championship again, and this obsession seemed to be taking a toll on both his physical and mental health.

Green Bay's 1960s offensive line was one of the best in NFL history, and it was anchored by tackle Forrest Gregg (75), whom Lombardi described as the finest player he ever coach. Here the future Hall of Famer and Packers coach clears the way for Jim Taylor in the first Super Bowl.
Robert Riger/Getty Images

> **"I don't know if I'm gonna get in that game tomorrow, but if I do, they'll never get old Max out. I've been studying film and I've found me a cornerback. I'm gonna have him for breakfast, lunch, and dinner."**
> —*Max McGee, before Super Bowl I*

a rage because of the comments and had to be restrained. Nonplussed, Lombardi commented that that was the attitude he was looking for. The team rallied, handing Baltimore a 42–27 defeat, and ending up tied with the Colts at 10–3–1.

The Packers won a playoff rematch over Baltimore 13–10, needing a Chandler field goal in overtime to seal the win.

More than 50,000 fans filled Lambeau Field on January 2, 1966, to watch the Packers battle for the championship against the Cleveland Browns and their unstoppable, league-leading rusher, Jim Brown. A snowstorm the morning of the game made travel to the stadium difficult, and the field was a muddy mess at the kickoff. The Packers defense was masterful, especially in the second half, shutting down the Browns offensive attack and limiting Brown to only 50 yards rushing in his final game (he retired unexpectedly after the Pro Bowl). When the final gun sounded, Vince Lombardi and the Packers had won another NFL championship, 23–12.

THE CHAMPIONS OF THE FIRST SUPER BOWL

Five months after the Packers' championship victory, Pete Rozelle made a monumental and unexpected announcement: The AFL and NFL had agreed to merge. Just a month before the June 8 agreement, merger seemed the last thing the leagues would

Super Bowl I ticket stub. *GreenBayAntiques.com/The Oneida Archive*

Pete Rozelle hated the name "Super Bowl" and as this sample shows, refused to even allow the name to be printed on "World Championship Game" tickets. The will of the fans eventually won out, though interest in the first Super Bowl was less than expected. Despite relatively cheap ticket prices, fewer than 75,000 fans—well below stadium capacity—actually showed up to L.A. Coliseum to watch the Packers beat the Chiefs. *Robert Riger/Getty Images*

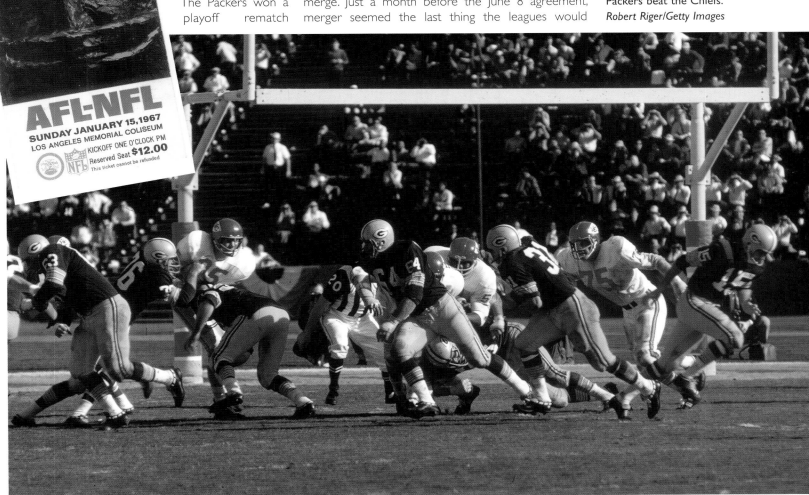

Ray Nitschke and Vince Lombardi on the sidelines at Milwaukee County Stadium during the Packers' December 23, 1967, playoff game against the Rams. Thanks to a stifling defense led by linebacker Nitschke, Green Bay dominated Los Angeles 28–7 in what was their first step toward winning a third straight championship.
Bettmann/CORBIS

discuss. The bidding war for draft choices had escalated to never-before-seen levels, and new AFL commissioner Al Davis retaliated by trying to sign NFL stars. The agreement reached by the organizations called for a joint draft, expansion to 26 teams by 1968, and formation of a single league—led by Rozelle—in 1970. Another exciting development was that the two leagues had agreed to play a "world championship" between the AFL and NFL champion, following the 1966 season.

With a clear prize—reaching and winning that championship game—for which to play, the 1966 Packers may have been one of the most committed and focused teams in Green Bay history. Bart Starr was superb, leading the team with aplomb and playing nearly error-free football: He threw only three interceptions to offset his 156 completions and 14 touchdowns. The Taylor-Hornung backfield was clearly

in its last season together, but other runners were stepping up, including Elijah Pitts and the new rookie halfback-fullback tandem of Donny Anderson and Jim Grabowski. The pair had been signed as the backfield of the future. Green Bay had spent $1 million to sign the talented runners, nicknamed the "Gold Dust Twins."

The defense again was the key to the season, holding opponents to fewer than 12 points per game. The Packers were especially unkind to enemy passing attacks. For the season, they sacked opposing quarterbacks 47 times and picked off 28 passes, returning six of those for touchdowns.

The Packers plowed through their 1966 opposition, losing only by one to the 49ers and by three to the Vikings, en route to a 12–2 record. They finished a full three games clear of the Colts and earned a slot in the championship game against the

Though he looks fairly harmless in this image recorded on the practice field, during games Henry Jordan was one of the NFL's most intimidating defensive players. He usually worked in tandem with fellow defensive tackle Dave Hanner, who would played conservatively and occupy blockers, allowing the aggressive Jordan to break into the backfield and completely disrupt the offensive plays.
Robert Riger/Getty Images

HENRY JORDAN
Defensive Tackle
1959–1969

Like fellow defensive lineman Willie Davis, Henry Jordan was also rescued from a backup role in Cleveland thanks to a 1959 trade by Vince Lombardi. Jordan had been a captain of the University of Virginia football team and also was an NCAA championship runner-up in wrestling. The Browns selected him in the fifth round of the 1957 draft, but his career stalled. With the move to Green Bay, Jordan moved into the starting lineup alongside Dave Hanner, giving the Packers' what was arguably the best defensive tackle tandem in the league. The two tackles' differing styles complemented each other well. Hanner played conservatively to hold the line, while Jordan used his quickness and aggressive rushing maneuvers to hassle the quarterback and disrupt play. Jordan was the most honored member of the 1960s defensive units that led the Packers to five championships. During that time, he was named All Pro six times and played in four Pro Bowls. After injuries forced the durable Jordan to retire after the 1969 season, he became the first executive director of Milwaukee's now-famous Summerfest lakefront festival. Sadly, he died in 1977 at the young age of 42 following a heart attack.

The end of the most famous play in what was arguably the most famous game in NFL history: With temperatures hovering below zero, Bart Starr lunges across the goal line on a quarterback sneak, giving the Packers a last-minute 21–17 victory over Dallas in the Ice Bowl, earning them the NFL title and a trip to Super Bowl II in warm Miami.
Focus On Sport/Getty Image

10–3–1 Cowboys, who had won their first Eastern Conference title. More than 74,000 Cowboy fans filled the Cotton Bowl to watch the Packers prevail in a back-and-forth game 34–27. Packer defensive back Tom Brown sealed the win with an interception in the end zone in the game's final seconds. Green Bay had earned the right to play in the world championship against the Kansas City Chiefs.

Many fans don't realize that this first world championship game was not a "Super Bowl," but rather the "AFL-NFL World Championship Game." Super Bowl was a term coined, in jest, by Lamar Hunt. Pete Rozelle hated the name and diligently fought its use (the game tickets did not have the words "Super Bowl" on them until the fourth championship), but the media and the public loved it. Ultimately, Rozelle was

"It was probably the most famous play in the most famous game ever played. And only one of the eleven guys who ran it knew what was going on."
—Packers center Ken Bowman on Bart Starr's quarterback sneak to win the Ice Bowl

forced to accept the term Super Bowl because the many fans he had helped attract to the game chose the name for him.

The lead-up to Super Bowl I found Vince Lombardi more nervous than he had been for any other game in

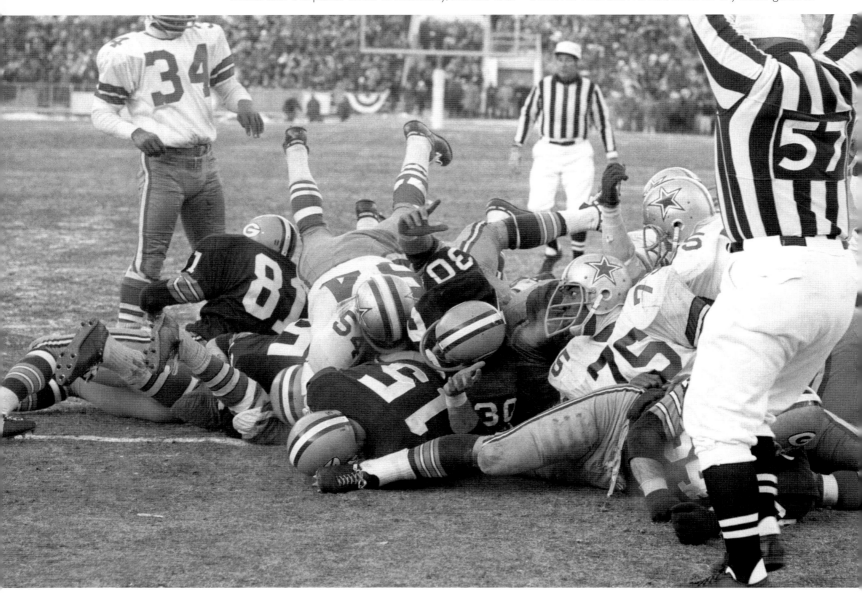

his career, but this was not just any game. There was immense pressure on Lombardi and the Packers to win—to prove that the NFL was the dominant league. Lombardi told his team they were representing the whole league, and that this would be the most important game they ever played.

The Chiefs kept the game close and trailed only 14–10 at halftime, but in the second half, the Packers defense picked up the pressure. A Willie Wood interception was quickly converted into a touchdown, and the Chiefs offense could never get on track. The Packers marched on to a convincing 35–10 victory,

allowing Pete Rozelle, the NFL owners, and Vince Lombardi to breathe a big sigh of relief. Bart Starr was masterful, passing for 250 yards and 2 touchdowns en route to being named the game's most valuable player. Little-used backup end Max McGee entered the game for the injured Boyd Dowler and delivered one of the best games of his career, catching seven passes for 138 yards and both of Starr's touchdowns. Years later, the fun-loving McGee admitted he had ignored Lombardi's 11 o'clock curfew and snuck out for a night of carousing before the game, not getting to bed until 7:30 a.m.

By the time Green Bay played in Super Bowl II in January 1968, backfield stars Jim Taylor and Paul Hornung were gone, but the team did not miss a beat. Young players, including Donny Anderson, shown carrying the ball in the championship against the Raiders, stepped up in their place and led the Packers to a 33–14 victory.
Bettmann/CORBIS

ANOTHER MASTERFUL COACHING JOB

Conditions for Super Bowl II in Miami on January 14, 1968, could not have been more different than two weeks earlier at the subzero Ice Bowl in Green Bay, but the outcome was the same—the Packers win. Here Donny Anderson follows the blocks of guard Gale Gillingham (68) and tackle Bob Skoronski (76) en route to a nice gain against the Raiders.

Focus On Sport/Getty Images

Despite having led his team to victory in the first Super Bowl, life was not destined to get any easier for Vince Lombardi. As the 1967 season approached, all fans could talk about was whether this Packer team could match Curly Lambeau's 1931 squad and deliver a third straight championship. Having fallen short of this goal in 1963, Lombardi put extra pressure on himself to match this accomplishment—especially important now that he coached home games in a stadium named for Lambeau. In addition, the 54-year-old Lombardi was suffering the effects of a lifetime dedicated to football and not taking care of himself. The mental strain was more obvious, but he also started to suffer physically. An arthritic hip caused him extreme pain, and medication taken for the condition caused severe stomach problems. He also started to suffer shortness of breath and mild chest pains. His wife worried that he would not survive the season.

Lombardi had already entertained thoughts of retiring, and even suggested the possibility in an interview prior to the 1966 championship game. Despite that suggestion, Lombardi was back in 1967 for at least one more season—and what a year it would be. Despite his mental and physical ailments, Lombardi delivered another masterful coaching job. He led the team through a challenging season that ended with an NFL championship game that would go down as the most memorable in team history, followed by a second trip to the Super Bowl.

With expansion to 16 teams, the NFL landscape had changed markedly. There were now four divisions of four teams; the Packers played in the Central (which became known as the "Black and Blue Division" for its hard-nosed football) along with the Bears, Lions, and Vikings. The four division winners made the playoffs and it would take two wins just to make it to the Super Bowl. The stakes had been raised—especially because 15 other NFL teams wanted a crack at the AFL champion.

Lombardi's biggest challenge entering 1967 was replacing one of football's all-time-greatest backfields. Jim

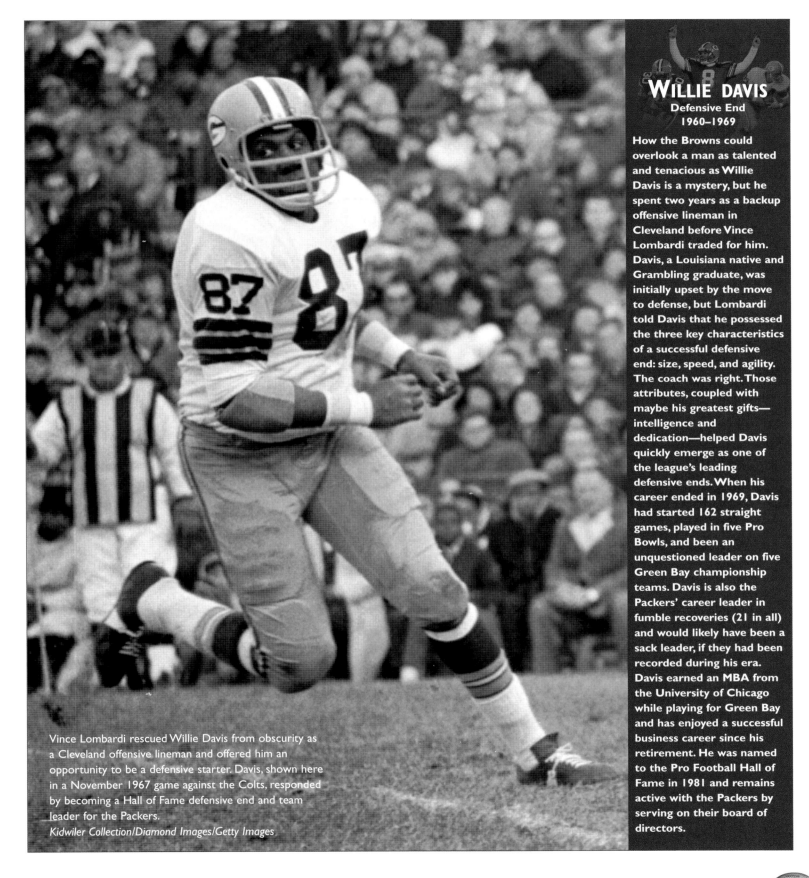

WILLIE DAVIS
Defensive End
1960–1969

How the Browns could overlook a man as talented and tenacious as Willie Davis is a mystery, but he spent two years as a backup offensive lineman in Cleveland before Vince Lombardi traded for him. Davis, a Louisiana native and Grambling graduate, was initially upset by the move to defense, but Lombardi told Davis that he possessed the three key characteristics of a successful defensive end: size, speed, and agility. The coach was right. Those attributes, coupled with maybe his greatest gifts— intelligence and dedication—helped Davis quickly emerge as one of the league's leading defensive ends. When his career ended in 1969, Davis had started 162 straight games, played in five Pro Bowls, and been an unquestioned leader on five Green Bay championship teams. Davis is also the Packers' career leader in fumble recoveries (21 in all) and would likely have been a sack leader, if they had been recorded during his era. Davis earned an MBA from the University of Chicago while playing for Green Bay and has enjoyed a successful business career since his retirement. He was named to the Pro Football Hall of Fame in 1981 and remains active with the Packers by serving on their board of directors.

Vince Lombardi rescued Willie Davis from obscurity as a Cleveland offensive lineman and offered him an opportunity to be a defensive starter. Davis, shown here in a November 1967 game against the Colts, responded by becoming a Hall of Fame defensive end and team leader for the Packers.

Kidwiler Collection/Diamond Images/Getty Images

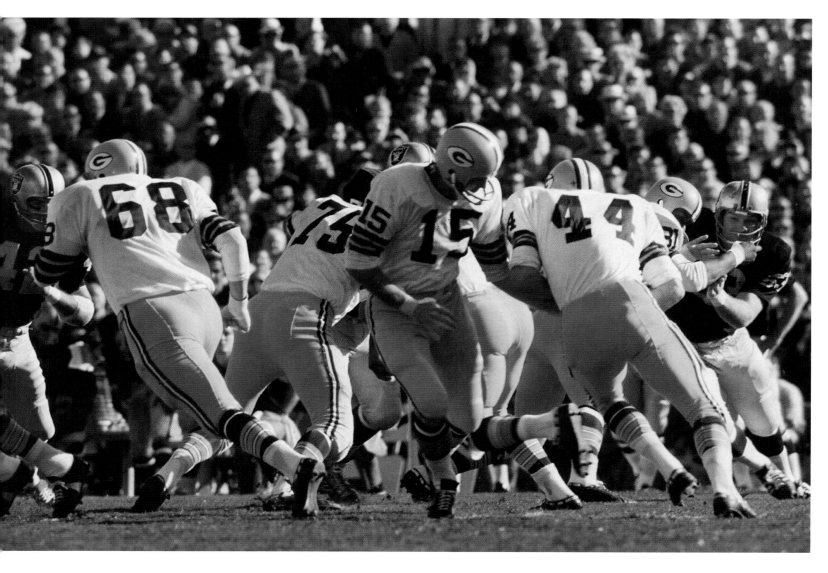

Bart Starr earned his second straight Super Bowl MVP award by playing a standard game for him: 13 for 24, 202 yards, 1 touchdown, no interceptions. The Packers took apart the Raiders in unspectacular, workmanlike fashion. After the game, Vince Lombardi admitted that his team did not play particularly well in winning 33–14.
Bettmann/CORBIS

Taylor, angry at the money paid to new draft picks, was traded to the expansion New Orleans Saints. Paul Hornung was selected by the Saints in the expansion draft, but was forced to retire after being diagnosed with a potentially dangerous back problem. Despite these losses, and a spate of injuries during the season, the Packers still racked up nearly 2000 yards on the ground, using a committee of runners, including Ben Wilson, who was obtained from the Rams, and rookie speedster Travis Williams, who also led the league in kickoff returns and turned four kicks into Packer touchdowns.

Offenses tend to get the most notoriety and many people forget that the Packers dominance in the 1960s was largely the result of their defensive mastery. The 1967 unit was the best in the NFL, especially in its ability to shut down opposing passers. The surprising Bob Jeter—a former receiver who had been converted to cornerback the previous season—led

the team with eight interceptions and earned a spot in the Pro Bowl.

The Packers struggled early in 1967, especially after Bart Starr was knocked out for most of three games with a shoulder injury, but they still found ways to win. By midseason the Packers were finally playing like a championship team, and they wrapped up the Central Division title on November 26 with a 17–13 win over the Bears. Then, their championship form disappeared, and they limped through the final three weeks with a close win over the Vikings and losses to the Rams and Steelers. The Rams returned to County Stadium on December 23 for a playoff game, and the banged-up Packers delivered one of their best performances of the season in winning 28–7. The win set up the Packers' December 31, 1967, NFL championship tilt at Lambeau Field against the Dallas Cowboys—the most celebrated game in team history.

Barely visible through a layer of mud, tackle Forrest Gregg lets out a victory roar from the sidelines near the end of Green Bay's 13–0 victory over the 49ers in San Francisco's Kezar Stadium. Gregg was a stalwart on the Packers' offensive line from 1956 to 1970, then returned to the team as head coach in 1984.
Robert Riger/Getty Images

FORREST GREGG
Offensive Tackle
1956–1970

"Forrest Gregg is the finest player I ever coached." When Vince Lombardi makes a statement like that, you know a player is special, but it was not the coach's statement that made the NFL take notice of Gregg. It was his performance on the field—which at one point stretched to 188 consecutive starts. The Texas native starred at Southern Methodist University and the Packers selected him in the second round of the 1956 draft. Gregg's career took some time to get going thanks to missing the 1957 season while fulfilling military commitments, but once he returned to the Packers, he never gave up his starting right tackle position. At 6-feet, 4-inches and 249 pounds, Gregg was undersized for the position, so he compensated by developing outstanding technique. He was also versatile; when injuries depleted the Packers during two different seasons, Gregg effortlessly shifted to the more athletic guard position to help out. Gregg played in eight straight Pro Bowls and started for five championship teams. He finished his career with a single year in Dallas (1971), and then jumped into coaching. He returned to Green Bay as head coach in 1984, and while he enjoyed mixed success in that role, he will always be remembered as one of the most important members of the Packers' family. He was elected to the Pro Football Hall of Fame in 1977.

The Packers earned their second NFL championship of the Lombardi era with a 16–7 win over the New York Giants on December 30, 1962, in Yankee Stadium. The teams faced difficult conditions—13 degree temperatures and 40 mph winds—and Bart Starr (shown looking for an open receiver) had difficulty throwing the ball. A gutsy performance by fullback Jim Taylor allowed Green Bay to grind out the win on the ground. *Time & Life Pictures/Getty Images*

ICE BOWLS AND SUPER BOWLS

The "Ice Bowl" will be forever remembered for both its weather (some of the most punishing conditions ever experienced during an NFL game) and its stunning finish, but the background stories were just as compelling. Dallas was an upstart, a recent expansion team challenging one of the league's traditional powerhouses. The Cowboys had maintained a steady ascent since their founding in 1960 and the team and its fans thought that their hour had arrived. Even more fascinating was the rivalry between the two head coaches. Vince Lombardi and Tom Landry had been the offensive and defensive coordinators, respectively, for the New York Giants in the 1950s. They respected but did not much like each other. Now the brash Lombardi and the calm Landry were two of the league's star coaches, but this NFL championship was taking the shape of a grudge match between the two men.

The morning of the game dawned clear and bitterly cold; the temperature reported during the game was as low as 13 degrees below zero. Lombardi had invested $80,000 in a General Electric heating system for the field, but it did not work as advertised in these adverse conditions—the turf was frozen, and the legend of "The Frozen Tundra" of Lambeau Field was born.

> "Many things have been said about Coach Lombardi and he is not always understood by those who quote him. But the players understand. This is one beautiful man."
> —*Jerry Kramer*

The legend of the Ice Bowl spectators is almost as great as the game played on the field. Despite the challenging conditions, Packer fans were not going to miss such an important football game and the stands were loaded to capacity with spectators wearing layer upon layer of clothing. A healthy number had even showed up early to go through their traditional pre-game tailgating ritual, complete with beer and brats on the grill. Even four decades later, fans still reminisce about their personal experiences at the game—though if all are to be believed there would have been many times more in attendance than the official count of 50,861!

The game was one for the ages. The Packers jumped out to a 14–0 lead, and it looked like the rout was on. Then two Packer turnovers were converted into Cowboy scores and at halftime it was a tight 14–10

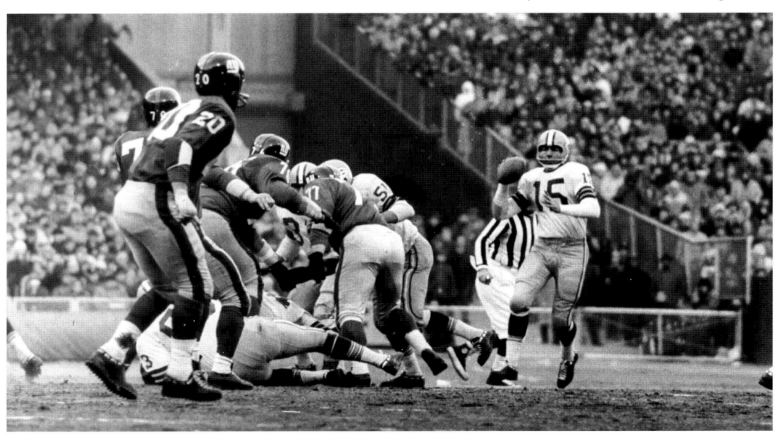

Sometimes waiting and watching is harder than playing: Packers Tom Moore (25), Herb Adderley (26), and Forrest Gregg (75) look anxious to get back on the field during a Green Bay home game on a warm September day.
Robert Riger/Getty Images

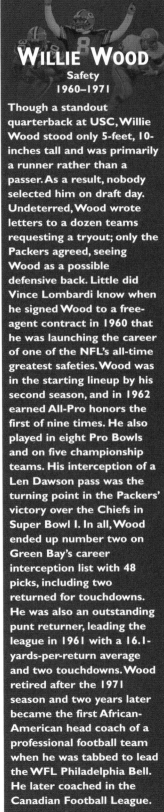

WILLIE WOOD
Safety
1960–1971

Though a standout quarterback at USC, Willie Wood stood only 5-feet, 10-inches tall and was primarily a runner rather than a passer. As a result, nobody selected him on draft day. Undeterred, Wood wrote letters to a dozen teams requesting a tryout; only the Packers agreed, seeing Wood as a possible defensive back. Little did Vince Lombardi know when he signed Wood to a free-agent contract in 1960 that he was launching the career of one of the NFL's all-time greatest safeties. Wood was in the starting lineup by his second season, and in 1962 earned All-Pro honors the first of nine times. He also played in eight Pro Bowls and on five championship teams. His interception of a Len Dawson pass was the turning point in the Packers' victory over the Chiefs in Super Bowl I. In all, Wood ended up number two on Green Bay's career interception list with 48 picks, including two returned for touchdowns. He was also an outstanding punt returner, leading the league in 1961 with a 16.1-yards-per-return average and two touchdowns. Wood retired after the 1971 season and two years later became the first African-American head coach of a professional football team when he was tabbed to lead the WFL Philadelphia Bell. He later coached in the Canadian Football League.

contest. In the second half, the momentum shifted in favor of the Cowboys, and Dallas took the lead on a 50-yard touchdown pass from halfback Dan Reeves (who would someday coach four teams to Super Bowl appearances—and losses) to Lance Rentzel. Bart Starr led the Packers on a last-ditch drive, completing five passes in the brutal conditions. With a first and goal on the Cowboys 1, the Packers failed to gain any ground in two running attempts. They used their last timeout with 16 seconds remaining—time for just one play.

Logic would have called for a chip-shot field goal attempt to send the game into overtime, but Lombardi would have none of that. Maybe the cold weather affected his judgment, or maybe he just had that much confidence, but Lombardi agreed when Starr said he could sneak it in himself. The play was not even in the playbook; it would be sandlot-style improvisation for the championship. "Then run it in. And let's get the hell out of here," were Lombardi's final instructions to his quarterback. Following the block of Jerry Kramer, Starr executed the quarterback sneak to perfection in what became one of pro football's most memorable plays.

After a game as amazing as the Ice Bowl, it's probably not surprising that the Packers final game of the season has taken a back seat in comparison—even though it happened to be Super Bowl II versus the Oakland Raiders. But the game has taken on a special significance of its own because it was Vince Lombardi's last game as head coach of the Packers. The press and people close to Lombardi guessed this might be the case (and, in fact, he had already told Pete Rozelle about his retirement plans), but it was not until the end of a team meeting three days before the Super Bowl that Packer players knew Lombardi was retiring. His voice breaking with emotion, the normally gruff Lombardi stammered, "I want to tell you how very proud I am of all of you." The players realized they were about to play their last game for Vince.

An excited crowd at Miami's sold-out Orange Bowl learned first hand on January 14, 1968, that the NFL was still pro football's dominant league. Green Bay ground out two methodical drives ending in field goals before exploding for a 62-yard Starr-to-Dowler touchdown pass. The Raiders responded with their own touchdown drive to keep the game close, but the Packers went to the locker room at halftime with a 16–7 lead. The second half wasn't even a contest as the Packer offense controlled the ball, and the defense kept the Raiders completely in check. With their 33–14 victory, the Packers were again on top of the football world. Despite the changes looming for the team, few would have guessed it would take three decades to return to this lofty position.

Despite considerable hype after the Packers made him a first-round draft pick, Donny Anderson (shown carrying the ball in Super Bowl I) never achieved the stardom predicted for him. Part of the problem may have been the Packers' fall from the NFL elite after Vince Lombardi's departure. Anderson played six quality years for the Packers, then was traded to St. Louis after yielding his role as lead halfback to John Brockington in 1971.
Bettmann/CORBIS

SAY IT ISN'T SO: LOMBARDI RETIRES AS COACH

Two weeks after the Super Bowl, Vince Lombardi made the announcement that Packer fans both expected and dreaded: He was retiring as head coach of the Packers. Lombardi was remaining with the team as general manager, and he had tabbed his top assistant, Phil Bengston, to succeed him as coach. Despite the fact that Lombardi was still going to be around, Packer fans knew things would not be the same. Though Lombardi retired primarily as a concession to his poor health, there were other good reasons for stepping down. The Packers were old compared to most NFL teams and were clearly on the decline. Without an aggressive overhaul of the lineup, fielding a winning team—let alone a championship contender—in 1968 was going to be serious challenge. Now the burden of making this happen, while also succeeding a legend, had been handed to Phil Bengston.

Bengston may have been as good a candidate as any in the NFL for this difficult assignment. He had been an All-American tackle at the University of Minnesota, then was a long-time college assistant for Missouri and Stanford. He moved to the pro ranks in 1951 as a 49ers assistant. Lombardi added him to his first Green Bay staff in 1959, and he put Bengston in charge of the defense in 1960. Throughout the Packers incredible run in the 1960s, the Bengston-led defenses had been consistently among the best in the league.

"Pro football is the difference between me being just another guy and having something today."
—Willie Davis

Bengston would have to take advantage of this opportunity while toiling in the shadow of Lombardi, who was ill-suited to being a full-time general manager. Despite the fact that he desperately needed a break from coaching, Lombardi hated being out of the spotlight, and he wanted more power in the NFL world, longing to be part owner of a franchise. Lombardi had previously approached the Packer executive committee about letting him purchase part of the team, but the team leadership was unwilling to tamper with Green Bay's publicly owned status. In the spring of 1968, a better opportunity presented itself when Lombardi became part of a group making a serious bid to buy the San Francisco 49ers. They were unsuccessful, but the effort made it clear that Green Bay was probably not in Lombardi's plans for the future.

Bengston had much of the 1967 Packers roster return for his first season; he was a popular choice among players for the job. Notable retirees were Max McGee and Don Chandler. The latter's departure proved a serious headache for the Packers, who had kicking problems throughout 1968. The "Gold Dust Twins"—Anderson and Grabowski—powered a solid Packer running game, but the offense was inconsistent and lacked the scoring punch of previous seasons. Injuries to Bart Starr kept the two-time Super Bowl MVP off the field for at least part of eight different games. The Packers dropped several close contests and won in consecutive weeks only once all season. The Central Division was evenly matched, but the Packers' 6–7–1 record was only good enough for third place.

To go from Super Bowl champion to a losing record was unthinkable in Green Bay, and Vince Lombardi received much of the criticism from fans, who could not understand why he had retired from coaching. What fans did not realize as the forgettable season was coming to a close was that Lombardi was already plotting his departure from Wisconsin. The Washington Redskins had made him a fantastic offer; Lombardi would become their vice president, general manager, and head coach, as well as part owner of the team. The ownership stake would allow him, by NFL rules, to break his contract with Green Bay. Though the Packers' board debated whether to fight the Redskins for Lombardi, in the end they realized the efforts would be futile, and they regrettably said goodbye to their famous coach.

Lombardi's departure was announced publicly on February 5, 1969. The reaction among Packer fans was swift and angry—most turned on their once-beloved coach, accusing him of being greedy and lacking loyalty. Their reaction was unfair, especially considering how business-oriented the NFL had become, and Lombardi

Paul Hornung follows the action intently from the sidelines during a 1966 game—his last season with the Packers.
Gerald R. Brimacombe//Time Life Pictures/Getty Images

Left: Hall of Famers in action: Green Bay center Jim Ringo (51) opens a gaping hole for fullback Jim Taylor. Ringo was one of the NFL's most durable players, at one point starting in 182 straight games. Vince Lombardi unexpectedly traded Ringo to the Eagles after the 1963 season—legend has it because he showed up for contract negotiations with an agent in tow.
Robert Riger/Getty Images

Below: The sight of an onrushing Ray Nitschke was not a pleasant one for this Rams ball carrier during his team's 24–13 loss to the Packers on September 25, 1966. Nitschke was the quintessential middle linebacker—athletic, fierce, and seemingly in love with delivering crunching hits on offensive players.
Focus On Sport/Getty Images

was making a brilliant business decision, but the move was unimaginable for many Packer fans, so deep was their devotion to their city and their football team.

Phil Bengston added the general manager title to his coaching duties, but he would prove a poor judge of college talent. The drafts he led yielded little new talent for the aging team, which faced more retirements, including offensive line stalwarts Jerry Kramer and Bob Skoronski. Still, the 1969 Packers had heart and they rallied from the off-season distraction to put themselves in the Central Division race at the season's midpoint. "The Pack Will Be Back," became the battle cry for the year, but in the NFL, it takes more than a slogan to win games. The aging team seemed to tire in November, and consecutive losses to Baltimore, Minnesota, and Detroit knocked them out of the playoff race. Injuries again felled Bart Starr and he gave way to backup Don Horn for the season's final four games. Though three of these games were Packer victories, they proved too little too late. Despite a respectable 8–6 record, Green Bay was kept out of the Central Division cellar by only a terrible Bears team.

While the 1960s had begun with considerable optimism for the Packers—and the results had exceeded even the most optimistic fan's expectations—the decade was ending on a different note. The Packers again found themselves lacking solid leadership, and the team's prospects for the next several years looked dim indeed.

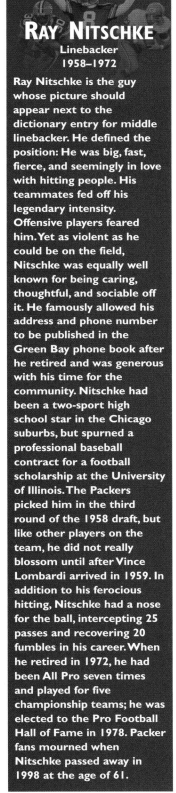

RAY NITSCHKE
Linebacker
1958–1972

Ray Nitschke is the guy whose picture should appear next to the dictionary entry for middle linebacker. He defined the position: He was big, fast, fierce, and seemingly in love with hitting people. His teammates fed off his legendary intensity. Offensive players feared him. Yet as violent as he could be on the field, Nitschke was equally well known for being caring, thoughtful, and sociable off it. He famously allowed his address and phone number to be published in the Green Bay phone book after he retired and was generous with his time for the community. Nitschke had been a two-sport high school star in the Chicago suburbs, but spurned a professional baseball contract for a football scholarship at the University of Illinois. The Packers picked him in the third round of the 1958 draft, but like other players on the team, he did not really blossom until after Vince Lombardi arrived in 1959. In addition to his ferocious hitting, Nitschke had a nose for the ball, intercepting 25 passes and recovering 20 fumbles in his career. When he retired in 1972, he had been All Pro seven times and played for five championship teams; he was elected to the Pro Football Hall of Fame in 1978. Packer fans mourned when Nitschke passed away in 1998 at the age of 61.

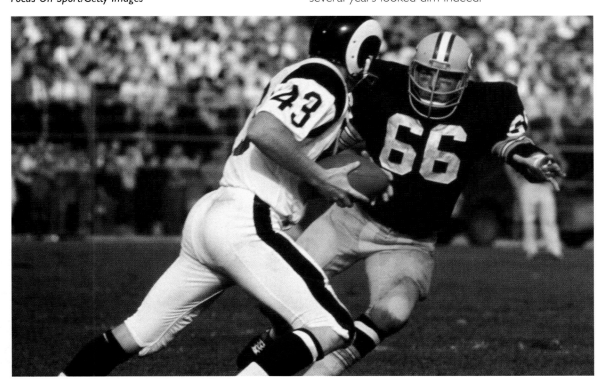

CHAPTER 6

THE 1970S: STRUGGLES, BUT A STARR COMES TO THE RESCUE

Right: **Green Bay made a clean break from the Lombardi era by hiring University of Missouri's Dan Devine as their head coach in 1971. Despite a playoff appearance in 1972 Devine found his style not as well suited to the pro game and he returned to the college ranks after the disappointing 1974 season.**
Michael Zagaris/Getty Images

Opposite below: **John Brockington—shown carrying the ball during his rookie season, 1971—burst onto the NFL scene in a big way. The former Ohio State star became the first player to rush for more than 1,000 yards in each of his first three years in the league.**
NFL/WireImage.com

Amazing things can happen over the span of a decade, and this was especially true with the National Football League in comparing 1970 to 1960. In 1960, a well-funded rival league threatened to topple the burgeoning NFL. Ten years later, the AFL had merged into the NFL and the former rivals were about to consummate their union with their first year of interleague regular-season play. At the start of the decade, football seemed to be growing in popularity, but by the 1970s, professional pollsters provided evidence that pro football had exploded and passed baseball as America's favorite spectator sport. Furthermore, aspects of pro football were becoming ingrained in American culture. The Super Bowl, as it was now officially called, was the biggest sporting (and party) event of the year. In 1970, another important institution was born with the start of ABC's Monday Night Football, giving football fans the promise of quality sports on television for one more day of the week (at least for four months out of the year).

The new post-merger NFL was big and complex and reached out to almost every corner of the lower 48 states. The league's 26 teams were broken into two 13-team conferences; Baltimore, Cleveland, and Pittsburgh moved to the new American Football Conference to keep the numbers even, while the remaining NFL franchises stayed in what became known as the National Football Conference. Unable to get consensus on how to achieve realignment in the new NFC, Pete Rozelle drew up five separate options on slips of paper, put them in an empty vase, and had one of his assistants reach in and select the plan that was finally implemented.

One potential post-merger problem had resolved itself the past two seasons. Some were concerned that keeping the NFL and AFL largely intact would result in two wildly mismatched conferences. The Packers' domination in the first two Super Bowls left the NFL thinking it was by far the better league. The next two championship games erased this misconception. First, the audacious Joe Namath guaranteed—and delivered—a Jets' win over the Colts in Super Bowl III, then the innovative Kansas City Chiefs dismantled the plodding and traditional Minnesota Vikings in Super Bowl IV. The NFL teams no longer had illusions they were going to mop up on the former AFL teams in the new combined league.

Even after realignment, the Green Bay Packers found themselves in a familiar place, playing in the NFC Central with the Bears, Lions, and Vikings. Under the league's new arrangement, there would actually be increased opportunities to make the playoffs. Winners of the three divisions in each conference automatically advanced, but so did a fourth team—the division runner-up with the best record—called the "wild card" qualifier by the NFL. Sadly, even with more slots available to make the playoffs, Green Bay would take relatively little advantage of the opportunities in the decade ahead.

A couple of weeks before the 1970 season started, Packer fans had to come to terms with their grief over a fallen hero. Though many people were angry when Vince Lombardi departed Green Bay for new

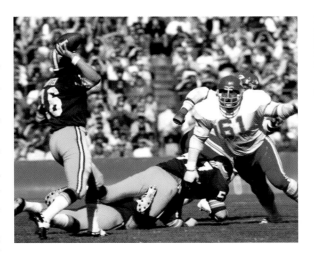

Dan Devine struggled to find the right quarterback while Packers coach. During this 1973 game against Kansas City (which ended in a 10–10 tie) Scott Hunter was the signal caller, but five other quarterbacks started various games during Devine's four-year tenure in Green Bay.
Vernon Biever/WireImage.com

opportunities with the Washington Redskins, all was forgotten and forgiven when word emerged that the legendary coach was dying with advanced colon cancer. Lombardi's one season coaching the Redskins had been fairly successful, and after posting a 7–5–2 record, it appeared he was going to work his

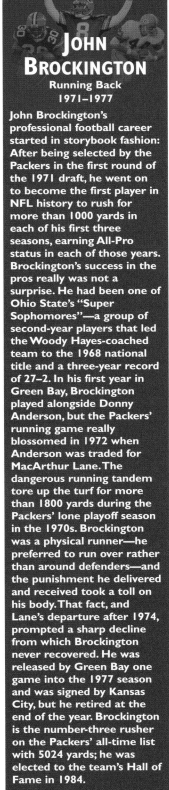

JOHN BROCKINGTON
Running Back
1971–1977

John Brockington's professional football career started in storybook fashion: After being selected by the Packers in the first round of the 1971 draft, he went on to become the first player in NFL history to rush for more than 1000 yards in each of his first three seasons, earning All-Pro status in each of those years. Brockington's success in the pros really was not a surprise. He had been one of Ohio State's "Super Sophomores"—a group of second-year players that led the Woody Hayes-coached team to the 1968 national title and a three-year record of 27–2. In his first year in Green Bay, Brockington played alongside Donny Anderson, but the Packers' running game really blossomed in 1972 when Anderson was traded for MacArthur Lane. The dangerous running tandem tore up the turf for more than 1800 yards during the Packers' lone playoff season in the 1970s. Brockington was a physical runner—he preferred to run over rather than around defenders—and the punishment he delivered and received took a toll on his body. That fact, and Lane's departure after 1974, prompted a sharp decline from which Brockington never recovered. He was released by Green Bay one game into the 1977 season and was signed by Kansas City, but he retired at the end of the year. Brockington is the number-three rusher on the Packers' all-time list with 5024 yards; he was elected to the team's Hall of Fame in 1984.

turnaround magic on another team. But the disease never gave him the chance, and Vince Lombardi died on September 3, 1970.

Everyone associated with pro football was affected by Lombardi's passing, in part because it marked the end of a truly memorable era for the game. This was especially true in Green Bay, Wisconsin, where Lombardi's death told fans in especially harsh terms that the Packers' most recent run of success was over. And while most fans understood that what they had enjoyed in the 1960s was a rare treat in pro sports, they also dreamed of once again rooting for a winner. But looking at the team scheduled to take the field in 1970, Packer fans probably figured those dreams weren't going to come true any time soon.

John Brockington carries the ball during the Packers' 20–17 victory over the Bears on October 8, 1972. After his amazing first three seasons, Brockington's effectiveness waned and he was eventually cut by Green Bay one game into the 1977 season. *Vernon Biever/WireImage.com*

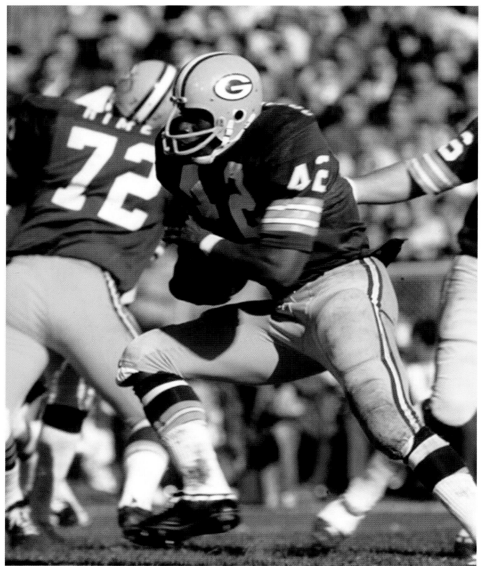

> ## "It really didn't matter who we handed the ball to. We could move the ball on anybody."
> —*Ken Bowman, on Green Bay's 1972 Brockington/Lane running game*

THE BENGSTON ERA COMES TO A QUICK END

The transition away from the Lombardi era was also evident looking at the Packers' roster at the start of the 1970 season. Willie Davis, Boyd Dowler, and Henry Jordan had retired. Herb Adderley and Elijah Pitts were among the players traded away. Fortunately, the draft had provided some decent replacements. The Packers used their extra first-round pick (obtained via a trade with the Bears for Pitts and others) to select defensive tackle Mike McCoy, who was a seven-year starter for Green Bay. The other first-rounder was Rich McGeorge, who played nine seasons at tight end for the Packers. Other notable draftees from 1970 included defensive back Al Matthews, linebacker Jim Carter, and defensive back Ken Ellis, but even this talented class could not stave off what turned out to be a disappointing season.

On September 20, 1970, a sellout crowd at Lambeau Field was appalled to witness a season-opening disaster—a 40–0 thrashing at the hands of the Lions. It was the first time the Packers had been shut out at home since 1949, and Bart Starr later recalled that the game offered something he never before experienced in Green Bay: angry, booing fans. It was a tough season for Starr, who again struggled with injuries. The fans were friendlier to him on October 18, however, when the team celebrated Bart Starr Day, with numerous dignitaries on hand, including President Richard M. Nixon. Unfortunately, the team also lost that day to the Rams, and limped along to a disappointing 6–8 record, including humbling losses to the Bears and Lions in the final two games. Not surprisingly, Phil Bengston announced his resignation after the last game. He had been a fine assistant for the Packers, but replacing Vince Lombardi and coaching a team in transition was a challenging and unforgiving task in which he probably had little chance of succeeding.

After Bengston's departure, the Packers' answer to the question "Now which way?" turned out to be "In a completely different direction." New head coach and general manager Dan Devine had been a coaching star in the college ranks for 16 seasons, compiling 120 career victories, first at Arizona State, then at the University of Missouri. The executive committee's route to hiring Devine on the heels of Bengston and Lombardi was eerily similar to the events of two decades earlier when college coaching veteran Lyle Blackbourn replaced a long-time NFL assistant (Gene Ronzani) who failed to fill the shoes of a coaching legend (Curly Lambeau). More than a few people questioned the wisdom of this hiring, and there were still whispers around the NFL about whether college coaches really were prepared to successfully make the jump directly to a head job in the pros.

Despite these concerns, Devine arrived in Green Bay with exceptional credentials. He was a Wisconsin native (born in the small town of Augusta) and a three-sport star at the University of Minnesota-Duluth. After graduating, Devine coached high school ball for two years, then moved to Michigan State as an assistant before being hired by Arizona State in 1955. Devine called himself a "fussbudget" in describing his attention to detail (including his requirement that players keep their shoes shined and pants pressed), but he was also an exceptional motivator who excelled at getting outstanding performances from his players.

Devine's regular-season debut with the Packers was a bust ... literally. Playing the Giants at Lambeau Field, the Packers were in the fourth quarter of a wild shootout when Devine was run over on the sideline at the end of a play and his leg broken. He had to be rushed to ironically named St. Vincent Hospital, and defensive line coach Dave Hanner took charge of the team. The Packers ended up losing 42–40. The gutsy Devine directed the team from a golf cart during the following week's practices, and he coached from the skybox during a Week 2 win over the Broncos. By the third week, he was back on the sidelines, coaching on crutches.

Devine was not the only person on the team who was hurting. Bart Starr had undergone experimental surgery to repair his damaged shoulder during the off-season. Ever loyal to the Packers, Starr hoped to return to form and help the team in its transition to a new coach, but he nearly bled to death because of post-surgical complications. When Starr returned to the lineup late in the season, his presence did not do much to boost the Packers' flagging fortunes.

The Packers experienced a few bright spots in 1971. Rookie quarterback Scott Hunter did a decent job in Starr's absence, and first-round pick John Brockington proved a sensational halfback, running for 1105 yards and averaging better than 5 yards per carry. Brockington and Donny Anderson formed what might have been the best backfield in the league, and Green Bay accumulated more than 2200 yards on the ground. But even though the offense was respectable, the once-dominant Packer defense showed little of its

In 1978, cornerback Willie Buchanon led the Packers with nine interceptions and was voted to the Pro Bowl. He is shown in pass coverage during that season's game in Tampa, a 17–7 Green Bay victory. Despite his outstanding season, Buchanon and the Packers could not agree on a new contract and he was traded to the San Diego Chargers.
Manny Rubio/WireImage.com

former greatness, yielding points in large batches. Emblematic of the change was Ray Nitschke, slowed by age, being benched in favor of Jim Carter, though Devine returned the veteran to the lineup for Ray Nitschke Day, a December 12 win over the Bears. That day offered a rare highlight, as the Packers finished in the NFC Central cellar for the second year in a row with a record of 4–8–2. Packer fans with sharp memories might have recollected that Lisle Blackbourn had led Green Bay to a very similar 4–8 record his first season, but fortunately some of the Blackbourn-Devine parallels were destined to break down in 1972.

WILLIE BUCHANON
Cornerback
1972–1978

Willie Buchanon is proof that life can be very busy for football players even after they retire. Buchanon has been a successful real estate broker in his hometown of Oceanside, California, for a quarter century, co-owns a marketing company that places ads on trucks around the country and donates half its earnings to underprivileged kids, is music minister at his church, and volunteers as an assistant high school track coach. But when this man played for the Green Bay Packers, he was part of a talented fierce-hitting secondary that caused problems for opposing passers. Buchanon had starred at San Diego State and was selected by Green Bay with their first-round pick in 1972; he immediately moved into the starting lineup. Buchanon was a tough player who made three Pro Bowl appearances and twice returned from broken legs suffered in 1973 and 1975. His best season came in 1978 when he led the team with nine interceptions (including four in one game) and was voted All Pro. Unfortunately, Buchanon and the Packers could not agree on a new contract, so the team traded him to San Diego, where he spent the rest of his career before retiring to his busy post-football life in 1982. Buchanon's son, William, is trying to carry on the family NFL tradition: A wide receiver out of USC, he spent 2006 on the Raiders' practice squad.

THE GOLDEN GIRLS

Packers cheerleaders? While the team currently has no official cheer squad, this has not always been the case. During the 1960s glory years and into the early 1970s, the Packers' sidelines were graced by the Golden Girls, a team of talented young cheerleaders who entertained Lambeau Field faithful with pom-pom, dance, and baton-twirling routines. These were not NFL cheerleaders in the sexy mold made popular by the Dallas Cowboys squad launched in the late 1970s. Instead, they were clean-cut young women from all over northeastern Wisconsin, the epitome of Midwestern wholesomeness and a perfect match for a small-city franchise like the Packers.

Coaching the cheer squad was the incomparable Mary Jane Van Duyse (standing on the right end in the top photo), the original Golden Girl, a nickname given to her, ironically, by a *Chicago Tribune* writer after he watched her perform during a Packers-Bears game. The talented baton-twirler and dancer had first performed at a Packers game in 1949; she became the head drum majorette of the team's popular Lumberjack Band in 1954. After Vince Lombardi was hired as coach, he suggested starting a cheerleading group to perform at games. Mary Jane naturally was tabbed to recruit and train the cheerleaders; besides her work with the team she ran dance studios in northeast Wisconsin and had an ample supply of students from which to select participants.

Starting with their debut in 1961, the Golden Girls became a fixture at Packers games and retain a cherished place in the hearts of fans who spent time at Lambeau Field during the storied Lombardi era. Their gutsy performance at the Ice Bowl is the stuff of legends: Despite the subzero temperatures, the cheer squad performed their routine wearing their standard gold sweaters, short skirts, and tights.

Most stayed the whole game, even when told they could leave; a few even suffered minor frostbite because of the frigid conditions.

Times change, even in the world of cheerleading, and the Golden Girls disbanded after the 1972 season. (Considering the team's dismal performance in the years that followed, the Packers could have used the squad on the sideline to add some spirit to the games!) That same year, Mary Jane married prominent businessman—and Packers fan—Bill Sorgel, and the couple enjoyed a storybook marriage until his passing in 2006. Meanwhile, Mary Jane retains close ties to the Packers and her former Golden Girls, thanks to periodic reunions and plans by the team's Hall of Fame to pay a special tribute to the squad in 2007.

Fred Carr: "What did we give up for [Hadl]?"
Jim Carter (imitating bandleader Lawrence Welk): "A one, a two, and a one, two, three."
—A locker room exchange discussing the infamous John Hadl trade

"WE SHOULD HAVE GONE TO THE SUPER BOWL"

The 1972 season, in fact, appeared to be a turning point for the post-Lombardi Packers. Joining Dan Devine on the sidelines was new assistant quarterbacks coach, Bart Starr. The Packers' legendary quarterback had spent an arduous off-season trying to rehab his shoulder, but to no avail. He announced his retirement before the season started and Devine convinced him to accept a one-year assignment tutoring young quarterbacks Scott Hunter and Jerry Tagge, the latter a first-round pick from Nebraska who had been a prep star in Green Bay. Starr admitted he had never thought much about being a coach, but he enjoyed the experience. After one year in coaching, Starr returned to his original post-football plan: running his automobile dealership in Birmingham, Alabama, and being a television commentator for NFL games on CBS.

With a year under his belt, general manager Devine aggressively re-made his roster. In addition to Tagge, notable draft picks included cornerback Willie Buchanon and kicker Chester Marcol, who were two of the best ever to play those positions for the Packers. Marcol even led the NFL in scoring his rookie season. Devine also pulled off a number of trades, the most noteworthy being when he sent Donny Anderson to the Cardinals for another running back, MacArthur Lane. Some thought the trade was curious, but it turned out to be a brilliant move. The veteran Lane was a devastating blocker for John Brockington, who enjoyed another 1000-yard season. Lane also added 821 yards on the ground and was the Packers' leading receiver.

With a rejuvenated defense leading the way, the young Packers played well, won a handful of close games, and found themselves sitting at 4–3 at midseason. Then, they picked their play up a notch and ran off two three-game winning streaks sandwiched around a loss to the Redskins. A December 10 pasting of the Vikings in Minnesota clinched the Central Division title, which the Packers took with an impressive 10–4 record. A rematch with the Redskins, owners of the NFC's best record at 11–3, awaited.

Years later, Macarthur Lane summed up his memories of the 1972 Packers. "We should have gone to the Super Bowl and won it. We had the best team." Lane can be forgiven for his selective memory—the 1972 Miami Dolphins, one of football's all-time greatest teams, finished undefeated and won the Super Bowl— but many people in Green Bay expected a different result than what transpired on the field in Washington. The Redskins keyed on the Packers vaunted running attack, shut it down, and beat the Packers easily, 16–3. In the process, Dan Devine stubbornly refused to abandon the run. Bart Starr later admitted he had unsuccessfully lobbied the head coach during the game to try passing more, and that was the only time he disagreed with a Devine coaching decision.

The Packers entered the 1973 season with high hopes and while sitting at 2–1–1 after Week 4 had every reason to believe they were still a playoff contender. Dan Devine, content with the previous season's team, had done little in the off-season to change his roster other than trade a couple of draft picks to Miami for quarterback Jim Del Gaizo. Yet this new addition was offset by a significant departure: As promised, Bart Starr said goodbye after one season as quarterbacks coach. His departure left the Packers with three young quarterbacks (Hunter and Tagge in addition to Del Gaizo) and apparently no one to teach them their difficult job. The position became a headache for Devine, who was unable to select a starter and stick with him. By the season's end, Hunter and Del Gaizo had each appeared in eight games, and Tagge in seven.

The rotating quarterbacks played havoc with the Packers' ability to gain yards and score points. Starting in Week 6, the offense was held to fewer than 100 yards for three straight games—all losses—and the season unraveled. John Brockington became the first man in NFL history to rush for more than 1000 yards in his first three seasons, but that was the only bright spot for a team that scored a paltry 14 points per game. A season-ending 21–0 shutout of the Bears kept the Packers out of the NFC Central cellar, but nobody was satisfied with the team's 5–7–2 record. Devine had put together a fairly talented team, but there were questions about his ability to manage that talent at the professional level.

THE WFL AND A DESPERATE TRADE

After a string of successful years, 1974 turned out to be a challenging one for the NFL. The amazing popularity of pro football and the money being earned by the NFL and its clubs had a natural effect: More people wanted a piece of the action, both wealthy investors who wanted to be owners and growing cities that thought they were worthy of a franchise. So, as had happened several times before, a rival league emerged—this time the World Football League (WFL). The WFL was led by Gary Davidson, who had previously served as president of the upstart American Basketball Association and World Hockey Association. It assembled 12 teams, including franchises in several non-NFL cities (for example, Memphis, Portland, Birmingham, and Honolulu), and started play in the summer of 1974.

The WFL was seemingly in financial trouble from its opening kickoff, but it managed to upset the NFL by signing away several high-profile players with the promise of more money. Of particular note was the signing of the Miami Dolphins' superstar trio of Larry Csonka, Paul Warfield, and Jim Kiick, by the Memphis Southmen, though the trio was not scheduled to start play until the 1975 season. As 1974 progressed, some WFL teams failed and others relocated, making it appear that there might never be a 1975 season.

Even as the WFL started play, the NFL was facing another public relations nightmare: players on strike and picketing training camps. The WFL had helped expose the fact that NFL players were underpaid compared to other pro athletes, and when the latest labor contract (signed after a brief strike in 1970) expired, those players walked in hope of gaining a larger chunk of the NFL revenues. Among their demands (there were 93 specific points), players were fighting for free agency—the right to sign with whatever team they wanted once their contract expired. The players' initial unity quickly broke down; eager to start camp, some crossed picket lines, though the first preseason games were played primarily by unknown rookies. The union finally gave in and suspended its strike in late August, allowing veterans to get in a couple of preseason games before the regular season. The players ended up playing without a contract until 1977.

The Packers might have been better off if the entire season had been played with rookies fresh out of college. The quarterback position continued to vex Dan Devine, and during the off-season, he dispatched Hunter and Del Gaizo and brought in Jack Concannon from the Bears to back up Jerry Tagge. Midway through the season, that duo together had managed just a single touchdown pass and the low-scoring Packers were lucky to have no worse than a 3–4 record. Desperate to win and knowing his job was probably on the line, Devine pulled off a rare midseason trade that would be remembered as one of the worst personnel moves in team (if not league) history. In return for aging and expendable quarterback John Hadl, Devine mortgaged Green Bay's upcoming drafts,

> ## "Who do they think he is, a Polish prince?"
> —*Bears coach Abe Gibron on the Packers protesting rough treatment of Chester Marcol during kickoffs*

giving the Los Angeles Rams two first-round, two second-round, and one third-round pick. Devine finally had an experienced quarterback, but at what cost?

While Hadl had once been an AFL superstar running Sid Gillman's revolutionary pass-happy offense in San Diego, he was 34 years old when he arrived in Green Bay, and his arm had lost some of its zip. Furthermore, Green Bay's offensive woes clearly extended beyond the person playing quarterback. Hadl contributed exactly three touchdown passes in Green Bay's final seven games and the team repeated its first-half-of-the-season performance in finishing with a 6–8 record.

Fans were calling for Dan Devine's job, but unbeknownst to team officials, the coach was going to relieve them of the need to fire him. Thinking his tenure in Green Bay was about to end, Devine had been secretly pursuing leads in college football. After the last game of the season, Devine resigned to become the head coach at Notre Dame—arguably NCAA football's top job. Despite the fact that Devine's pro coaching career was largely a failure, he was still a talented coach. He led Notre Dame for five seasons, leading them to three bowl victories, plus a national championship in 1977. That championship squad was led by Joe Montana, maybe the greatest quarterback in football history—an amazing irony considering how Devine struggled with quarterbacks while coaching the Packers.

LOMBARDI'S QUARTERBACK BECOMES HEAD COACH

On December 24, 1974, the Packers' executive committee gave Green Bay fans what they hoped would be a Christmas present that they could cherish for years to come by hiring Bart Starr as the team's new head coach and general manager. Since Starr had been Vince Lombardi's coach on the field, team officials hoped he could use his impeccable leadership skills and football knowledge—learned from one of the game's masters—to help a team only seven years removed from a Super Bowl victory recapture some of its lost glory.

To some people, hiring Starr was a brilliant masterstroke, a way to reconnect with the team's greatest era, but to others it was a huge mistake. Starr was a wonderful person and one of the most respected men in pro football, but his coaching experience was limited to his single season as an assistant. Furthermore, the Green Bay job had become one of the toughest in football. After Lombardi's departure, the team's organization had deteriorated and it lacked the sharp football minds necessary to keep up with a rapidly changing game. More critical, the Packers' talent had dropped off, some of their best

players were mired in contract disputes, and thanks to Devine's costly trade for John Hadl, the draft might not provide much help for a couple of years.

Considering these circumstances, accepting the job was not an easy decision for Bart Starr. He admitted in his autobiography, *Starr: My Life in Football*, that all of his close friends in football urged him to turn down the opportunity. Long-time Packer Bob Skoronski summed it up best in terms with

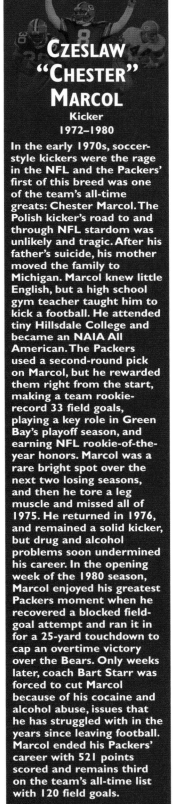

CZESLAW "CHESTER" MARCOL
Kicker
1972–1980

In the early 1970s, soccer-style kickers were the rage in the NFL and the Packers' first of this breed was one of the team's all-time greats: Chester Marcol. The Polish kicker's road to and through NFL stardom was unlikely and tragic. After his father's suicide, his mother moved the family to Michigan. Marcol knew little English, but a high school gym teacher taught him to kick a football. He attended tiny Hillsdale College and became an NAIA All American. The Packers used a second-round pick on Marcol, but he rewarded them right from the start, making a team rookie-record 33 field goals, playing a key role in Green Bay's playoff season, and earning NFL rookie-of-the-year honors. Marcol was a rare bright spot over the next two losing seasons, and then he tore a leg muscle and missed all of 1975. He returned in 1976, and remained a solid kicker, but drug and alcohol problems soon undermined his career. In the opening week of the 1980 season, Marcol enjoyed his greatest Packers moment when he recovered a blocked field-goal attempt and ran it in for a 25-yard touchdown to cap an overtime victory over the Bears. Only weeks later, coach Bart Starr was forced to cut Marcol because of his cocaine and alcohol abuse, issues that he has struggled with in the years since leaving football. Marcol ended his Packers' career with 521 points scored and remains third on the team's all-time list with 120 field goals.

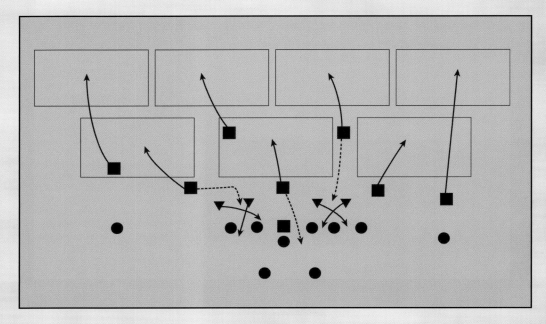

Packers' safety Johnnie Gray reacts to a play during a December 1975 game against the Los Angeles Rams. Safeties had an important role in the 1970s Green Bay defense, responsible for patrolling the deep zone in pass coverage, moving up to take an aggressive position against the run, or even blitzing on occasion. *NFL/WireImage.com*

KEY PLAY: THE 4–3 DEFENSE AND THE TWO-DEEP ZONE

By the 1970s, in response to the explosion of the passing game, most teams had shifted to the 4–3 defense; the Packers under Bart Starr and defensive coordinator Dave Hanner followed this trend. Many of the innovations involved in the use of this formation had been pioneered during the previous decade by Dallas Cowboys coach Tom Landry, Vince Lombardi's primary rival. But even Lombardi students Starr and Hanner could not deny the effectiveness of some of the trends introduced by Landry, including:

• **Emphasizing a patient read-and-react philosophy for defenders**

• **Using the "flex," in which the strong-side defensive end and weak-side tackle played back from the line of scrimmage to give them extra time to react to a play**

• **Employing a two-deep zone, with linebackers, corners, and safeties responsible for pass coverage in a section of the field, rather than on a specific receiver (the boxes in the diagram show typical two-deep zone coverage responsibilities)**

By the 1970s, even though most teams were employing the simple 4–3 formation, there was nothing simple about how defenses were being run. Linemen would often use "stunts"—varying rush directions, including crossovers and spins (shown on the diagram)—to confuse blockers. Linebackers—and/or cornerbacks or safeties—would often "blitz," an all-out rush into the offensive backfield, in varying combinations, from various angles, sometimes on delayed timing. (Dashed lines on the diagram illustrate a few blitz options.) Even the placement of the 4–3 relative to the line could be varied, with the tackles and linebackers shifting into the "over" and "under" alignments.

Despite using cutting-edge strategies, the Packers' defensive success—or lack thereof—in the 1970s was determined in large part by the quality of the players they put on the field, and in this area they came up short. At the end of the decade, Starr dismissed Hanner, abandoned the 4–3, and embraced the 3–4. The Packers responded in the 1980s by fielding some of the weakest defensive teams in NFL history.

which Starr could not disagree. "You have nothing to gain … you're not prepared for the job … you don't have the experience." Despite his good friend's candid comments, Starr could not refuse the chance to turn around the football team to which he had given so many years of his life and that held such an important place in his heart.

Compounding Starr's problems during his rookie season as a coach was the loss or productive drop-off of several key players. When linebacker Ted "The Stork" Hendricks (the team's best defensive player in 1974) refused to sign a new contract, Starr traded him to Oakland. Kicker Chester Marcol tore a leg muscle and spent 1975 on injured reserve. Willie Buchanon broke his leg and missed all but two games. Running back John Brockington went into a slump from which he never recovered. And John Hadl, while competent,

never regained the form that made him a star in San Diego. A few rookies—most notably defensive backs Steve Luke and Johnnie Gray, nicknamed the "Hit Brothers"—made their mark, but they could not offset the fact the Packers were old and overmatched by most NFL teams. They lost their first four games and were never a factor in the Central Division race, ultimately finishing 4–10 and tied for last with the equally mediocre Bears.

Facing his first off-season as a coach and general manager, Bart Starr knew that getting a better quarterback was the key to the Packers' future. He settled on former Kansas State star Lynn Dickey, languishing on the Houston Oilers' bench behind Dan Pastorini. Starr negotiated what turned out to be a very good trade for Green Bay, sending Houston Ken Ellis (who was demanding a trade

What a difference a decade can make: In the mid-1960s the Packers dominated pro football, while the Miami Dolphins were an AFL expansion team. By the time of this October 1975 game at Lambeau Field (a 31–7 Miami victory), the Dolphins and running back Mercury Morris had enjoyed several years among the NFL elite, while the Packers were stumbling to a 4–10 record.
Bruce Bennett Studios/Getty Images

"I ask for your prayers and patience; we will earn everything else."
—*Bart Starr to Green Bay fans on becoming the Packers' head coach*

anyway), John Hadl, and third- and fourth-round draft choices for Dickey. Because he played during a forgettable era for the Packers, and because his career was interrupted by a serious injury, Dickey may rank as one of the most overlooked players in team history. His career passing statistics, including 23,322 yards and 141 touchdowns, put him among the top 100 NFL quarterbacks of all time in many categories, and his numbers were on par with those posted by Bart Starr—even though Starr played many more seasons than Dickey.

But when you are a quarterback, the only statistic that matters is whether you can lead your team to victory, and on that matter, Lynn Dickey did not help the Packers much in 1976. The offense sputtered throughout the season, scoring only 212 points, and in one forgettable game (a 28–7 loss to the Bengals) generated only 36 yards. John Brockington was no longer effective and gained only 406 yards on the ground. A three-game winning streak in October temporarily buoyed fans' hopes, but the team could not maintain the momentum and finished 5–9 and alone on the bottom of the Central Division.

The Packers showed no improvement in 1977; in fact, they seemed to be getting worse. Starr had replaced offensive coordinator Paul Roach in the off-season, but to no avail. The 1977 offense was one of the poorest in the league and scored only 11 touchdowns the entire season. The season hit a low point when Lynn Dickey's leg was shattered on the last (and meaningless) play of a 26–7 loss to the Rams. It would take the young quarterback two years of recovery and rehab before he returned to the field.

When the 1977 Packers finished with a 4–10 record (the expansion Tampa Bay Buccaneers kept them out of last place), Bart Starr wondered if he would get a new contract. His first three-year deal was

Not many current-day Packers fans remember Barty Smith—shown ripping off a nice chunk of yardage against the Bears—but he was a talented fullback for the Packers throughout much of the 1970s. He led the team in both rushing (554 yards) and receptions (37) in 1977.
Focus on Sport/Getty Images

LARRY McCARREN
**Center
1973–1984**

University of Illinois alum Larry McCarren was only lightly regarded when he came out of college; the Packers selected him in the 12th round of the 1973 draft and parked him in a spot on the taxi squad that season. Not a big player—he played at 6-feet, 3-inches and 247 pounds—McCarren was smart, hardworking, and tough. By 1974, he had worked himself into the starting lineup and began a stretch of playing 162 consecutive, a streak that earned him a nickname: "The Rock." The moniker came as much for his penchant for playing through pain, especially in 1980 when he stayed in the lineup despite preseason hernia surgery and a midseason broken hand. Late in his career, McCarren finally received the league-wide recognition he deserved in being named All Pro from 1981–1984. A neck injury finally forced McCarren to retire after 1984, but he easily shifted to a new career—broadcasting. Today "The Rock" is one of Wisconsin's best and best-known media personalities, serving both as sports director for a Green Bay television station and as color commentator for Packers radio broadcasts. Fans of his popular TV show, *Larry's Locker Room*, wave foam replicas of his distinctive hand with its trademark splayed pinky, a trophy (poorly healed from a broken bone) earned during his days as one of the league's top centers.

up, and the team had won a total of 13 games. Any other coach would probably have been shown the door, but Bart Starr was not just any coach. He was still a hero in Green Bay, and the executive committee gave him another contract—and another chance—to rekindle the greatness of the Lombardi era.

STARR BUILDS FOR THE FUTURE
As a quarterback, Bart Starr was noted for being patient and cool under fire, and these traits also served him well as a coach and general manager. Despite his team's poor record, he remained committed to the idea of adding young players and building for the future, and as 1978 approached, Starr was ready to reap the rewards of his efforts to remake the Packers roster. Recent drafts had yielded several talented players. Tackle Mark Koncar, the first-round pick in 1976, joined an improving offensive line, anchored by center Larry "The Rock" McCarren. The 1977 draft yielded defensive bookends Mike Butler and Ezra

"The Rock"—center Larry McCarren, number 54—manhandles a San Diego defensive lineman during the Packers' 24–3 win over the Chargers on September 24, 1978.
Vernon Biever/WireImage.com

Johnson in the first round along with eight other players who made the team. Eighth-round pick David Whitehurst, from little-known Furman University in South Carolina, took over as the Packers starting quarterback after Lynn Dickey went down.

The 1978 draft was just as rewarding, yielding eight more players who made the regular-season roster. The team's second choice, linebacker John Anderson, was a great one, but their first choice—wide receiver James Lofton—was the best pick of the Starr era. The speedster from Stanford turned out to be one of the most gifted players in NFL history. Through 16 seasons (the first nine with the Packers), Lofton caught 764 passes, including 75 for touchdowns. His 14,004 career

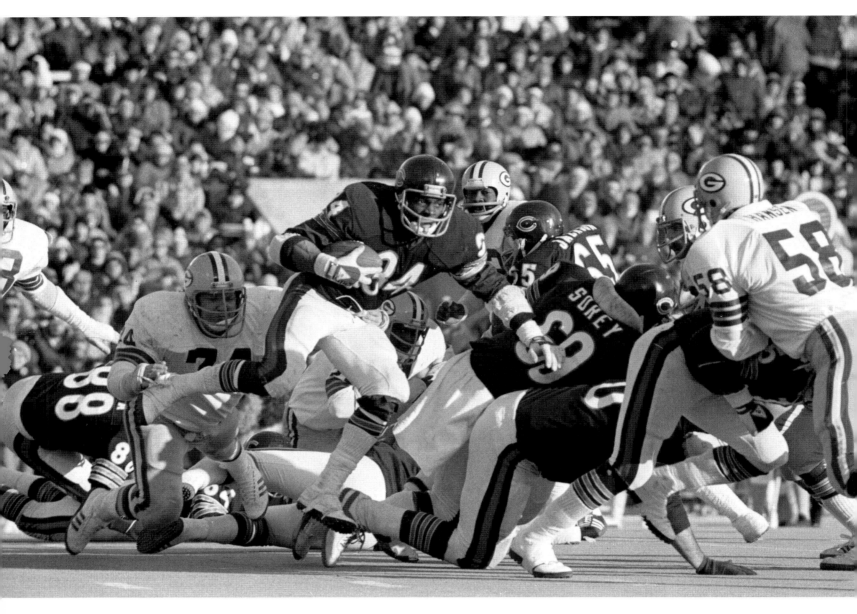

By the late 1970s, the Packers' porous defense had trouble stopping other teams. Scenes like the Bears' Walter Payton surging past Green Bay defenders during a 21–10 Chicago victory on December 12, 1977, became all too common, eventually leading to the firing of Packers defensive coordinator Dave Hanner. *Bettman/CORBIS*

receiving yards rank third all-time in the NFL, trailing only Jerry Rice and Tim Brown.

Lofton made an immediate impact on the Packers, leading the team with 46 catches and 6 touchdowns, and second-year running back Terdell Middleton followed the now-robust offensive line to a 1000-yard season. Thanks to the infusion of young talent, the offense nearly doubled its scoring output from 1977. Seven weeks into the 1978 season, the revived Packers were 6–1, all alone in first place, and seemingly bound for the playoffs. Years later, Starr admitted he was surprised at this early success, and that his young team was not as good as its record indicated. Fulfilling their coach's low expectations, the team could only muster two more victories the rest of the season. They stayed

in the hunt for a playoff spot until the final week, but ultimately lost the division race to Minnesota. Both teams had identical 8–7–1 records, but the Vikings' 21–7 victory over the Packers on October 22 proved the tiebreaker. (The rematch in Green Bay ended in a 10–10 tie.) Atlanta secured the NFC wild card spot with only a 9–7 record. The Packers' near miss was frustrating, but the executive committee seemed vindicated in its decision to stick with Bart Starr.

The 1978 team that seemed to be on the verge of a breakout was nowhere to be seen in 1979—a season that most Packer fans would just as soon forget because of injuries, poor play, and embarrassing gaffes on and off the field. While the offense remained decent and fans were heartened by the late-season return of

Lynn Dickey and the emergence of rookie tight end Paul Coffman (signed as a free agent), the defense was missing in action. Teams ran at will on the Packers, racking up nearly 3000 yards on the ground. James Lofton continued to excel in catching 54 passes, but found himself at odds with Green Bay fans, who booed him after he fumbled during a close loss to the Jets. Lofton lost his cool and flashed the crowd an obscene gesture. He went further after the game, commenting that "[the fans] can shove it as far as I'm concerned."

Lofton also had a locker room run-in with Bart Starr after a loss to the Vikings, but that incident was a minor one during a season the coach probably wanted to forget. (And both men later said the incident helped them build a much closer relationship.) In particular, the press started to question whether Starr was the right man for the job. Obviously feeling the pressure, Starr had an angry exchange with a reporter following a Packers' loss to the Buccaneers—who were on their way to winning the Central Division in only their fourth NFL season.

The Packers, meanwhile, stumbled home with a disappointing 5–11 record in Bart Starr's sixth season as head coach. The year came to particularly sad end when Starr fired defensive coordinator and long-time Packer Dave "Hawg" Hanner, who had been with the organization as a player or a coach for 28 years. Yet this move seemed merely cosmetic. The Packers' organization had many shortcomings and had fallen far behind the elite NFL franchises, particularly in the science of evaluating talent. Bart Starr was a good man who worked extremely hard to succeed, but he seemed overmatched by the challenging dual roles of head coach and general manager. With the 1980s looming, the Packers were nowhere close to the team that Starr had once guided as a quarterback, and the prospects for improvement appeared dim. It was a tough time to be a Packer fan.

> **"Lynn Dickey dealt with pain nearly every day of his career. I have never seen anybody quite like him ... Most people wouldn't go to a tea party with some of the injuries he had."**
> —*Packers' trainer Dominic Gentile*

In 1976 Bart Starr traded for Houston backup Lynn Dickey in his quest to find the Packers a talented starting quarterback. The coach's instincts about Dickey were correct, but he had trouble keeping him healthy. A horrific leg injury in 1977 sidelined Dickey for two years—but the tough quarterback was the starter again before the end of 1979.
Getty Images

THE 1980S: FORMER PLAYERS FAIL TO FIND COACHING SUCCESS

The 1982 season resulted in Green Bay's strongest performance of the decade. Here linebacker Mike Douglass wraps up Falcons' fullback William Andrews during the Packers' 38–7 pasting of Atlanta on December 26. Though the season was shortened by a strike, the Packers made the most of the nine games played, qualifying for the "Super Bowl Tournament" and winning their first-round playoff game over the Cardinals. *Bruce Bennett Studios/Getty Images*

After a decade marked by relative calm in the wake of the AFL-NFL merger and by continuing growth in both the popularity of the sport and the revenues it generated, pro football faced the 1980s with changes abounding. Even as football had elevated itself into—and in the process changed—American culture, forces were in turn conspiring to change the culture of football. Developments in the 1970s hinted at some of the challenges that lie ahead.

While for many years the NFL had primarily been about "the game," the league was becoming increasing concerned with "the money"—the business side of the sport that now threatened to overshadow what transpired on the field. In fact, the money and the game had always maintained a necessary coexistence, but now the business side of football had taken on a whole new meaning. Rather than franchises struggling to make a few bucks to cover payroll, they were each generating millions of dollars from a variety of revenue streams—tickets, television, merchandise, advertising, and so on—and really the teams were functioning much more like a single powerful unit than ever before. The National Football League had evolved into a multi-billion dollar entity that now operated more like General Motors or IBM than a mere sports organization. By 1980, the "corporatization" of pro football was in full swing.

This new corporate approach manifested itself in a variety of ways, most visibly in stadiums. For years, NFL teams had been happy to camp out in venues built primarily for baseball, and even as new stadiums appeared in the 1960s and 1970s, most were generic

multipurpose facilities built to house both baseball and football. Then two teams—the Dallas Cowboys and Kansas City Chiefs—became the envy of every other franchise with gleaming new stadiums built expressly for football. Suddenly other NFL teams wanted *their* own stadiums, complete with moneymaking amenities

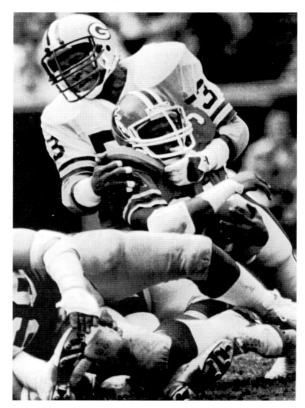

"I am fascinated by the unwillingness of coaches and scouts to step up to the table and accept responsibility for wasting a draft choice ... Our selection of Rich Campbell over Ronnie Lott in 1981 was a colossal blunder."
—*Bart Starr*

like luxury boxes for rich corporate tenants. The irony in this development is that few of the franchises had any intention of building these stadiums themselves; they wanted their home cities to foot the bill. Many cities were more than happy to at least consider the huge tax burden of building a new football stadium, if the alternative was losing their NFL team—a threat that would become very real in the years ahead.

This threat existed because the demand for NFL teams exceeded the number fielded by the NFL. Like any good corporate franchisor, the NFL looked to grow itself into the best new markets for its product, though it had become very careful with regards to this process. Unlike the league's first years when somebody with decent references and $50 for an entry fee could join the league, the NFL now studied potential cities and owners carefully. It became a hotly contested beauty contest of sorts, with overjoyed winners and angry losers—with the winners being required to post multi-million dollar expansion fees to the NFL before they started spending the real money now necessary to establish a team. Tampa Bay and Seattle were the winning cities in the late 1970s, though many more metro areas were waiting in the wings hoping to join the NFL, one way or another.

Even as the NFL and its owners were making tremendous amounts of money, the players were not sharing in the wealth in an equivalent way and many were very angry about this fact. The AFL-NFL bidding wars of the 1960s had improved players' pay, but in 1980 there was still no free agency that allowed players to sign with the highest bidder once their contract expired. Something called the "Rozelle Rule" enforced this situation. A team *could* sign a veteran after their contract with another club expired, but they were required to provide compensation to the other club—usually high draft picks. This situation stymied player movement and gave teams the upper hand in contract negotiations. Free agency had been an important issue in the 1974 strike, and though a new collective bargaining agreement signed in 1977 promised no player walkout until 1982, the issue promised to rise again in the years ahead.

Lynn Dickey, shown during a November 1982 game against the Jets, directed a potent Packers passing offense in the early 1980s that racked up yards and touchdowns with ease.
Ronald C. Modral/Getty Images

For many football fans at the start of the 1980s, the shifting landscape of the NFL was disconcerting. They loved the game and found all the corporate talk about labor issues and stadium financing a major distraction. And when, in the years ahead, these issues kept players off the field or took their teams away, they were understandably angry.

Fans in Green Bay were angry, too, but their dissatisfaction was simpler to pinpoint: The Packers had fallen far behind other franchises and were not playing good football. Lombardi-era hero Bart Starr had promised success, but delivered very little of it. After another poor performance in 1979, the team's prospects for 1980 looked pretty poor. Most fans would have welcomed a little corporate-style upgrade at this point in the team's history, but it was not going to occur in the next decade.

NEW DECADE, SAME OLD TEAM

The Eighties version of the Packers looked a lot like the Seventies version—a team mired in mediocrity

LYNN DICKEY
Quarterback
1976–1977, 1979–1985

Ask Packers fans to name the team's greatest quarterbacks and the conversation usually tails off after Favre and Starr—but what about Lynn Dickey? Dickey, who threw for 21,369 yards and 133 touchdowns, is at number three in most career passing categories. Unfortunately, Dickey had several strikes against him, the first being that he spent his first four years as a backup in Houston after starring at Kansas State. Head coach Starr made a shrewd trade that brought Dickey to Green Bay as the starter, but in 1977 he experienced the second strike against him when he missed two years recovering from a severely broken leg. Dickey's toughness and resiliency was legendary, and by 1980, he was healthy and finally living up to his potential But then there was the third, and maybe most important, strike: Dickey played for mostly mediocre teams. But Green Bay's inability to win, especially in the 1980s, had little to do with offense—the Packers could score points by the bushel and Dickey led the way. In 1983, he enjoyed his finest season in leading the league with 4458 yards and 32 touchdowns and was named All Pro for the only time in his career. Nagging injuries and a new coach, Forrest Gregg, finally conspired to end Dickey's career. Gregg cut him before the 1986 season and he retired. Dickey joined the Packer Hall of Fame in 1992.

Bart Starr took over as Green Bay general manager and head coach in 1974, but over nine seasons he never achieved the success he had enjoyed as the team's on-field signal caller. Here he is shown on the sidelines during one of only two playoff games he coached in, the Packers' January 16, 1983, loss to the Dallas Cowboys by a score of 37–26.
Ronald C. Modra/Getty Images

and controversy. The new decade got off to a terrible start when Green Bay's top draft pick, Penn State defensive lineman Bruce Clark, refused to sign with the Packers and instead inked a contract with the Toronto Argonauts of the Canadian Football League. Bart Starr was blindsided by the development and blamed Clark's agent for using the youngster in a scheme to help his other clients, but whatever the reason, Starr took a beating in the press. The preseason offered more problems. The Packers went winless, and during the last game, defensive end Ezra Johnson was observed munching a hot dog on the sidelines while his teammates were still on the field in a losing effort. The resulting outcry looked like it might cost Starr his job, but instead defensive line coach Fred von Appen took the fall for Ezra's voracious appetite.

The regular season was not much better, but it offered some special highlights for Green Bay fans. A healthy Lynn Dickey finally showed his potential and exploded for a team record 3529 yards passing (though he also led the league in interceptions with 25). James Lofton had a Pro Bowl season, catching 71 passes and leading the league in receiving yards. And

former first-round pick Eddie Lee Ivery returned from a knee injury that scuttled his rookie year to rush for more than 800 yards. The Packers shook off the hot dog controversy to win their opening game over the Bears 12–6. Chester Marcol scored the game-winning touchdown in overtime when he recovered his own blocked field goal attempt on the rebound and ran it in the 25 yards for the score.

Marcol's touchdown run may have been the high point of the season for the Packers. While Green Bay was exciting offensively, they were frightening on defense. The dismissal of defensive coordinator Dave Hanner and a switch to the 3–4 formation seemingly rewarded opponents with a license to score at will: The Rams put 51 points on the scoreboard in Week 3 and the Bears humiliated the Packers 61–7 in a late-season rematch of the overtime thriller. Injuries were another problem, with 27 different players missing games because of various ailments.

Throughout the disappointing season, fans were wondering if this was going to be Bart Starr's last year in Green Bay. When the board of directors gave him a public vote of confidence in midseason (often not a

In six seasons, Bart taught me about priorities. When I mention faith, family, and football, I stole it from him."
—*James Lofton, talking about Bart Starr during his Pro Football Hall of Fame induction ceremony*

good sign) and the team proceeded to finish tied for last in the Central Division at 5–10–1, most thought the end was near. The executive committee surprised everybody—Starr included—when they kept him on as coach, but took away his general manager title. What would have been logical at this point would have been to hire an experienced football insider to take over as GM, deal with personnel issues, and let Starr focus on coaching—or, alternatively, to make Starr the general manager and hire a new coach—but the executive committee basically did nothing but take away a title from Starr. He was still overwhelmed by a challenging job and no reinforcements were in sight. The Packers organization seemed hopelessly unaware of how successful teams were being managed.

The organizational model of choice in 1980 was undoubtedly "America's Team"—the Dallas Cowboys. President and general manager Tex Schramm, head coach Tom Landry, and vice president of player personnel Gil Brandt were a dynamic trio. Brandt's peerless scouting network and computerized talent-evaluation system consistently gave Landry—who focused on coaching—the players to compete for championships. The Cowboys had qualified for the playoffs nine out of 10 seasons during the 1970s and played in five Super Bowls, winning two. Schramm, Landry, and Brandt worked together for an unprecedented 29 years, departing the Cowboys only after Jerry Jones bought the team and cleaned house in 1989.

Bart Starr had no general manager or director of player personnel to help with roster building, which may have explained what happened in the 1981 draft. Even though Lynn Dickey had enjoyed a breakout season, and Starr admitted that his gut told him to take Ronnie Lott, the coach used his number six pick in the draft to take California quarterback Rich Campbell. Campbell threw a grand total of 68 passes during an entirely forgettable career. Lott became arguably the greatest defensive back in NFL history. Two years earlier, Starr had passed on Joe Montana (and readily admitted his error); now he had given the 49ers the other key player for their championship teams of the 1980s.

There was no championship in the offing for the

In 1983, the Packers' passing game was second to none. Quarterback Lynn Dickey—shown (below) looking for an open receiver during the October 23 game against the Vikings—amassed a league-leading 4,458 yards and 32 touchdowns. He had a talented receiving corps to throw to, including backup tight end Gary Lewis (left), shown hauling in a Dickey pass during the same game, which the Packers lost in overtime, 20–17.
Ronald C. Modra/Sports Imagery/Getty Images

PACKERS TRADITIONS
TRAINING CAMP

The Green Bay Packers' training camp is one of the most-anticipated events of the year for the team's fans. While some NFL squads conduct their preseason practice in relative obscurity, the Packers practice in the shadow of Lambeau Field in front of large crowds (though the team stays at St. Norbert College in nearby DePere, Wisconsin). Thousands of fans flock to Green Bay starting in July to watch the daily (sometimes twice daily) workouts. As long as the weather is good, practices are conducted on Clarke Hinkle field, which lies adjacent to busy Oneida Street just a short walk from Lambeau Field. There are bleachers that offer seating for around 600, but many fans crowd the fences for a view of the action. The nature of the training camp only reinforces the close relationship between the Packers and their fans. Most of the attendees enjoy attending preseason practice as much (or maybe more than) games because it allows them a close look at and, sometimes, access to their favorite players. One of the most entertaining traditions at the Packers' training camp is watching the players ride bikes provided by local kids to and from practice. Riding the bikes dates back to a 1961 suggestion by none other than Vince Lombardi who thought it would be a good way for players to build closer bonds with fans. A newer preseason tradition is the "Family Night" intrasquad scrimmage at Lambeau Field, an event geared toward younger fans who might not otherwise get to see the team play in person. The game is the most popular NFL preseason scrimmage, drawing more than 60,000 fans in recent years.

Green Bay defensive end Kabeer Gbaja-Biamila follows a time-honored training camp tradition as he rides eight-year-old fan Max Berger's (left, holding "KGB's" helmet) bike to the practice field on August 2, 2006. *Allen Fredrickson/Reuters/Corbis*

1981 Packers, though the team showed some improvement, particularly late in the season. The first half of 1981 looked painfully familiar to Packers fans, who were overwhelmingly in favor of firing Starr, according to a poll published by the Racine (Wisconsin) *Journal Times.* The draft had yielded little new talent, Eddie Lee Ivery was again sidelined with a major knee injury, and more player problems emerged, including starting offensive tackle Mark Koncar taking umbrage at criticism leveled at him by Starr and walking out on the team for a short time.

Starr did not quit in the face of adversity. A rare midseason trade with the Chargers brought John Jefferson, who teamed with James Lofton to give the Packers one of the league's best receiver tandems. When the team's struggles continued, Starr reached out to the fans to help turn around Green Bay's fortunes. "Packer Support Sunday" on November 1 came off as a giant community pep rally and seemed to energize the team. With a number of strong performances, Green Bay's record went from 2–6 to 8–7, with a wild card playoff spot in reach. Needing a win over the Jets in their final game to clinch a trip to the postseason, the Packers stumbled and lost 28–3 to finish with a .500 record—but for the first time since 1978 there was at least some guarded optimism for the upcoming season.

A STRIKE UNDERMINES A PROMISING SEASON

Unfortunately, Green Bay fans would never learn the full potential of the 1982 team for reasons beyond the Packers' control. The year started positively, with the signing of a new $2.1 billion television contract in March, but ended up being a difficult one for the NFL. The problems started when the NFL lost a highly publicized lawsuit that allowed the Oakland Raiders to relocate to the Los Angeles Coliseum. After the Rams moved to Anaheim in 1978, the L.A. Coliseum Commission went looking for a new tenant and found a willing party in Al Davis, the Raiders' president. In trying to move to L.A. without asking the league, he got the fight that he seemed to be trying to provoke— a long drawn-out one in court. When a jury ruled in favor of the Raiders on May 7, 1982, they made their way south for the upcoming season.

The impacts of this court case were felt throughout the decade because it allowed a sort of "franchise free agency" that prevented the NFL from stopping teams that wanted to relocate. Owners unhappy with their stadiums or with other gripes could simply abandon their home cities for greener pastures. The saddest example of what NFL fans faced happened in the early morning hours of March 29,

1984, when Colts owner Robert Irsay ordered the team's office and training facility equipment loaded into a convoy of moving vans and driven to Indianapolis. The team had a new home and Baltimore fans were devastated. Events like this only reinforced just how important Green Bay's public ownership of the Packers had become. The team might have lagged in adapting to corporate-style management, but at least it would not be guided by the whims of a single owner, and seemed destined to stay put in Green Bay.

Four days after the Raiders' relocation verdict, pro football made more headlines. On May 11, yet another rival league announced its formation and intention to start play the following season. The United States Football League (USFL) was a different kind of challenger to the NFL—it was well financed, innovative, and intent on playing football in the *spring*. The USFL planned to field a league with 12 teams and counted some of America's wealthiest men—including Donald Trump—among its owners. To show it was serious, the USFL made a major push to sign a number of top-level college players to lucrative contracts. As a result, several future NFL stars began their football careers in the USFL, including Reggie White, Steve Young, Jim Kelly, and Herschel Walker.

The 1982 season started under the shadow of a threatened player walkout, but the Packers started right where they had left off in 1981 by playing spirited football. The season opener provided the biggest come-from-behind win in team history when the Packers erased the Rams' 23–0 halftime lead and won 35–23. When the Packers beat the Giants in the following week's Monday Night Football Game, the

Above: Tight end Paul Coffman drags a Giants tackler during Green Bay's 27–14 victory over New York on October 4, 1981. Coffman made an unlikely rise from undrafted free agent to Pro Bowler during his eight seasons with the Packers. *Takashi Makita/WireImage.com*

Below: Walter Payton and the Bears gave the Packers fits during Chicago's 1985 Super Bowl season, but on this play the gang-tackling Green Bay defense seems to have the upper hand. Despite stopping the star runner here, the Packers lost the November 3 contest at Lambeau Field 16–10. *Jonathan Daniel/Getty Images*

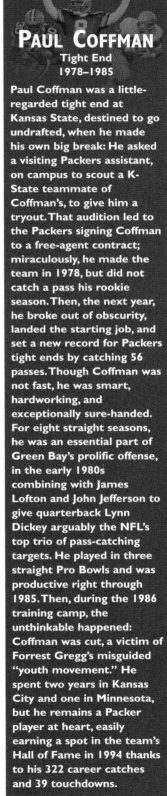

PAUL COFFMAN
Tight End
1978–1985

Paul Coffman was a little-regarded tight end at Kansas State, destined to go undrafted, when he made his own big break: He asked a visiting Packers assistant, on campus to scout a K-State teammate of Coffman's, to give him a tryout. That audition led to the Packers signing Coffman to a free-agent contract; miraculously, he made the team in 1978, but did not catch a pass his rookie season. Then, the next year, he broke out of obscurity, landed the starting job, and set a new record for Packers tight ends by catching 56 passes. Though Coffman was not fast, he was smart, hardworking, and exceptionally sure-handed. For eight straight seasons, he was an essential part of Green Bay's prolific offense, in the early 1980s combining with James Lofton and John Jefferson to give quarterback Lynn Dickey arguably the NFL's top trio of pass-catching targets. He played in three straight Pro Bowls and was productive right through 1985. Then, during the 1986 training camp, the unthinkable happened: Coffman was cut, a victim of Forrest Gregg's misguided "youth movement." He spent two years in Kansas City and one in Minnesota, but he remains a Packer player at heart, easily earning a spot in the team's Hall of Fame in 1994 thanks to his 322 career catches and 39 touchdowns.

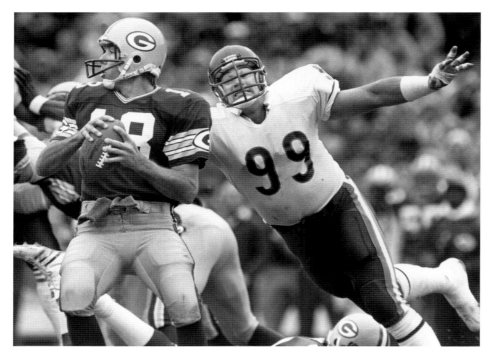

With Lynn Dickey struggling and plagued by injuries in 1985, Forrest Gregg started looking at other quarterbacks. Former Seahawk Jim Zorn saw action in several games, including the Packers' 16–10 loss to the Bears on November 3; here he is about to be sacked by Chicago's Dan Hampton. By the next season, Gregg has dumped both Dickey and Zorn in favor of the relatively inexperienced Randy Wright.

Jonathan Daniel/Getty Images

Forrest Gregg's Packers gained a reputation as the "bad boys" of the NFL for their behavior off and on the field. The November 3, 1985, game against the Bears was one to forget. The contest was marred by five unsportsmanlike conduct penalties and Green Bay cornerback Mark Lee (22)— shown arguing with an official— was tossed out.

Jonathan Daniel/Getty Images

season was looking bright—until the next day when the players went on strike. The nation went without football for 57 days, a bleak time for a country that was in love with the sport. The players put on exhibition games to raise money for the union, but the networks would not televise the contests. NBC tried broadcasting Canadian Football League games, but the American audience was not impressed. "It looked like high school football," complained one fan.

Ironically, the NFL's rich new TV contract had galvanized the players' strike. They wanted a bigger piece of the revenue pie, and made several demands including free agency, which they failed to obtain when this dispute was finally settled on November 16. But the players gained several key concessions from the owners, in particular the right to obtain copies of every player contract. Salaries became public knowledge and players (and their agents) gained more leverage in negotiations by citing the money earned by comparable NFL performers at the same positions.

The NFL scrambled to salvage its season and settled on an interesting solution. They eliminated divisions and had teams play seven more regular-season games to determine qualifiers for a "Super Bowl Tournament." Eight teams from each conference were seeded according to their records from the nine-game regular season and started playoffs to determine the Super Bowl entrants.

During the strike, Bart Starr was able to manage the tense relationship between players and management and kept his team focused on conditioning and the rest of the season even while they were on strike. As a result, the Packers hit the ground running when the season resumed and they finished in third place in the NFC with a 5–3–1 record, easily qualifying them for the playoffs.

The Packers validated their entry in the Super Bowl Tournament by hammering the St. Louis Cardinals 41–16 in the first playoff game played at Lambeau Field

> "I think blue collar workers can relate to me because I've had to work my way up the corporate ladder, so to speak ... I've never had anything given to me."
> —*Paul Coffman*

since the 1967 Ice Bowl against the Cowboys. Dallas happened to be the Packers' opponent in the second round of the 1982 playoffs, but the game was played at flashy Texas Stadium, not on the Frozen Tundra. The Packers put up a good fight and racked up 468 yards of offense, but Lynn Dickey's three interceptions proved critical errors in a 37–26 loss.

Bart Starr seemed to finally have turned a corner in his coaching career, and fans were starting to again rally behind him. During the off-season, he secured a two-year contract extension from new Packers president Robert Parins, but admitted that meeting with the former judge gave him an "uneasy feeling." Starr addressed his weak defense by drafting Tim Lewis in the first round. Lewis would intercept five passes as a rookie and be named All-Pro in his second season, so it was a solid pick. But that gain was offset by the critical loss of defensive end Mike Butler to the USFL. Parins, who had taken over negotiating player contracts, failed to close the deal, much to Starr's chagrin.

When the season finally started, it was apparent the NFL had probably never seen a team quite like the

1983 Green Bay Packers. They could move the ball and score seemingly at will, but they also conceded points just as easily. Almost every game had the look of a shootout. When the dust finally settled and fans caught their breath, the Packers had scored 429 points, given up 439 points, and finished tied for second in the Central with an 8–8 record. Along the way, Lynn Dickey led the league with an incredible 4458 yards passing and 32 touchdowns, and four players (James Lofton, John Jefferson, Paul Coffman, and Gerry Ellis)

Above: **Eddie Lee Ivery was highly regarded when the Packers picked him in the first round of the 1979 draft, but he missed most of two seasons with knee injuries. The speedy runner bounced back and led the team in rushing in three different seasons, including 1985; he is shown carrying the ball during that year's game against the Rams.**
Stephen Dunn/Getty Images

Like his predecessor Bart Starr, former Packers' player Forrest Gregg failed to rekindle the success of the Lombardi era as head coach. Unlike Starr, Gregg brought considerable coaching experience to the job, but after four frustrating seasons he departed Green Bay to take over as coach at his alma mater, Southern Methodist University.
Getty Images

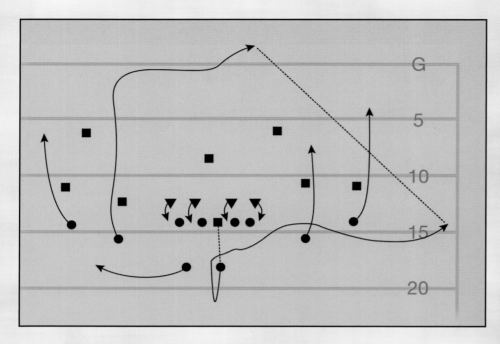

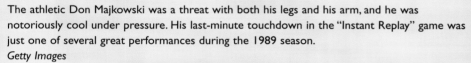

The athletic Don Majkowski was a threat with both his legs and his arm, and he was notoriously cool under pressure. His last-minute touchdown in the "Instant Replay" game was just one of several great performances during the 1989 season.
Getty Images

KEY PLAY: A MAJIK TOUCHDOWN WINS THE INSTANT REPLAY GAME

There were far too few Packers highlights during the 1980s, but the November 5, 1989, Lambeau Field contest against the Bears might have offered Green Bay fans their biggest thrill of the decade. Exciting quarterback Don "Majik" Majkowski had injected some life back into a moribund team, but on this day the Packers found themselves trailing 13–7, sitting on the Bears' 14-yard line, and with time left for just one more play. Green Bay came to the line in spread formation with a single back, paired wideouts on each side, and Majkowski back in the shotgun. Everyone in the stadium knew a pass was coming. On the snap, the four receivers took off for the end zone; the lone back swung out into the left flat as the outlet receiver. The Bears rushed four linemen and quickly put pressure on Majkowski, who was forced to step up in the collapsing pocket to avoid a sack. With no receivers open, he started scrambling forward and to the right. He flirted with the line of scrimmage for several yards before unleashing a desperation pass just as he reached the sideline, back toward the center of the field. For a right-handed thrower, this scrambling cross-body pass was the toughest kind to execute, but Majkowski's effort was true, finding his favorite target, Sterling Sharpe. From his left flanker position, Sharpe had followed the flow of the play and found an opening in the coverage two yards deep in the end zone. The Packers had scored the tying touchdown—or so everyone thought until they saw the penalty marker on the field. Line judge Jim Quick had flagged Majkowski for passing beyond the line of scrimmage. It so happened that 1989 was the first season of instant replay, and the call was directed to the booth official for review. What followed were probably the longest minutes in Packers' history as the Lambeau faithful nervously awaited the call. And then it came: "After further review, we have a reversal, touchdown!" The crowd exploded, and with Chris Jacke's extra point, the Packers won 14–13 in what became known as the "Instant Replay Game."

each caught more than 50 passes.

The most exciting game of the season was a rare Monday night contest at Lambeau Field against the Redskins on October 17. The two teams scored points like they were playing pinball, racking up more than 1000 yards of offense and trading touchdowns with ease against defenses that might have as well have stayed on the bench. Jan Stenerud's short field goal with less than a minute left proved the winning margin, but only because Washington missed its own field goal on the game's last play. Fans still agree the 48–47 Packer victory was the most exciting game in the storied history of Monday Night Football.

The critical moments of the season actually came at the end of the last game. The Packers were clinging to a 21–20 lead over the Bears, with a win likely rewarded by a playoff berth. As Chicago successfully drove for a field goal, Starr managed the clock poorly and the Packers had no time to respond when they got the ball back. They lost the game 23–21, and the next day Bart Starr lost his job after nine seasons as the Packers' head coach. Starr's dismissal was businesslike and unceremonious. Despite the limited success of his coaching tenure, it was a sad way for the Packers to end their relationship with a man who had meant so much to the franchise for so many years. Fortunately, in the future, with different leadership in place, Starr was able to rekindle his relationship with the team and its fans, and he remains an important part of the Packer family.

ANOTHER LOMBARDI PROTEGE TAKES THE REINS

Considering Judge Parins' cold and businesslike firing of Bart Starr, it would have been logical for the Packers to hire a coach that allowed a clean break with the past and forged a new identity independent of the Lombardi era. Yet the Packers went right back to their glory years in hiring Starr's former teammate, Forrest Gregg, as their new coach.

Unlike the inexperienced Starr, Gregg was a seasoned coaching veteran when he joined the Packers. After concluding his Hall of Fame playing career with a single season (1971) in Dallas, Gregg

The 1980s edition of the Bears-Packers rivalry did not provide many highlights for Green Bay fans. The decade was marked by scenes they wanted to forget: Charles Martin bodyslamming Jim McMahon, William "Refrigerator" Perry's touchdown run, and as seen here Walter Payton deftly eluding gangs of would-be Packers tacklers.
Focus On Sport/Getty Images

THE CHEESEHEADS

Most Wisconsinites will tell you that "cheesehead" is a term for describing anybody that resides in their state. They use the term with affection and pride; most are quick to proudly point out Wisconsin's status as "America's Dairyland" (as the state's auto license plates announce) and its prodigious output of cheese. Yes, Wisconsin loves its cheese. But the cheesehead moniker has been elevated to legendary status in the hands of Packers fans, thanks to the creativity of Milwaukeean Ralph Bruno. In 1987, stung by Chicago fans' *insults* **of Wisconsin residents being a bunch of "cheeseheads," Bruno carved a wedge-shaped block of foam from an old sofa and painted it yellow. He proudly wore it on his head to a Milwaukee Brewers–Chicago White Sox game, and a sensation was born. Today, the giant foam wedge of cheese, manufactured in huge numbers by Foamation Inc, has become almost as important a wearable statement of Packers loyalty as a replica jersey. It has also spawned a whole family of foam, cheese-like wearables, including various hats, ties, and even bras. Scan the crowd shots of any televised Packers game and you are sure to see the latest in cheesehead fashion.**

The cheesehead has become a fashion standard for many Packers fans. This gentleman in the stands at Lambeau for the September 25, 2005, game against Tampa Bay uses his foam headwear to make a declaration about Green Bay's publicly owned status that is unique in the NFL.
Paul Spinelli/Getty Images

joined the Chargers' staff as an assistant in 1973 and moved to Cleveland as offensive line coach in 1974. He was promoted to the Browns' top spot the next year and held the job for three seasons, but he resigned with a game left in 1977. He coached the CFL Toronto Argonauts in 1979, but returned to the States as head coach of Cincinnati in 1980. While Gregg enjoyed success with the Bengals, leading them to Super Bowl XVI, he could not resist the opportunity to turn around the fortunes of his former team.

In addition to their coaching resumes, Starr and Gregg were very different in terms of personality. While everyone agreed that Starr was a nice man who cared about his players, pro athletes were changing in the 1980s, and issues regarding temperamental players had been a problem throughout his tenure. Gregg, on the other hand, usually elicited one word when people were asked to describe him: disciplinarian. While quiet, thoughtful coaches such as Tom Landry were still respected and often successful, the 1980s also saw its share of traditional "throwback" coaches—Mike Ditka and Bill Parcells, for example—who practically bullied their teams into winning. Gregg, as a strict disciple of this Lombardi-like approach to coaching, was probably viewed by the Packers' executive committee as the perfect person to restore order, and winning football, to Green Bay.

Gregg inherited a potent offense, but he still made changes, shifting to a more run-oriented attack that nicely complemented the passing game. The key to this change was remaking the offensive line, in particular inserting big (6-feet 6-inches and 300 pounds) guard Ron Hallstrom, a first-round pick in 1982, into the starting lineup. He took advantage of the opportunity offered by Gregg to craft a stellar pro career that spanned 12 seasons.

Much of Forrest Gregg's focus was on upgrading the defense, which was coordinated by Dick Modzelewski. The draft delivered some fresh talent for

Opposite above: **In 1986 Randy Wright emerged as the Packers starting quarterback, but with mixed success. He held the job at the beginning of 1988—his is shown passing under pressure during a loss to the Bears early that year—but a groin pull forced him to the sidelines and opened the door for Don Majkowski, who eventually usurped Wright as the starter.**
Jonathan Daniel/Allsport

Opposite below: **Future Hall of Fame receiver James Lofton picks up yards after hauling in a Lynn Dickey pass during the Packers playoff game against the Dallas Cowboys on January 16, 1983. Lofton scored two touchdowns, but the Packers lost 37–26.**
Jonathan Daniel/Allsport

the unit. First-round pick Alphonso Carreker became the Packers' starting left defensive end and safety Tom Flynn, taken in the fifth round, led the team with nine interceptions. With the new players and leadership, the defense was vastly improved, yielding only 309 points and ranking in the middle of the league.

The Packers were slow to adapt to Gregg's changes and finished the first half of the season with a single victory. Then things started to click for Green Bay and the team suffered only one loss the rest of the way, finishing with a second straight 8–8 season. The record did not deliver a playoff spot, but it left fans feeling optimistic that a turnaround was in progress. A disappointing development during the season was an injury that forced center Larry McCarren out of the lineup after he had played in 162 straight games. "The Rock"—one of the team's most popular players—was forced to retire over the off-season, but he remained in Green Bay and today is a local television sports director and broadcaster for the Packers' radio network.

UPGRADING THE TEAM AND THE STADIUM

Because Gregg was a former tackle, it is not surprising that upgrading the Packers offensive line was one of his top priorities. Gregg devoted his top two picks in the 1985 draft to offensive lineman, but he got a couple of good ones: Arizona State tackle Ken Ruettgers and San Diego State guard Rich Moran reliably anchored the left

JAMES LOFTON
Wide Receiver
1978–1986

When the Packers selected James Lofton, a Stanford All American, in the first round of the 1978 draft, they knew he was a gifted receiver. They also knew he was smart (an academic All American) and athletic (NCAA long jump champion), but they probably did not realize how big of an impact Lofton would have in Green Bay. He became the key player in the pass-happy Packers' offense, playing in the Pro Bowl seven times, including a string of six straight appearances beginning in 1980. Lofton was tough and fiery and determined to win, but the Packers did little of that during his years with the team. Despite that, he still compiled impressive career numbers: 530 catches (number two all-time), 9656 yards (the Packers' record), and 49 touchdowns. Lofton turned out to be one of football's most durable receivers, playing for 16 seasons. He was traded to Oakland after the 1986 season, and later enjoyed four amazing years in Buffalo, where despite being one of the league's oldest receivers he was also one of the best, again reaching the Pro Bowl in 1992 and posting an outstanding performance in Super Bowl XXVI. After finishing up his career with short stints with the Rams and Eagles, Lofton retired after the 1993 season. He was elected to the Pro Football Hall of Fame in 2003 and today is an assistant coach with the San Diego Chargers.

which increased Lambeau Field's capacity to 56,926 and provided a lucrative new revenue stream to the team.

The 1985 season ended up being a challenging one for Gregg and the Packers—in particular for quarterback Lynn Dickey, who struggled through poor games and injuries. Gregg benched him during the season's third game, turning instead to second-year backup Randy Wright, who did not fare much better. Gregg also signed veteran Jim Zorn, the former starter in Seattle who had been supplanted by Dave Krieg. The three quarterbacks shared time throughout the season, with Dickey still getting most of the snaps, but the situation was clearly unsettling for the offense.

Meanwhile, the Chicago Bears were steamrolling through the NFL en route to a 15–1 record and a Super Bowl championship, so the Central Division was never a contest. Despite this fact and a poor 3–6 start, the Packers never gave up and won five of their last seven games to finish 8–8 for the third straight season. The highlight in this stretch was one of the most memorable games in Green Bay history: the December 1, 1985, "Blizzard Bowl" or "Snow Bowl." Nearly a foot of snow, howling winds, and an inspired Packer squad greeted the Tampa Bay Buccaneers who looked way out of their element in losing 21–0. Only 19,856 fans showed up for the game, but considering the conditions and the fact that area roads were largely impassable, the number is indicative of just how dedicated Green Bay fans really are. Many arrived at the game on snowmobiles.

Forrest Gregg looked at back-to-back .500 seasons

Green Bay won only four games in 1988, Lindy Infante's first season, but one of the victories included a 45–3 rout of New England at Milwaukee. Packers defensive back Ron Pitts (now a Fox Sports announcer) is shown returning a punt during that game.
Caryn Levy/Allsport

side of the Packers' line for much of the next decade.

While Gregg overhauled the football team, the Packers' board was overseeing the first major upgrade to Lambeau Field since 1970. Earlier expansions had increased capacity to 56,263, but the facility lacked the moneymaking luxury boxes that had become commonplace in so many other NFL facilities. This problem was rectified at the start of the 1985 season with the debut of 72 private suites in the stadium,

The kicking game was a problem for Lindy Infante in 1988. He started the season with Max Zendejas (shown placing the ball for a kickoff during Green Bay's October 9 game against New England), but cut him after he missed an easy field goal against the Redskins. Three kickers shared time the rest of the season, none with much success.
Karen Levy/Allsport

"Forrest looked down at me and said, 'And you, you're nothing but a low-life scum-of-the-earth worm rookie. In our opinion, you don't even exist.' I stopped laughing."
—*Brian Noble, remembering the coach's response to his laughter during a team meeting*

A fish-eye view from one end zone of a jam-packed Lambeau Field during a 1988 game. By this point in time the legendary stadium had been expanded with 72 private suites and boasted a capacity of 56,926.
Richard Hamilton Smith/CORBIS

as a major disappointment and dedicated the off-season to a major overhaul of the Packers. His first move was to fire offensive coordinator Bob Schnelker, a 32-year NFL coaching veteran—but the big shocks came during the 1986 preseason. Gregg, convinced he had to go with youth over experience, cut several Packer veterans, most surprisingly Lynn Dickey and Paul Coffman. Dickey had gone through protracted contract negotiations before reporting to camp and though 36 years old, appeared to be the best quarterback on the roster. His departure left the unproven Randy Wright as the starter. Coffman's release was even more mystifying. The tight end had caught 49 passes the previous season. He was picked up by the Chiefs, and played three more NFL seasons.

The young replacements offered the Packers little help in 1986. Randy Wright passed for more than 3200 yards and 17 touchdowns, but he was mistake-prone and the Packers' offense struggled to score points. Injuries also took a harsh toll, with Rich Moran and

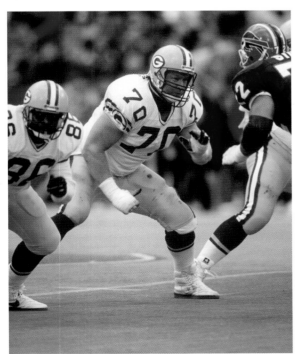

John Anderson missing most of the season and Tim Lewis suffering a career-ending neck injury. The losses started to pile up, but even worse were highly publicized incidents of player misbehavior. In October, James Lofton and Eddie Lee Ivery were accused of sexual assault after an incident at a Milwaukee strip club, but never charged. In December, Lofton was again accused of sexual assault, this time by a dancer at a Green Bay nightclub, and this time he was charged. Though he was later acquitted of the charges, the situation led to Lofton being traded to the Raiders.

A sad on-the-field incident during the November 23 game against the Bears came to represent the entire season for the Packers. Frustrated defensive lineman Charles Martin body-slammed the Bears' Jim McMahon, an obvious cheap shot that knocked the quarterback out for the rest of the season. Because the embarrassing play was witnessed by a large television audience and repeated on highlight broadcasts across the country, the Packers soon became known as the "bad boys" of the NFL. Though this reputation—gained because of the transgressions of just a few players—was undeserved, the Packers were a bad football team. The 4–12 campaign was not over quickly enough for many fans.

Many of the team's problems could be traced to its archaic organizational structure, which had lagged behind other franchise's embrace of modern corporate principles. This fact was a direct result of the Packers' odd public-ownership structure, which helped keep the team in Green Bay, but also kept it somewhat

Offensive lineman Keith Uecker gained notoriety in 1987 by being the only Packers regular to cross the picket line and play for the "replacement" teams during the players' strike. He is shown in action the following season pass blocking against the Bills. Today he is an assistant coach for Wayne State University in Detroit.
Rick Stewart/Allsport

Sterling Sharpe—shown diving in an attempt to grab a pass just beyond his reach—was a tremendously talented receiver who deserves considerable credit for the Packers' resurgence in the 1990s. Sadly, he missed out on the team's Super Bowl appearances when a neck injury cut short his career after the 1994 season.
Focus on Sport/Getty Images

isolated from the NFL mainstream. The executive committee took an important step to correct this problem in January 1987 when Tom Braatz, a veteran of the Atlanta Falcons' organization, was hired as executive vice president of football operations. For the first time, the team had an executive other than the head coach to build and manage the team.

Braatz' first draft was a mixture of misses and hits. The top-pick was running back Brent Fullwood, who was let go after a couple of mediocre seasons, but a couple of other choices from 1987 would make significant contributions to the Packers. Johnny Holland became a quality linebacker for the Packers for seven seasons. More significant was Braatz' 10th-round selection of unheralded Virginia quarterback Don Majkowski. The "Majik" man was destined to create a lot of excitement in Green Bay, and might have enjoyed a longer career if not for injuries and the emergence of another quarterback named Favre—but that's a story for another chapter.

Unfortunately, more player-related problems created additional embarrassment—in particular, cornerback Mossy Cade being sent to prison for two years after being convicted of sexual assault. Players who were not misbehaving were staging contract holdouts, including quarterback Randy Wright and first-round pick Fullwood. That such chaos was happening on the watch of a law-and-order coach like Forrest Gregg was perplexing to Green Bay fans, who found their loyalty tested by both the bad behavior and the losing teams. Yet another strike in 1987 tested their devotion to the sport of pro football.

The NFL players walked out again after the second game; the Packers were 0–1–1 at the time. The league responded by calling in replacement players—including some who had spent time in training camps but were cut before the season started—to cross the picket lines. The NFL played three weeks of decidedly mixed-quality football before the regular players gave in and came back to

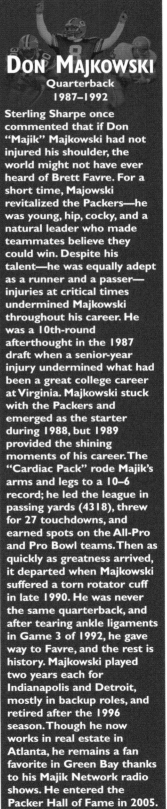

Below: Linebacker Tim Harris was a defensive stalwart for the Packers for five seasons, starting in 1986. The dangerous pass rusher went to the Pro Bowl in 1989 after recording a team-record 19.5 sacks.
Richard Hamilton Smith/CORBIS

Above: Boasting blonde locks and lots of swagger, Don Majkowski gave Green Bay a much-need injection of confidence. In 1989, his first full season as starting quarterback, he led the Packers to a 10–6 record.
Ronald C. Modra/Sports Imagery/Getty Images

DON MAJKOWSKI
Quarterback
1987–1992

Sterling Sharpe once commented that if Don "Majik" Majkowski had not injured his shoulder, the world might not have ever heard of Brett Favre. For a short time, Majowski revitalized the Packers—he was young, hip, cocky, and a natural leader who made teammates believe they could win. Despite his talent—he was equally adept as a runner and a passer—injuries at critical times undermined Majkowski throughout his career. He was a 10th-round afterthought in the 1987 draft when a senior-year injury undermined what had been a great college career at Virginia. Majkowski stuck with the Packers and emerged as the starter during 1988, but 1989 provided the shining moments of his career. The "Cardiac Pack" rode Majik's arms and legs to a 10–6 record; he led the league in passing yards (4318), threw for 27 touchdowns, and earned spots on the All-Pro and Pro Bowl teams. Then as quickly as greatness arrived, it departed when Majkowski suffered a torn rotator cuff in late 1990. He was never the same quarterback, and after tearing ankle ligaments in Game 3 of 1992, he gave way to Favre, and the rest is history. Majkowski played two years each for Indianapolis and Detroit, mostly in backup roles, and retired after the 1996 season. Though he now works in real estate in Atlanta, he remains a fan favorite in Green Bay thanks to his Majik Network radio shows. He entered the Packer Hall of Fame in 2005.

work without a new contract. Green Bay fared better than many franchises during the replacement weeks. Forrest Gregg created a respectable team that won two of its three games, and the Packers attracted more than 35,000 fans for each of its two home contests. Four of the replacements—Steve Collier, Jim Bob Morris, Patrick Scott, and Max Zendejas—stuck with the regular team for a time after the strike ended, with Scott and Zendejas sticking around until 1988.

The Packers might have been better off if the entire season had been played with replacements, because the team's losing ways returned along with the regular roster. Even though Green Bay finished 5–9–1, Forrest Gregg sounded optimistic in declaring that the Packers would soon be a winning team again. What he did not explain was that he was not going to be the coach of these winning teams. Instead, he resigned in January 1988 to become the head coach and athletic director at his alma mater, Southern Methodist University in Dallas.

With quarterback Don Majkowski at the helm, Green Bay's 1989 team became the "Cardiac Pack," noted for its close games and come-from-behind wins. The November 26 contest against the Vikings in Milwaukee—during which "Majik" audibles at the line of scrimmage—was no different: Green Bay needed a fourth-quarter touchdown to secure a 20–19 win.
Getty Images

A NEW COACH AND A BREAK WITH THE PAST

The Packers finally made a clean break from the past when they hired Lindy Infante as their new head coach in February 1988. Infante had a long coaching resume; most recently he had been the Browns' offensive coordinator, but he had also been the head coach of the USFL Jacksonville Bulls. More importantly, Infante had no previous ties to the Packers, and he was viewed as one of the league's leading offensive innovators, important because Green Bay's scoring output had slumped considerably during Gregg's tenure.

Coaches are one thing, but talent is another, and Green Bay still had a lot of catching up to do with the rest of the league. The 1988 draft, though, delivered one of the best players to ever wear the green and gold. The Packers took South Carolina receiver Sterling

Sharpe with the seventh pick in the draft, and he immediately validated that lofty position. Sharpe led the team in receiving his rookie season, and he was clearly something special. His fearlessness and strength in the middle of the field became legendary. He would take and deliver vicious hits, rarely dropping the ball, then pop back to his feet ready for the next play.

Sharpe's play was the primary highlight of the 1988 season, during which the team struggled to adapt to Infante's new offense and the coach had difficulty settling on a quarterback. Randy Wright began the season as the starter, but he gave way to Majkowski, who was exciting but erratic. Wright was reinstalled, but an injury sidelined him, and Majkowski returned for the final game, a 26–17 win in Arizona over the recently relocated Cardinals. Lindy Infante's first season ended with a disappointing 4–12 record.

"Don Majkowski ... had he been able to stay healthy ... you might never have heard of Brett Favre ... Don was cool, the Marlboro Man, the Lone Ranger, Little Joe Cartwright."
—Sterling Sharpe

The 1980s had been a largely forgettable decade for the Packers, but 1989 was destined to become a memorable year for both the franchise and the National Football League. On the league front, Pete Rozelle announced his retirement, well deserved after 29 successful years at the helm, but nonetheless a shock to a league that was embroiled in constant change. As Rozelle's successor, the league picked an able insider, Paul Tagliabue, but the shift in leadership

during a critical time was unsettling to the owners.

The biggest unresolved issue was free agency, which the players' union began to push incessantly. The NFL, determined to stave off a full-blown insurrection, gave in to the creation of what came to be known as "Plan B" free agency. Teams were allowed to protect 37 players on their roster, but the remaining players were allowed to sign with other teams without compensation. The plan amounted to little more than a shuffling of second-tier players, but for rebuilding teams like the Packers, it presented a legitimate opportunity to improve. The Packers took full advantage of Plan B, signing 20 free agents, more than any other team.

The draft still remained the best route to improvement, and 1989 offered a special opportunity to the Packers. Thanks to their poor record, they held the number two selection in the draft. When the Cowboys selected Troy Aikman with the first pick, the

Some consider tackle Tony Mandarich the biggest draft-day bust in NFL history. The Packers made Mandarich—shown blocking the Rams' Kevin Greene —the number 2 overall pick in 1989, but he had difficulty cracking the starting lineup, struggled when he became a starter, and was out of football after the 1991 season.
Getty Images

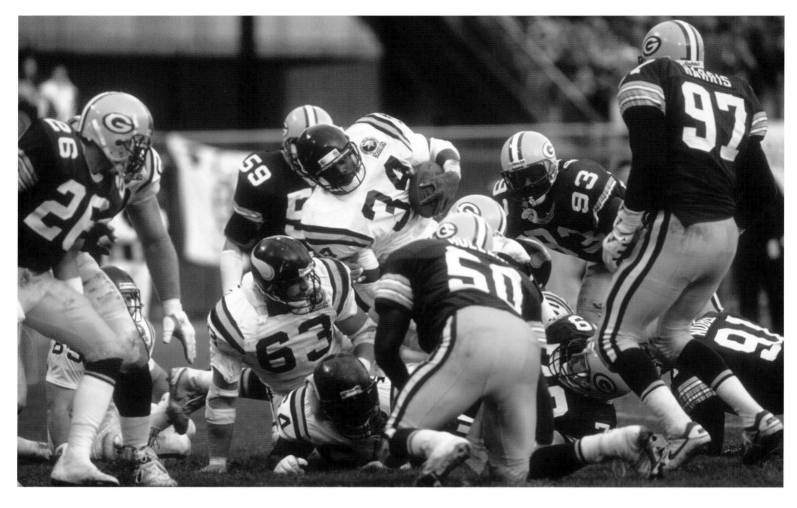

The Packers wrap up Vikings running back Herschel Walker during Green Bay's 20–19 victory over Minnesota on November 26, 1989. The two teams ended up tied with identical 10–6 records, but Minnesota won the title by merit of a tiebreaker and the Packers were left out of the playoffs.
Getty Images

Packers followed with a man that many people thought was a lock for greatness: massive Michigan State offensive tackle Tony Mandarich. (For the record, the players picked next were Barry Sanders, Derrick Thomas, and Deion Sanders, all future superstars.) Mandarich arrived in training camp under a cloud of rumors over steroid use, on which the NFL was cracking down. He struggled from the start and seemed to lose much of his legendary bulk, seemingly confirming the rumors. He spent 1989 on the sidelines and eventually cracked the starting lineup, but was out of football after the 1991 season. Mandarich has gone down as one of the biggest busts in NFL history. His failure on the field cast doubt on Tom Braatz' ability to judge NFL talent.

Shortly after the Packers made one of the NFL's biggest draft-day blunders, they more than compensated by making one of the league's smartest organizational moves of all time. On June 5, 1989, Bob Harlan was named the team's new president and chief executive officer. He had ably served the team in various capacities for 18 years, but as president, Harlan

blossomed, leading a revival of the Packers that ultimately returned them to the upper echelons of the NFL. But those days were still in the future. First, the Packers had to play year two of Lindy Infante football, which ended up being a lot of fun for fans.

In 1989, Don Majkowski became the "Majik Man" in throwing for 4318 yards and 27 touchdowns, Sterling Sharpe emerged as one of the league's top receivers with 90 catches, and even Brent Fullwood had a decent year, running for more than 800 yards. Despite their effective offense, the Packers' defense was not that good, and the team yielded nearly as many points as it scored. But because the team had a knack for pulling out close games, people started calling them the "Cardiac Pack." It became fun to watch the Packers again.

The season's most memorable game came on November 5 against the Bears. A scrambling Majkowski threw what appeared to be the winning touchdown pass to Sharpe in the last minute, only to be flagged for throwing beyond the line of scrimmage. The call went to review by the relatively new instant

Above: Despite having his career cut short by a neck injury, Sterling Sharpe remains Green Bay's all-time leader in pass receptions (595 in only seven seasons) and he ranks number two in both career receiving yards and touchdowns.
David Stluka/Getty Images

Right: In 1988 Lindy Infante took over the reins as Green Bay's head coach. Considered an offensive innovator, Infante briefly breathed life into the Packers leading to 1989's 10–6 record. Things went downhill after that and Infante was dismissed in 1991 after two successive losing seasons.
Getty Images

replay system, and the Lambeau Field crowd waited for what seemed like an eternity before the penalty was overturned. The Packers ended up with a 14–13 victory and rode a wave of enthusiasm to a 10–6 record. When the Vikings beat the Bengals on the season's final Monday Night game, Minnesota won the division on a tiebreaker, despite also having a 10–6 mark. Green Bay had been denied the playoffs, but they seemed to have turned a corner, and were playing an exciting brand of football. The fans had every reason to be excited about the 1990s. Little did they know just how excited.

STERLING SHARPE
Wide Receiver
1988–1994

Was Sterling Sharpe the greatest Packers receiver of all time? That seems a ridiculous question for a team that once featured Don Hutson and James Lofton, but it's a legitimate one to ask. If not for a neck injury that prematurely ended his career, Sharpe might have posted numbers that far surpassed those two Hall of Famers. Sharpe ranks as the Packers' leader in career receptions (595), number two in yards gained (8134), and number two in touchdowns (65)—in only seven seasons. He also owns the franchise's single-season record with 112 catches in 1993. Sharpe was a first-round pick out of South Carolina in 1987 and established himself as Green Bay's top pass-catcher his rookie season. His style was very physical for a receiver; he was fearless going across the middle from his flanker spot and he was not afraid to punish defenders. Most observers credit Sharpe with almost single-handedly carrying the Packers' offense during his career, especially during Mike Holmgren's early years, when Brett Favre was still learning to be a great quarterback. The league recognized Sharpe's gifts and rewarded him with five Pro Bowl appearances. A neck injury ended Sharpe's career after the 1994 season, but he remains one of the most popular personalities in football thanks to his many years as a television analyst—ironic because he never had a good relationship with the media while a player. Sharpe entered the Packer Hall of Fame in 2002.

CHAPTER 8

THE 1990S:
TITLETOWN RISES AGAIN

Sterling Sharpe after a catch during the Packers' 17–3 victory over the Pittsburgh Steelers on September 27, 1992. Sharpe practically carried the Green Bay offense on his shoulders in the early 1990s, only to miss out on the Super Bowl glory thanks to a career-ending neck injury.
Time & Life Pictures/Getty Images

Though pro football remained America's favorite sport, the 1990s would test the loyalty of fans like never before. The concept of permanent relationships between teams and cities had been challenged in the 1980s and would be thrown out completely in the decade ahead. Great stadiums—complete with numerous luxury boxes—became a must-have for every franchise, and teams started using the threat of relocation to get cities to pony up the money for new or renovated playing facilities. When

"God truly blessed me by sending me Mike Holmgren and sending me Brett Favre ... I can just go out and do my thing."
—*Sterling Sharpe*

cities did not cooperate, owners started following the lead of the Raiders' Al Davis and the Colts' Robert Irsay, and they moved. During the 1990s, Houston relocated to Tennessee (eventually becoming the Titans); the Rams moved from Los Angeles (actually Anaheim) to St. Louis; the Browns departed Cleveland for Baltimore and became the Ravens; and Al Davis gave up on the L.A. Coliseum and returned to Oakland.

Meanwhile, new commissioner Paul Tagliabue and the players union, led by Gene Upshaw, finally agreed on a plan for player free agency, which would start in 1993 and be accompanied by a salary cap for all teams that would go into effect in 1994. The plan was not perfect, and both owners and star players had misgivings about its effects, but it ended up providing many positive benefits: It gave the players a larger share of revenues, it maintained financial and competitive parity among the teams, and it ended much of the labor strife that had previously plagued the league. When pro baseball, basketball, and hockey all suffered through damaging strikes in the years ahead, the NFL owners and players looked like geniuses.

Though free agency appeared to be good for the game, there was mixed opinion about whether it really was good for fans. In their rush to take advantage of the new system, players started moving from team to team, following the richest offers. Fans were dismayed, time and time again, to watch their favorite players suddenly playing for hated rivals. Free agency changed the relationship between fans and players. Comedian Jerry Seinfeld summed up it up best with his joke that in the era of sports free agency fans were basically rooting for uniforms, not players.

Even as free agency seemed to undermine the relationship between fans and players, it also provided wonderful opportunities for teams looking to improve their talent base. While the college draft remained the NFL's most important means of restocking rosters, free agency allowed teams to shore up weak spots that could not be addressed through the draft—and quickly, since teams were signing veteran players who promised to offer an immediate impact. While spending money on free agents was not a guaranteed improvement program—and could be very expensive—some teams used the system masterfully.

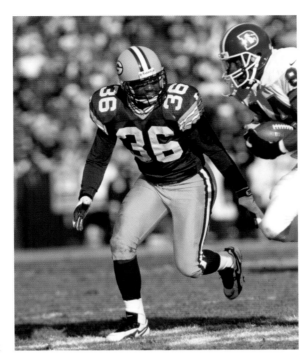

Safety LeRoy Butler accumulated career statistics that should make him a strong candidate for the Pro Football Hall of Fame. An aggressive hitter, Butler is shown zeroing in for a tackle during the Packers' 41–6 rout of the Broncos on December 8, 1996.
David Stluka/Getty Images

As free agency dawned, few teams used it to greater advantage than the Green Bay Packers.

THE MAGIC OF 1989 FADES AWAY

Stepping back to 1990, the concept of free agency (beyond the Plan B version) was still a few years off, and Green Bay fans did not care because the Pack was back—or so it seemed. It looked like they finally had the right coach in Lindy Infante. Even new team president Bob Harlan was convinced of that fact and rewarded Infante with a contract extension. Plus, the Packers had found a dynamic, winning quarterback in Don "Majik" Majkowski. Life was good.

Or it was good until player problems starting draining the team's energy before the season even started. Contract holdouts were especially devastating. Four of the Packers' starting offensive linemen held out and missed parts of training camp. And Don Majkowski decided that he'd better take advantage of his breakout season and held out for a new contract until shortly before the season opener. He missed the first two games, replaced by second-year man Anthony Dilweg, grandson of Packer legend Lavvie Dilweg. The young quarterback responded in the first game by

LeRoy Butler
Safety
1990–2001

When LeRoy Butler was a child, doctors were unsure if he would ever walk, let alone play football. Because of severely misaligned feet, Butler suffered through five years of surgeries and wheelchair confinement. Then one day a miracle happened: The wheelchair tipped over, Butler's casts broke, and he stood up and walked. Now nothing could stop him. He was a star cornerback at Florida State and initially stayed at that position with the Packers after they selected him in the second round of the 1990 draft. But when he switched to strong safety in 1992 under the tutelage of defensive coordinator Ray Rhodes, Butler developed into one of the NFL's best defensive backs. Butler credited Rhodes with helping him develop a nasty attitude on the field—a difficult task for one of the nicest men in the NFL. Butler's smarts, honesty, and refreshingly positive attitude made him a huge favorite with both fans and the media; the latter flocked to him for what were guaranteed to be the best quotes emerging from the Packers' locker room. Butler performed at a high level for many years, in the process earning Pro Bowl status four times. Butler was a devastating tackler, but his aggressiveness finally ended his career in 2001 when he shattered his shoulder making a relatively routine play. He hoped to come back, but had to call it a career prior to 2002. Butler was elected to the Packer Hall of Fame in 2007.

Don Majkowski fires a pass during the 1992 season opener against the Vikings. Majkowski was a tremendous talent who might have been the Packers' quarterback for years if not for injuries. A 1990 shoulder ailment robbed him of arm strength, but torn ankle ligaments in 1992's third game forced "Majik" to give up his job to Brett Favre and he never won it back.
Time & Life Pictures/Getty Images

leading the Packers to a 36–24 win over the Rams and earning NFL Player of the Week honors. The second game, a loss to the Bears, did not go as well and he gave way to Majkowski. Despite his great Packer bloodlines, Dilweg's time in Green Bay proved short and he was out of football by the 1991 season.

In addition to the quarterback problems, the running game was anemic with only one back, little-known Michael Haddix, rushing for more than 300 yards during the season. Former first-round pick Brent Fullwood was jettisoned early in the campaign after he pulled himself out of a game complaining of illness, then was spotted out on the town partying only hours later. Packer fans started having flashbacks to the Forrest Gregg years. The Packers' record only intensified the sense of déjà vu. Green Bay lost its last five games to finish 6–10.

Despite the presence of Tom Braatz to oversee team personnel, the Packers appeared to not be making up much ground on the rest of the league. The 1990 draft was a case in point. With two first-round

picks, the Packers selected linebacker Tony Bennett and running back Darrell Thompson. Bennett was a solid player who had a decent career with the Packers and Colts, but Thompson was a disappointment who never lived up to his potential. The 1990 draft did provide two bright spots. Linebacker Bryce Paup, a sixth-round pick from Northern Iowa, was a hard-working pass-rush specialist who eventually became a Pro Bowler. And cornerback LeRoy Butler from Florida State developed into one of the best defensive backs in the NFL after switching to strong safety. He was also a fan favorite, upbeat, outspoken, and always entertaining. He spent his entire 12-year career with the Packers and was elected to the team's Hall of Fame in 2007.

The 1991 draft was another bust for Green Bay. Braatz erred again with his first-round pick, selecting cornerback Vinnie Clark. The former Ohio State star could not crack the lineup in his rookie year and lasted only two seasons with the Packers. Without a decent influx of new talent, the team was clearly regressing. Even worse, Don Majkowski suffered a torn rotator cuff late in 1990 and entered 1991 with questions about his arm strength and his durability. The Packers used Plan B free agency to sign former Bears quarterback Mike Tomczak. The fact the Packers were signing their rival's castoffs instilled little confidence in Packer fans, who seemed prepared for the worst as the season began.

The Packers managed to meet their fans' low expectations in stumbling to a 1–6 record to open the season. Because the defense was improved, Green Bay was competitive and kept the games close. But their running game was again terrible, and coupled with another injury to Majkowski, the team had almost no offensive punch. The fans were disgusted. Bob Harlan had seen enough.

The first axe fell on November 20 when Harlan dismissed Tom Braatz with five games left in the season. Fans might have been happier to see Infante go at that point, but most did not realize what Bob Harlan had in mind. Improving the Green Bay Packers might eventually involve hiring a new coach, but first the

franchise had to get competitive with the rest of the league by upgrading its front office. Harlan achieved that goal with one brilliant move: One week after firing Braatz, he introduced the world to Green Bay's new executive vice president and general manager, Ron Wolf. Fans did not realize it at the time, but the Packers' return to greatness had officially begun.

WOLF AND HOLMGREN ARRIVE TO RECAPTURE THE GLORY

Ron Wolf turned out to be the right person for the Packers at the right time. He was an experienced administrator and recognized as one of the most gifted judges of NFL-quality talent. Wolf started his career as a talent scout for the Oakland Raiders in 1963 and had worked with good teams and bad. He enjoyed considerable success in his two stints with the Raiders, playing a key role in building championship teams during the 1970s and 1980s. In between those successes, he was vice president of operations for the expansion Tampa Bay Buccaneers. He was fired after

The Brett Favre legend started in 1992's third game—in which he is pictured unleashing a pass—when he replaced an injured Don Majkowski and led the Packers to a come-from-behind 24–23 victory over the Bengals. His 35-yard touchdown pass with 35 seconds remaining secured the win.
Tom Hauck /Allsport

Brett Favre's erratic play in his early years frustrated Mike Holmgren, but the coach stuck with his talented quarterback, providing the training and discipline that would turn him into one of the league's all-time greats. Here the two confer on the sidelines during Super Bowl XXXI.

Getty Images

just two years (the team had won just two games in that time), but he left the Bucs with a roster that would soon take them to the playoffs.

That Wolf accepted the Green Bay job was surprising. He had been director of player personnel for the Jets for only a year and was happy in that role. Plus, in 1987 he had interviewed for the Packers' position eventually filled by Tom Braatz, but took himself out of the running. What was different the second time around? Bob Harlan was now the president, and Wolf thought he was an "honest, decent" man, who seemed to be taking the once-struggling franchise in the right direction. Plus, Wolf was being offered complete control of football operations. The team would be completely his to turn into a winner. It was a compelling challenge for the competitive Wolf.

Ron Wolf's first order of business was to evaluate his head coach, whom he watched lead the team to a disheartening string of four losses. His decision was a tough one, because he liked and respected Lindy Infante, but also because the Packers would still owe the coach $1.65 million even if they let him go. In the

end, the Packers said goodbye to Infante the day after a season-ending victory over the Vikings left them with a 4–12 record. Wolf thought a change was in order, and he wanted a coach with a stronger personality to lead his team.

Though the press teased Green Bay fans with the notion that Wolf would hire his friend, Bill Parcells, as the next head coach, he really had only one candidate on his radar: 49ers offensive coordinator Mike Holmgren. It took two weeks to work out his hiring when the 49ers blocked the process, protesting the results of an unrelated trade between the teams earlier in the season. San Francisco forced the Packers to give up a second-round draft choice to hire their new coach. The draft pick ended up being a great deal.

Holmgren, seen as one of the league's rising coaching stars, was exactly the type of tough leader Wolf needed to orchestrate the turnaround of a team that had not won consistently for a quarter century. He also had a sharp offensive mind and a reputation as an able tutor of young quarterbacks. He had been a quarterback himself at USC, though he never cracked the starting lineup. He became a high school coach

"Mike's capacity for patience was huge … It's not an easy thing to admit, but as tough as he was on me, I'll be forever grateful."
—Brett Favre, talking about Mike Holmgren

after graduation, then was a college assistant at pass-happy Brigham Young before becoming a 49ers assistant under Bill Walsh and George Seifert. During his tenure in San Francisco, he worked closely with two of the NFL's all-time greatest quarterbacks, Joe Montana and Steve Young, and he grew accustomed to winning, as the team consistently reached the playoffs and even won two Super Bowls. Despite his impressive resume, coaching the Packers would be a major challenge for Holmgren. This was his first head-coaching job since leaving the prep ranks, and he was inheriting a dispirited and relatively untalented team.

THE TRADE THAT CHANGED HISTORY

With his new coach hired, Ron Wolf's next order of business was upgrading the team. The 1992 draft would provide his first test in the new job, and would end up establishing a trend that would continue throughout his years in Green Bay: making a so-so first-round pick, but discovering amazing talent in later rounds that other teams had apparently overlooked. In 1992, the Packers used the number five overall pick to select the diminutive but brash cornerback Terrell Buckley, who ended up being somewhat of a disappointment. "T-Buck" never delivered the results his mouth promised, but he was not exactly the "bust" some called him. His career spanned 14 seasons, and he had some particularly good years with Miami.

It was after the first round that Wolf worked his magic in 1992. The third round delivered Robert Brooks, the team's leading receiver for several years and a recent inductee into the Packer Hall of Fame. Edgar Bennett, destined to be a 1000-yard rusher, was picked in the fourth. Future Pro Bowl tight end Mark Chmura came in the sixth. And quarterback Ty Detmer was Wolf's ninth-round choice. Most teams thought the Heisman Trophy winner was too small for the NFL. After playing backup for two years with the Packers, he

Wide receiver Robert Brooks—a fan favorite during his years in Green Bay—acknowledges the cheers of the Lambeau Field crowd after scoring his second touchdown of the game during the Packers' 39–13 rout of the Eagles on September 9, 1996.
Tim Zielenbach/AFP/Getty Images

went on to start for four different NFL teams during a solid eight-year career.

Even more important than his draft-day work was a trade that Wolf pulled off in February 1992, sending the Packers' extra first-round pick (obtained in an earlier trade) to the Falcons for their third-string quarterback, Brett Favre. "Who?" was the first question out of most fans' mouths on learning of the trade. There was general disbelief and even grumbling in Wisconsin that Wolf had sacrificed such a high draft pick for a guy who had thrown only five passes (completing none) in his rookie season in Atlanta, and who was best known for his appreciation of that city's night life.

Years later we can appreciate the fact that Wolf, in obtaining Favre, may have pulled off the greatest trade in NFL history, but what at the time was seen as a high cost was necessary because at least two other teams wanted Favre. Wolf made the trade with confidence. When scouting Favre during his college days at Southern Mississippi, Wolf saw some traits he thought gave the young quarterback the potential for greatness: tremendous arm strength, an uncanny ability to avoid the rush, and confidence and charisma that made him a natural leader. There were other things in

ROBERT BROOKS
Wide Receiver
1992–1998

When the brilliant Sterling Sharpe was forced to retire after the 1994 season and no replacement could be acquired, there was panic in Packer country. Who could possibly fill Sharpe's shoes? The person was already in the starting lineup, number-two receiver Robert Brooks. After joining the Packers as a third-round pick out of South Carolina in 1992, Brooks contributed as a quality kick returner and steadily improved as a receiver, but he toiled in the shadow of the All-Pro Sharpe. When given the opportunity, Brooks proved he was ready to be a star. In 1995, he caught an amazing 102 passes for 1497 yards (still a team record) and 13 touchdowns, including a 99-yard scoring strike from Favre in a Monday Night Football win over the Bears that remains the longest pass reception in NFL history. In 1996, when both Brooks and the Packers were at their peaks, the receiver's season was abruptly ended by a devastating knee injury. Some thought Brooks would never play again, but in 1997 the resilient pass-catcher returned to the starting lineup, caught 60 passes, and was named NFL Comeback Player of the Year. The next year his production declined thanks to a chronic back problem, and he retired after the 1998 season. In 2000, he briefly attempted a comeback with the Broncos, but gave up football for good after appearing in four games. Brooks was named to the Packer Hall of Fame in 2007.

PACKERS TRADITIONS

THE LAMBEAU LEAP

Jumping into the stands after a touchdown has become cliché in the NFL these days, but there was a time when the act really meant something— when it was a spontaneous celebration of the joy of football and the bond between players and fans, when it really was the "Lambeau Leap." Not surprisingly, the first leap was a spontaneous act of joy on the part of one of the most joyous Packers of all time, safety LeRoy Butler. It was spawned during a December 26, 1993, game in which the Packers were pasting the Raiders with a 28–0 shutout. Butler hit a Raiders ball carrier, the football popped loose, and Reggie White picked it up and starting running for the end zone. The slow White knew he was not going to score so, reacting instinctively, he pitched the ball to the speedy Butler, who raced down the sideline for the touchdown. In the euphoria of the moment, Butler jumped into the bleachers, and Packers fans mobbed him in celebration. During the 1995 season, the high-scoring and high-leaping Robert Brooks popularized the craze, and during the 1996 Super Bowl year, just about every player who scored a TD made a wild run for the stands. The leap remains a post-touchdown tradition for many Packers, though some of the ugly attempts and near injuries have proven the celebration is not for everyone. Brett Favre, for example, has avoided the leap. It's not that he does not love scoring or rubbing elbows with the fans; it is just that he clearly knows the limits of his leaping ability.

Wide receiver Antonio Freeman celebrates his 57-yard touchdown pass from Brett Favre with a well-earned Lambeau Leap into the arms of adoring Packers fans. Green Bay won the December 20, 1998, game over Tennessee 30–22.
Joe Picciolo/AFP/Getty Images

Favre's background that intrigued Wolf. He had grown up in a football household (his father, Irv, was his high school coach), and he had a natural grasp for and love of the game. Plus, he was tough and durable, which he proved after surviving a severe car crash just weeks before the start of his senior season at Southern Mississippi. Complications forced doctors to remove part of his intestines and he lost 30 pounds, but just five weeks after the surgery, he was back at quarterback and leading his team to an 8–4 record.

Despite Favre's arrival, Mike Holmgren entered his first season as the Packers' head coach with Don Majkowski as his starting quarterback—but only about half of the players from the previous season; Ron Wolf had cleaned housed. Holmgren took this reshaped roster and immediately instilled a new attitude, that nothing less than winning was going to be acceptable. Helping him remake this team was a coaching staff that was among the most talented ever assembled. Among those joining offensive coordinator Sherman Lewis and defensive coordinator Ray Rhodes were assistants John Gruden, Steve Mariucci, and Andy Reid. Rhodes and the latter trio were all destined to be future NFL head coaches.

As expected, Holmgren installed the pass-oriented "West Coast Offense" that had been pioneered by Holmgren's former boss, Bill Walsh, in San Francisco. The Packers promptly lost their first two games. The next week, when things seemingly could not get much worse, the Packers fell behind the Bengals at Lambeau and Majkowski went down with a serious ankle injury. Enter Brett Favre, who struggled mightily in his first few series. By the fourth quarter, everything clicked, and he led the team to three touchdowns, including a 35-yard scoring strike with just seconds to go that won the game for Green Bay, 24–23. Favre started the next game, and every game after that through the 2006 season, an NFL-record 237 straight regular season games at the time this book was being written.

With Favre at the helm, the Holmgren-coached Packers showed flashes of greatness as the season progressed, but there was still a lot of work to be done. The ground game lacked a go-to runner and generated only seven touchdowns all season. In fact, even with Favre racking up more than 3200 yards through the air, the team's scoring punch was anemic, posting only 276 points all year. The defense was improved over the Infante years, though it gave up 20 more points than the offense scored. More importantly, the Packers' defense was developing a reputation for physical play, symbolized by hard-hitting Chuck Cecil, who earned a spot in the Pro Bowl. The safety usually ended every game bloodied because his crunching tackles tore open the skin on the bridge of

"You could see how important the game was to him. He was hurt, but he wasn't going to let his team lose. I knew that I wanted to play with a guy like that."
—*Reggie White, on playing for the Eagles against Brett Favre*

his nose. Fans loved him, but a *Sports Illustrated* cover story in 1993 asked the question, "Is Chuck Cecil too vicious for the NFL?"

The Packers visited Minnesota in 1992's last game, needing a win over the Vikings to earn a playoff spot. They were manhandled 27–7 and missed the postseason, but still finished 9–7. Fans who should have been disappointed reacted differently than with previous near misses (such as 1989). There was a profound sense that things in Green Bay had truly changed for the better, and that folks could afford to

be more patient than in the past, because better days lay on the horizon.

REGGIE WHITE CHOOSES GREEN BAY

With 1993 came the dawn of free agency, though few people thought the Packers could be serious contenders for the best players. The team's location in a small city, its quarter century since winning a championship, and its reputation for having a weak organization were all strikes against it. Yet, within the franchise there was an attitude, spearheaded by Bob Harlan, Ron Wolf, and Mike Holmgren, that the Packers were going places and that players would be smart to join them for the ride. The most coveted player in the free agent market was Philadelphia defensive end Reggie White, the type of talented and charismatic player who could help transform a team like the Packers, but numerous clubs sought his services. White spent a month being wined and dined by at least 10 different NFL teams. He only visited Green Bay during a short side trip between other stops, but he was

Reggie White caused a stir when, as 1993's most-coveted free agent, he chose the Packers over a number of other teams. The match was a good one as he helped lead Green Bay to the Super Bowl championship he coveted. Here White is shown playing against his former team, the Eagles, during only his second game with the Packers.
Time & Life Pictures/Getty Images

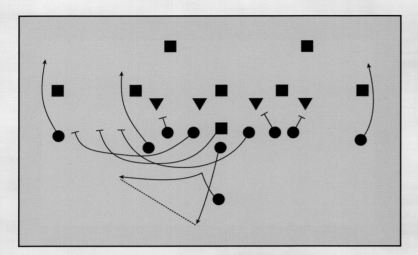

KEY PLAY: THE SCREEN—A RUN THAT STARTS AS A PASS

The Packers under Mike Holmgren were one of the all-time greatest teams in the execution of one of football's most elegant plays: the screen pass. The screen is actually a short pass to a running back executed off a faked long pass, and its success boils down to perfect timing and salesmanship, as well as athletic linemen and a courageous quarterback who can stand cool under fire. In effectively running the screen, the Packers lined up in standard pass formation, for example with two wideouts and a single back behind Brett Favre. On the snap, Favre dropped back looking long, the receivers took off on streak routes, and the line started pass blocking—all selling a downfield pass. Then the shift began. After blocking for a three count, the center and guards peeled off to form a wall. The running back (Edgar Bennett and Dorsey Levens were especially effective in this role), after holding in the backfield momentarily, drifted to a spot behind the forming wall of linemen. Brett Favre—standing firm in the face of an onslaught of rushers released by their blockers—waited until the precise instant that the defense was committed and the offensive players assembled, to deliver a short pass with a delicate touch. On the catch, the back was off and running behind the blocking of the pulled linemen.

Above: Brett Favre can throw the ball harder than most NFL quarterbacks, but he also has a light touch with the ball when he needs it; here he gently lofts a screen pass to a Packer running back waiting behind a row of blockers in the flat.
Steve Boyle/NewSportCORBIS

Right: Edgar Bennett, shown during the Packers' January 8, 1995, playoff loss to the Cowboys, was deadly on the receiving end of a screen. He was the team's number two receiver for three straight seasons, starting in 1993.
AFP/Getty Images

impressed by the simple, football-focused presentation offered to him, and he liked Wolf, Favre, and the coaching staff.

When, in April 1993, the Packers announced signing White to a four-year $17 million contract (the third highest in NFL history), the rest of the league was stunned—and the Packers' reputation changed almost overnight. The city that had once been considered a place to which players were banished for poor play was now seen as a desirable destination for quality players—even African-American stars, some of whom were uncomfortable playing in a small city with a relatively small minority population. There was also recognition that White desperately wanted to win a Super Bowl, and in selecting the Packers, he endorsed the idea that another championship was in their future.

Packers' safety LeRoy Butler celebrates Green Bay's first outright Central Division championship in more than two decades after the Packers defeated Pittsburgh 24–19 on December 24, 1995. The victory at Lambeau could not have been more unlikely: On the game's last play, wide-open Steelers receiver Yancy Thigpen inexplicably dropped an easy touchdown pass that would have won the game for his team.
Getty Images

Right: Wheaties cereal celebrates the Packers Super Bowl XXXI victory with a commemorative box sold in 1997.

Handout/Reuters/CORBIS

Mike Holmgren is carried off the field following the Packers' 35–21 victory over the Patriots in Super Bowl XXXI. Holmgren deserved to celebrate; he had expertly guided Green Bay's steady rise to the top of the NFL over the course of five sometimes-challenging seasons.

Getty Images

People around the NFL began to take notice of the Packers and—more importantly—the players started to believe they were destined for great things.

With the addition of White, the Packers entered the 1993 training camp with more optimism than had been seen in years. Wolf had continued to reshape the roster with lower-profile free-agent signings and the draft, the 1993 version of which was typical for him: weak at the top with gems in the lower rounds. Wolf had two first-round picks; linebacker Wayne Simmons was a solid be not spectacular performer for several seasons and safety George

Teague was a disappointment. Third-rounder Earl Dotson became a reliable fixture at right tackle for many years. Sixth-round cornerback Doug Evans moved into the starting lineup in his second year and soon earned All-Pro honors. If not for the presence of Brett Favre, fifth-round pick Mark Brunell might have been the Packers' next great quarterback; after one season as a backup in Green Bay, he became a three-time Pro Bowler with Jacksonville.

Signing Reggie White might have been a miracle, but miraculous turnarounds in the NFL usually take some time, and this would prove to be the case in Green Bay. While some fans might have expected the All-Pro defensive end to deliver a Super Bowl in his first season, Mike Holmgren knew better. He had a young team that still needed work before it was ready for the big time. In particular, Brett Favre struggled in his first full season as starting quarterback. He passed for 3303 yards and delivered Sterling Sharpe a league-leading 112 passes, but he took far too many risks and made numerous mistakes. As a result, Favre also led

> **"I think it's time that the Lombardi Trophy goes home to Lambeau Field, where it belongs."**
> —**Bob Harlan, after the Packers' Super Bowl XXXI victory**

the league in interceptions, with 24. His "gunslinger" mentality on the field made for exciting football, but it also tested his coach's patience.

Reggie White's presence transformed the Packers' defense into one of the best units in the league. When offensive struggles contributed to a three-game losing streak early in the season, a spirited performance by White led to a victory over the Broncos and the start of a three-game winning streak, which elevated the Packers into contention for the division title. A victory over the Raiders in the season's next-to-last regular season game clinched a playoff spot for the 9–6 Packers. They were tied with the Lions and traveled to Detroit for the season finale, with the Central Division going to the winner. The Lions posted a come-from-behind 30–20 win to take the division title, but the game set up a rematch between the two teams in the first round of the playoffs one week later.

The result of the previous week's game was completely forgotten by the end of the Packers' first playoff game in more than a decade. The game turned into a wild shootout, with both teams scoring touchdowns on interception returns; Packer rookie George Teague returned his pick 101 yards for a score. As would happen so many times in years to come, the game came down to an unlikely Favre-led drive capped by a spectacular touchdown pass—in this case, a scrambling, 40-yard heave to Sterling Sharpe with less than a minute left that gave the Packers a 28–24 win.

The following week, the Packers visited Dallas, and thanks to turnovers, spotted the Cowboys a 24–3 lead. Green Bay never backed down, with Favre passing for two touchdowns, but lost 27–17. The Cowboys—the best team in football—went on to a dominating Super Bowl victory over the Bills, their second in a row. While the Packers should not have been embarrassed to lose to such a good team, the Cowboys swagger in winning rubbed Green Bay players and fans the wrong way. Knocking Dallas off their perch became a focus for the Packers, but it would take a few years to achieve that goal.

THE PACKERS SAY FAREWELL TO MILWAUKEE

In the spring of 1994, Bob Harlan made a momentous and controversial announcement: The following season

Packers defensive end Reggie White has the Lombardi Trophy in hand as he runs around the Louisiana Superdome, celebrating the Packers' 35–21 Super Bowl XXXI victory over the New England Patriots.
Don Emmert/AFP/Getty Images

would be the last one in which the Packers played their annual trio of "home" games at Milwaukee County Stadium. No one could dispute the fact that Wisconsin's largest city had played an essential role in the franchise's survival. Even though the team was headquartered in Green Bay, Milwaukee provided the urban fan base and media coverage that allowed the small-city franchise to stand on equal footing with the NFL's big-city-based clubs. But money forced the Packers to reevaluate the arrangement.

For many years, Milwaukee had offered higher game attendance and revenue than was obtainable in Green Bay, but County Stadium was never very football friendly and after 40 years in operation it was run down and lacking the amenities found in modern NFL stadiums. Furthermore, several Lambeau Field expansions had negated any previous advantage offered by County Stadium—which lacked luxury boxes and seated only 55,000 fans. The next Lambeau Field upgrade, due to be completed for 1995, would add 90 new luxury boxes and push capacity beyond 60,000. The Packers would be giving away money if they continued to play in Milwaukee. To placate fans from the south, Bob Harlan generously offered Milwaukee season-ticket holders three games at Lambeau Field (always the second, fifth, and seventh home games of the year). Most were satisfied with the arrangement and were content to make the drive north to Green Bay to watch the games in a much better football facility.

Despite the fact many fans were eager to book travel to Miami to watch the Packers play in the next Super Bowl, the reality in 1994 was that the team would have to surpass some excellent NFC teams—namely the Cowboys and 49ers—before they reached the championship game. Brett Favre turned in a masterful performance in 1994, passing for 3882 yards and 33 touchdowns while throwing only 14 interceptions, but

Desmond Howard may have been the unlikeliest Super Bowl MVP, but his performance as a kick returner in the 35–21 victory over New England helped seal Green Bay's championship. During the game, Howard amassed 244 kick-return yards, including a 99-yard kickoff return touchdown in the fourth quarter.
Rhona Wise/AFP/Getty Images

After following the lead block of fullback William Henderson (33), running back Dorsey Levens (25) stretches for a first down during the second quarter of Green Bay's 20–3 Monday Night victory over San Francisco on November 29, 1999.
Lazlo Fitz/AFP/Getty Images

Reggie White retired in April 1998, changed his mind a few days later, and came back for one more season with the Packers. Here he is shown playing in his last regular-season game with Green Bay, a 16–13 win over the Bears in Chicago on December 27, 1998.
Getty Images

injuries and inconsistent defensive play hindered the Packers. The injury bug hit before the season started when the team's top draft pick, guard Aaron Taylor, was lost for the season during a mini-camp practice. In fact, the draft offered little help for the 1994 Packers. Running back Dorsey Levens and wide receiver Bill Schroeder were notable picks, but Levens was a little-used backup in 1994 and Schroeder was cut in training camp and would not make the team until 1997.

The 1994 season was a roller-coaster ride for Green Bay fans. At the midway point, the team had a .500 record and one of the league's top defenses. During the second half of the season, the defense faltered, and the team suffered through consecutive losses to the Bills, Cowboys, and Lions, leaving the Packers 6–7 with three games to play. The team responded with a rout of the Bears, an exciting Favre-led comeback win over the Falcons in the Packers' last Milwaukee game, and an easy win in Tampa Bay to finish with its third straight 9–7 record and a wild card playoff berth.

The Packers' first home playoff game in a dozen years was a rematch with the Lions and their incomparable running back, Barry Sanders, who had led the league in rushing with more than 1800 yards.

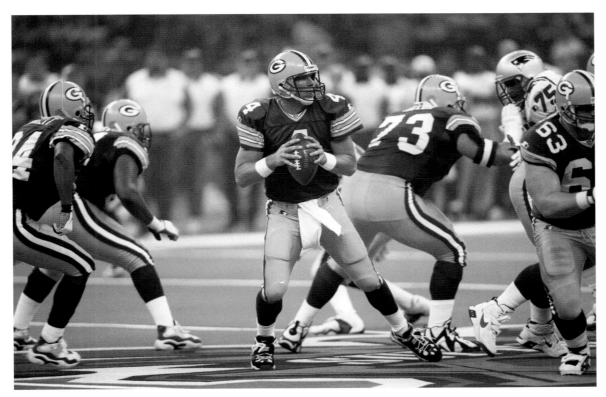

Brett Favre drops back to pass during Green Bay's 35–21 victory over New England in Super Bowl XXXI. Favre was masterful in leading the Packers' to the title, throwing for 246 yards and two long touchdown passes.
Wally McNamee/CORBIS

The Packers' defense smothered Sanders, holding him to negative rushing yards, and the offense controlled the ball in workmanlike fashion, resulting in a 16–12 Packer victory. Green Bay was hungry for what came next—another trip to Dallas—but were not prepared for what they encountered. The Cowboys' Troy Aikman put on a masterful performance, and the game was out of reach by halftime; Dallas went on to win 35–9. The game merely added more fuel to the fire of the growing Packers-Cowboys rivalry.

The off-season started with a thunderbolt of bad news. Sterling Sharpe, who had struggled with a neck injury all season, was diagnosed with a congenital spinal condition that doctors thought put him at risk for paralysis. He was urged to retire immediately. Though Sharpe initially refused to accept the diagnosis, the Packers took a businesslike approach to the situation in February 1995 and cut their star receiver. Sharpe never played again, confirming the wisdom of the team's decision, but it was a sad way to end the career of a man who was one of the best receivers to ever play for the Packers. In the ultimate irony, Sharpe—

who had maintained a very icy relationship with the media as a player—went on to a very successful career as a football analyst for ESPN.

The 1995 draft displayed Ron Wolf's exceptional gifts for uncovering overlooked football talent, with visionary picks throughout the list. First-rounder Craig Newsome immediately became a starting cornerback for the Packers. In the third round, Wolf took William Henderson, a ferocious blocking fullback still with the team 12 seasons later, and Antonio Freeman, a receiver who soon became Brett Favre's favorite target. Fifth-round pick Travis Jervey went to the Pro Bowl for his special-teams play, and seventh-round pick Adam Timmerman became one of the top guards in the NFL. Few personnel directors could match Wolf's top-to-bottom success on draft day.

The 1995 season saw several of Wolf's additions to the team enjoy breakout performances, in particular Robert Brooks, Mark Chmura, and Edgar Bennett. Brooks and Chmura stepped up and more than filled the gap left by the departure of Sterling Sharpe in catching 102 and 54 passes, respectively. Bennett was not a flashy runner, but he showed exceptional toughness in grinding out yards en route to the first 1000-yard season by a Packers rusher since 1978. Holmgren's teams were some of the best ever at executing the screen pass, with Bennett and Dorsey Levens following the Packers' athletic, pulling linemen for consistent gains at critical times.

BRETT FAVRE
Quarterback
1992–Present

What if Ron Wolf had not traded a first-round pick to Atlanta for Brett Favre in 1992? That question is unimaginable to Packer fans, who have enjoyed 15 seasons of entertaining football thanks to this gutsy, emotional, and talented quarterback from Kiln, Mississippi. Favre had enjoyed an outstanding college career at Southern Mississippi, but his injuries suffered in a 1990 automobile accident scared off some NFL teams. The Falcons picked Favre in the second round of the NFL draft and kept him as a third-stringer before Wolf rescued him from obscurity. Favre was skilled but raw when forced onto the field by Don Majkowski's ankle injury early in 1992, but he responded by leading the Packers to a come-from-behind victory in his first game. The next week he began pro football's most amazing streak: 237 straight regular-season starts and counting, forever securing his status as the NFL's most durable quarterback. It took Favre a couple of seasons to hone his skills, but he soon proved nearly unstoppable. His career highlights are numerous and still accumulating: NFL all-time completions leader (5021); second in career touchdown passes (414) and passing yards (57,500); eight Pro Bowls; three straight MVP awards (1995–1997); and two Super Bowl appearances. Through it all, Favre has endured nagging injuries, personal tragedies, coaching changes, and too much speculation on his retirement. But after an outstanding 2006 season, Favre quieted that talk by announcing his commitment to 2007 and to leading the Packers back to the playoffs, welcome news for Green Bay fans.

The season started off slowly, with too many close games and another loss to the Cowboys. When Brett Favre was knocked out of the game with an ankle injury during a loss in Minnesota, the Packers were only 5–4 and fans panicked. But as became typical for the resilient Favre, a week's rest was all he needed to get ready for the next game, a victory over the Bears. The Packers picked up their play and clinched the playoffs after game 15, a win over the Saints. They played the Steelers in the season finale with the division title on the line and nearly lost—but Pittsburgh receiver Yancy Thigpen's inexplicable drop of what would have been the winning touchdown on the game's last play handed the Packers the Central Division crown with an 11–5 record.

On December 31, the Packers hosted the Falcons in the first round of the playoffs and dominated all phases of the game in winning 37–20. The "reward" for this impressive win was a trip to San Francisco to play the defending Super Bowl champs; the Packers were a big underdog. When a crushing tackle by Wayne Simmons forced a 49ers fumble that was scooped up and returned for a touchdown by Craig Newsome, the Packers gained an edge they never relinquished. With their bruising 37–17 win, the Packers sent a message that they had finally arrived. Only one obstacle remained between them and the Super Bowl: the Dallas Cowboys.

For three quarters, the Packers had the fans in Texas Stadium believing change had finally come, but Green Bay's 27–24 lead would not hold up. Troy Aikman coolly led his team on a long drive to take the lead, and the

Fullback William Henderson, usually used as a blocker or receiver out of the backfield, gets a rare carry and turns it into yardage in Green Bay's 35–19 win over the Bears on December 5, 1999.
Jonathan Daniel /Allsport

> **"The league fathers have to keep Green Bay. It's the pro football Mecca. It's where it started."**
> —*Ron Wolf*

Cowboys went on to win 38–27. Two weeks later, Dallas won yet another Super Bowl. Despite the fantastic season, the near miss was frustrating for the Packers. Brett Favre was named NFL Most Valuable Player, but it was little consolation for a player, a team, and a city that were hungry for a championship.

SUPER BOWL CHAMPIONS ONCE AGAIN

With the Packers seemingly on the verge of greatness, Ron Wolf became more active than ever on the personnel front, using trades and free-agent signings to add more depth to the roster. Joining the team in 1996 were safety Eugene Robinson, defensive tackle Santana Dotson, receiver Don Beebe, and kick returner Desmond Howard; all would play key roles in the season ahead. But just when it looked like the team was ready for a Super Bowl run, stunning news emerged from Green Bay in May: Brett Favre admitted he was addicted to pain killers and at the NFL's insistence was entering a treatment center to deal with the problem. A month and a half later he emerged a different person (and married to his long-time girlfriend, Deanna), but was the same football player who had been the MVP in 1995. "My main focus is winning the Super Bowl," he announced at a July news conference. It was time to get the 1996 season started.

And what a season this would be—the Packers were focused and firing on all cylinders from the start, racing to an 8–1 record. Their only loss was to the Vikings at the Metrodome, a stadium that continued to hold a strange hex on Mike Holmgren and Brett Favre. Even a spate of injuries to the receiving corps (Robert Brooks suffered a season-ending injury in mid-October and both Freeman and Chmura missed several games) could not slow the Packers' potent passing attack. The depth assembled by Wolf proved priceless. Tight end Keith Jackson, acquired the previous season, and Don

At 6-foot, 2-inches and 340 pounds (or more), defensive tackle Gilbert Brown was one of the biggest Packers of all time. Nicknamed "The Gravedigger," Brown could be moved by few offensive lineman, meaning that running up the middle against the Packers was nearly impossible when he was on the field.
Getty Images

Green Bay fullback William Henderson is upended by Broncos' linebacker Bill Romanowski in the first quarter of Denver's 31–24 victory over the Packers in Super Bowl XXXII.
AFP/Getty Images

Beebe became the number two and three receivers. By year's end, Favre had thrown for 3899 yards and a team-record 39 touchdowns.

On the other side of the ball, the defense was downright stifling, giving up only 210 points for the year. Reggie White's sack numbers were down, but only because offenses regularly double-teamed him, which opened up opportunities for other Packers. LeRoy Butler was particularly effective, blitzing out of his strong safety position. Though the Packers had a two-game "mini slump" (including yet another loss to the Cowboys), they rallied to win their last five games. Their 13–3 record easily gave them the Central Division title, plus a first-round playoff bye.

San Francisco came to town for a playoff rematch on January 4, 1997, and the result was a sloppy, error-filled game played on a muddy field. Desmond Howard opened the scoring with a long punt return for a touchdown, and the Packers jumped out to a 21–0 lead. The 49ers came back to cut the margin to just seven, but the Packers won going away, 35–14. The following week the Carolina Panthers (who had knocked off the Cowboys) came to town for the NFC championship, and the Packers turned in a dominating performance en route to a 30–13 victory. Green Bay running backs Dorsey Levens and Edgar Bennett were superb, together rushing for 201 yards. After nearly three decades, the Green Bay Packers were returning to the Super Bowl.

New Orleans' Superdome was the site for Super Bowl XXXI, and the Crescent City was deluged with Packer fans hungry for a victory. The AFC representative was the New England Patriots, coached by Bill Parcells—the man who some thought *could*

have been the Packers coach, which offered an interesting side story to the media. The Packers were focused and cool entering the game, and jumped out to a quick lead after a long Favre touchdown pass to Andre Rison and a Chris Jacke field goal. New England responded with two touchdown drives to grab a 14–10 lead, but Brett Favre's 81-yard strike to Antonio Freeman (the longest touchdown pass in Super Bowl history) gave the Packers a lead they never relinquished. The Packers' stars—Favre and Reggie White—rose to the occasion with big games, but the Super Bowl MVP award went to Desmond Howard, who accumulated 244 return yards, including a 99-yard kickoff return for a touchdown. When the clock expired, the Packers had earned a 35–21 victory and

In the 1990s, the excitement returned to Lambeau Field— along with winning football. For the first time since the 1960s, Packers fans could unfurl banners like this declaring Green Bay "Titletown USA" and they would not be stretching the truth.
Getty Images

the right to take the championship trophy, named in honor of Vince Lombardi, home to its rightful place in Titletown, USA.

ANOTHER STOCK SALE, ANOTHER SUPER BOWL

With the championship back in Green Bay, fans had every excuse to celebrate and the team threw one heck of a party. Loaded on buses slowed to a crawl by crowds approaching 100,000, the players spent three hours waving to fans as the motorcade wound through the city. Their destination was Lambeau Field where another 60,000 spectators waited for the official celebration. The amazing thing about the event was the terrible weather: Returning to Green Bay the day after the game, the team was greeted by typical January-in-Wisconsin weather—20 degrees and subzero windchills. Neither fans nor players appeared bothered by the conditions as they reveled in the joy of the title.

Later in 1997, Bob Harlan took advantage of the enthusiasm created by the championship to announce yet another Packers stock sale to the public, though

the circumstances behind the move were different than earlier stock sales. Yes, the team needed to raise money, but rather than being a move of desperation to save the franchise, the Packers hoped their stock sale would generate a cash reserve that would help the team remain on equal footing with the rest of the league. Free-agent signings and maintaining and upgrading 40-year-old Lambeau Field had tapped the team's cash, and the Packers hoped fans would provide them a new source of money.

Predictably, numerous fans could not wait to own a piece of the team, even though at $200 per share it was not cheap, and there were no promises of dividends or ever getting that money back. True Packers fans just wanted to own part of the team they loved. In the end, 106,000 new shareholders pumped $24 million into the franchise—less than Harlan had hoped, but surely more than any other team in the league could have raised with a similar scheme.

The Packers' new stockholders could have been forgiven if they thought the Super Bowl championship was the beginning of another Lombardi-style dynasty.

The 1990s provided a sharp contrast to the 1980s with regards to the Packers-Bears rivalry, as Green Bay proved the dominant team throughout the new decade. Here Green Bay linebacker Bernardo Harris breaks up a pass intended for Chicago's Ryan Wetnight during the Packers' 16-13 victory at Soldier field late in the 1998 season.
John Zich/AFP/Getty Images

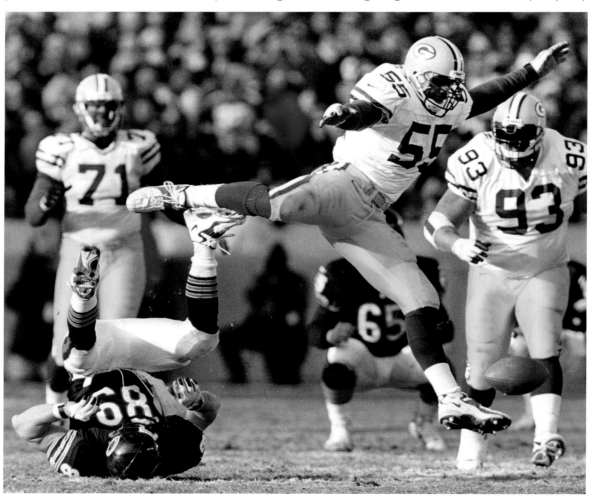

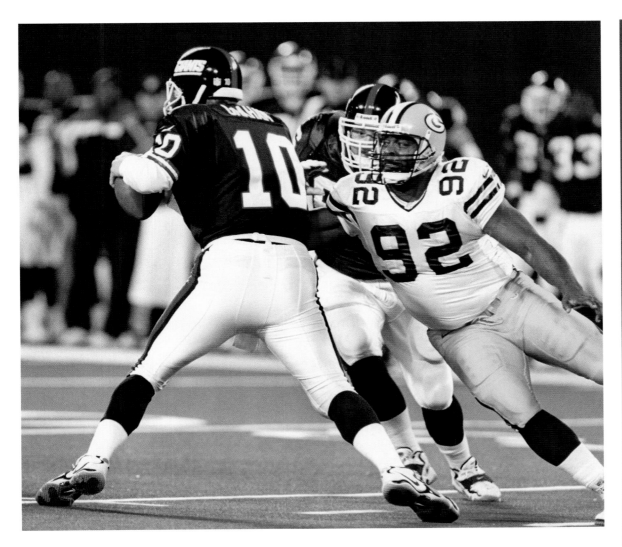

REGGIE WHITE
Defensive End
1993–1998

Reggie White's tenure in Green Bay was relatively short, but during that time, he may have had the greatest impact on a franchise as any single player in NFL history. When White joined the Packers, he was one of the NFL's top defensive players, but just as importantly, he was a vocal leader with a fervent desire to win. His teammates followed the charismatic White all the way to a victory in Super Bowl XXXI. White starred at the University of Tennessee, but started his pro career by playing two seasons for the USFL Memphis Showboats. White became a star during eight seasons with the Philadelphia Eagles, appearing in seven straight Pro Bowls, and he created a stir in 1993 when he became the NFL's first high-profile free agent. Ron Wolf shocked the league by signing White to the third-richest contract in NFL history, but the "Minister of Defense" (White was an ordained minister) and the Packers seemed to be a match made in heaven. White was voted to the Pro Bowl in all six seasons with the Packers, and he became the team's career sack leader with 68.5. He retired after 1998, but made a relatively disappointing one-season comeback with Carolina in 2000 before leaving the game for good. Four years later, football fans were shocked when the seemingly unstoppable football star died unexpectedly as a result of a lung disorder. He was posthumously inducted into the Pro Football Hall of Fame in 2006.

But dynasties would prove hard to build in the free-agency era—even as the new system gave, it could also take away. Free agency took away Desmond Howard and kicker Chris Jacke, and key contributors Keith Jackson and defensive end Sean Jones retired, but otherwise the team remained remarkably stable. Back-to-back titles were the goal.

While some teams succumb to complacency after winning the big game, the 1997 Packers showed no sign of letting up, especially under the relentless push of Mike Holmgren, now established as one of the NFL's top coaches. Brett Favre—fresh off a second NFL MVP award—maintained his incomparable passing statistics, leading to 1000-yard seasons for receivers Antonio Freeman and Robert Brooks. When Edgar Bennett was lost for the year thanks to a preseason injury (which also ended his Packer playing career), Dorsey Levens carried the rushing load by himself, gaining 1435 yards. The defense backed off its amazing performance of 1996 but was still one of the better units in the league.

Reggie White—"The Minister of Defense"—was the greatest defensive end in the history of pro football, especially when it came to rushing the quarterback. White is shown zeroing in on Giants' quarterback Kent Graham in 1998, in the process recording one of the 198 sacks he amassed during his NFL career with the Eagles, Packers, and Panthers.
Getty Images

The Packers steamrolled through their schedule with relative ease. Though a November loss to the Indianapolis Colts (coached by Lindy Infante and to that point winless) caused concern, the Packers responded the next week by routing the Cowboys 45–17. The balance of power had indeed shifted in the NFL.

The Packers entered the playoffs with a second consecutive 13–3 record and were installed by many as the favorite to win it all. After a first-round bye, Green Bay hosted Tampa Bay on January 4, 1998, and

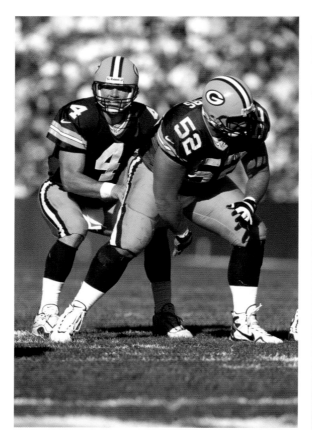

Right: **Brett Favre takes the snap from center Frank Winters during a 1999 games against the Bears at Lambeau Field. Winters was a tenacious lineman and a starter for the Packers from 1992 through 2002. In addition to protecting the Packers' star quarterback, he was one of Favre's best friends on the team**
David Stluka/Getty Images

Far right: **Life is tough in the trenches: Center Frank Winters (52) has wrapped up a Bears lineman, but ball carrier Dorsey Levens (25) has already been tackled for a short gain.**
Jonathan Daniel /Allsport

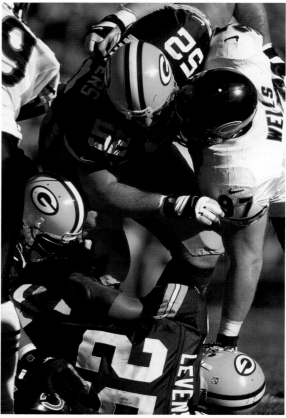

responded with a listless 21–7 victory in which the defense saved the day for the misfiring offense, plagued by interceptions, fumbles, penalties, and dropped passes. The following week, the Packers traveled to San Francisco, their third straight year of facing the 49ers in the playoffs. Most observers thought this game was the real NFL championship since these NFC powers were clearly the class of the league. The Packers defense delivered a memorable performance, shutting down the 49ers run game and maintaining constant pressure on quarterback Steve Young. The result was an impressive 23–10 Packers victory and another trip to the Super Bowl.

Despite the fact the Denver Broncos had also compiled a 13–3 regular season record, oddsmakers did not take them seriously and established the Packers as a clear favorite for Super Bowl XXXII in San Diego. Maybe they let history color their thinking a little too much—the Broncos had lost in four previous trips to the championship game, and the AFC had lost an embarrassing 13 straight Super Bowls. The reality was that Denver was a good team led by one of the NFL's all-time greats—quarterback John Elway—and they were hungry for a championship.

The game ended up being a classic, hard-fought, seesaw affair. The Packers took a quick lead on a Favre

touchdown pass to Freeman, but the Broncos responded with three unanswered scores en route to a 17–14 halftime lead. In the second half, Broncos running back Terrell Davis (suffering with a severe migraine headache) proved the difference maker. After the Packers tied the game in the fourth quarter, Davis took control and ran in what proved to be the winning touchdown with a minute and a half remaining. Favre quickly drove the Packers down the field in response, but his attempt at yet another miracle comeback was thwarted. The Broncos were Super Bowl champs with a 31–24 victory.

HOLMGREN ON THE WAY OUT

The 1998 Packers ended up proving that staying on top in the NFL is every bit as challenging as getting to the top. They averted disaster in the spring when Reggie White retired—then unretired—in the space of just two days, citing the miraculous healing of his ailing back. But there were other problems that could not be avoided. Like other championship teams, the Packers faced the prospect of paying more money to—or losing as free agents—players who thought their Super Bowl performance had earned them raises. In 1998, Dorsey Levens held out, missed the preseason, signed a rich new contract, then broke his leg in the second

Far left: **A second-round pick in 1997, safety Darren Sharper scored three defensive touchdowns his rookie season. By the next year he was in the starting lineup and on his way to becoming a Pro Bowl performer.**
David Stluka/Getty Images

Left: **Antonio Freeman became Brett Favre's favorite target by default in 1996 after Robert Brooks was injured, but he made the most of his opportunity, remaining the Packers' top pass catcher through the end of the decade.**
David Stluka/Getty Images

game. He was replaced by a cast of unknowns, and the Packers' running game suffered in his absence. With more pressure on the passing game to deliver, Brett Favre threw more interceptions, but he still played like the quarterback who had been the league MVP the previous three seasons.

The Packers opened the season like they were bound for their third straight Super Bowl winning four straight, but when the Vikings broke their 25-game home win streak on Monday Night Football, the loss seemed to take the wind out of their sails. Another problem emerged when the media began to speculate that Mike Holmgren was in his last year with the team. It was no secret that he coveted a combined general-manager/head-coaching role, not possible in Green Bay with Ron Wolf in place. Wolf even speculated to the media in November that Holmgren would probably leave after the season.

With the Vikings posting a league-best 15–1 record, the Central Division title was out of the question, but the Packers played well enough to finish 11–5 and earn a wild card playoff spot. How times had changed: Though this was the team's sixth straight trip to the postseason, fans viewed the year as a disappointment compared to the previous campaigns. Waiting for the Packers in the playoffs were the 49ers;

Fullback William Henderson was one of the most unheralded Packers, but for years he was one of the most important. A punishing blocker and talented pass-catcher, Henderson played Green Bay from 1995–2006 and during that time amassed more than 300 receptions coming out of the backfield.
David Stluka/Getty Images

Ray Rhodes, previously a Packers defensive coordinator and Eagles head coach, succeeded Mike Holmgren in 1999. Rhodes was not a good fit for the job and lasted for only one disappointing 8–8 season.
Getty Images

it was an unfortunate draw. San Francisco was hungry to gain revenge for the Packers' three straight playoff wins over their West Coast rival.

The game in San Francisco was an exciting shootout featuring two of the league's best offensive teams, but Packers fans will always remember it for the Green Bay defense's inability to stop an inevitable pass from Steve Young to Terrell Owens with 3 seconds to play. The 25-yard touchdown strike gave the 49ers a 30–27 victory. Just five days later, Packers fans' worst nightmares were realized when Mike Holmgren resigned to become head coach and general manager of the Seattle Seahawks. On top of that, Reggie White also announced his retirement and this time he was not coming back. Not only would there be no Super Bowl, there were serious questions about the team's future. It would prove to be a long, cold winter in Wisconsin.

RAY RHODES: ONE YEAR AND DONE

After Holmgren's departure, Ron Wolf acted quickly and decisively, hiring the hard-nosed Ray Rhodes as his new coach. Rhodes was a former NFL player and the first African-American to coach the Packers. He seemed to be a logical choice for the job, having spent two successful years as Green Bay's defensive coordinator and four years as the Eagles' head coach. The Packers did not need rebuilding, so Wolf thought it only logical to bring in a tough, experienced

Holmgren protégé to continue the legacy of success. While the hiring looked good on paper, Rhodes never settled into the Green Bay job. Though he was intense, he was not as much a disciplinarian as Holmgren, and the team responded with loose, error-ridden play. Another problem was the defense, reeling from the retirement of Reggie White, which never found its rhythm and gave up an average of 21 points per game. And, most importantly, there was Brett Favre's thumb, which was injured in the season opener. Though he never missed a game, Favre had trouble effectively gripping the ball the entire season and threw more interceptions (23) than touchdowns (22).

Despite his gutsy play, Favre was not happy with the direction the team was taking, and he was not shy about sharing his feelings with Ron Wolf as the Packers slid into mediocrity late in the season. The general manager did not need to be told that he had made a mistake; even before the season ended, he privately decided to make a change. Just hours after the Packers beat the Cardinals to finish 8–8—and out of the playoffs—Wolf fired Rhodes. Players and fans alike expressed shock that Wolf had given his coach only one year, but most observers realized the change was necessary before the team slid even further. Though they were no longer championship caliber, the Packers still had one of the league's most exciting quarterbacks. With Brett Favre around, there was always reason to be hopeful for the future.

Opposite: Antonio Freeman races down the sidelines toward the end zone after hauling in a Brett Favre pass during the Packers' 31–3 win over San Diego on October 24, 1999. Freeman ended his Packers' career with an impressive 431 receptions—57 for touchdowns.
Getty Images

ANTONIO FREEMAN

Wide Receiver
1995–2001, 2003

The Packers have been fortunate to have a legacy of wide receivers who stepped up their game to make up for the loss of a valuable teammate. Antonio Freeman is a perfect example. When Robert Brooks went down with a knee injury in 1996, Freeman became Brett Favre's top target and played a key role in leading the Packers to Super Bowl XXXI. During that game, Freeman snagged an 81-yard scoring strike that stood for several years as the longest touchdown pass in Super Bowl history. The Baltimore product attended Virginia Tech and was picked in the third round of the 1995 draft by Green Bay. Freeman's primary role his rookie season was returning punts and kickoffs, but once he took over for Brooks, he began a string of four straight seasons leading the Packers in receptions. His single Pro Bowl season was 1998, when he led the NFL in receiving yards (1424) and caught 14 touchdown passes. Freeman caught two TD passes in the losing Super Bowl XXXII effort against Denver, but his most memorable moment on the national stage came during overtime of a November 2000 Monday Night Football home tilt with the Vikings. Freeman juggled a Favre pass while rolling on the ground, somehow secured the ball, then rose to his feet and ran past the stunned Minnesota defenders to score the winning touchdown. A contract dispute after that season sent Freeman to the Eagles for one year, but he finished his career with the Packers in 2003.

THE 2000S:
MIXED RESULTS,
BUT HOPE FOR THE FUTURE

Green Bay rookie tight end Bubba Franks—the Packers' first-round draft pick in 2000—gets a good taste of life in the NFL when he is upended by Dolphins' safety Brian Walker during an October 28 game in Miami. Despite the hit, Franks held on to the ball for a 23-yard reception.
Reuters/CORBIS

The dawn of the new millennium found the National Football League entrenched not only as America's leading sporting institution, but also as a central component of the country's culture and one of its leading forms of entertainment. Yes, entertainment—football had fully moved beyond the realm of being a mere game. The Super Bowl had become one of the year's biggest excuses for a party. Even the most casual fans eagerly gathered for not only the game, but for Super Sunday's whole experience, including the grandiose halftime shows (which became a source of unwanted controversy)

"People will come up to me, grown men, and tell me stories about following the Packers when they were three years old ... Some will have tears in their eyes when they talk about the team."
—*Brett Favre*

and the television commercials, which cost sponsors millions to air and spawned their own mini-competition to see who could produce the funniest or most memorable ad.

Meanwhile, as other forms of entertainment scrambled to deal with new technology, unsure of how to handle competition from the Internet and video games, the NFL embraced the new media—and expanded its reach even further. The Internet seemed tailor-made for football, providing fans with a vast electronic world to mine for data and news about their favorite teams, along with a venue to take their role of armchair coach to even greater levels, thanks to chat rooms and message boards. And while many arms of the entertainment industry (along with parents, educators, etc.) were lamenting the growth of video games, the NFL was laughing all the way to the bank

thanks to products such as EA Sports' Madden NFL (named for the former Raiders coach and current sportscaster). New legions of young fans were being introduced to football, not by playing in the backyard, but by playing the video game as their favorite NFL team. Switching back and forth between real Sunday games and their video contests became seamless and natural for this new generation, who proved just as devoted to football as their parents and grandparents.

The first years following 2000 proved relatively stable for the prosperous NFL. Wholesale franchise relocation (or threats of) seemed to be a thing of the past. With the 2002 startup of the Houston Texans, the league reached the 32-team makeup that Pete Rozelle had once suggested as ideal. Along the way, the NFL had appeased rejected fans in Cleveland, Baltimore, and Houston with expansion franchises. Though there were still cities interested in hosting football, and the league had never solved the Los Angeles problem (the nation's second largest city still lacked a team), the NFL

Safety Darren Sharper moves up to tackle Saints running back Deuce McAllister during the Packers' September 15, 2002, game in the Louisiana Superdome. Sharper was voted to his second Pro Bowl at the end of this season. *Getty Images*

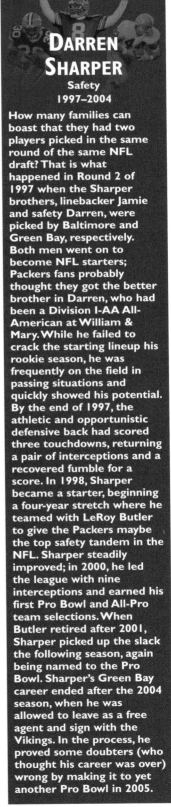

DARREN SHARPER
Safety
1997–2004

How many families can boast that they had two players picked in the same round of the same NFL draft? That is what happened in Round 2 of 1997 when the Sharper brothers, linebacker Jamie and safety Darren, were picked by Baltimore and Green Bay, respectively. Both men went on to become NFL starters; Packers fans probably thought they got the better brother in Darren, who had been a Division I-AA All-American at William & Mary. While he failed to crack the starting lineup his rookie season, he was frequently on the field in passing situations and quickly showed his potential. By the end of 1997, the athletic and opportunistic defensive back had scored three touchdowns, returning a pair of interceptions and a recovered fumble for a score. In 1998, Sharper became a starter, beginning a four-year stretch where he teamed with LeRoy Butler to give the Packers maybe the top safety tandem in the NFL. Sharper steadily improved; in 2000, he led the league with nine interceptions and earned his first Pro Bowl and All-Pro team selections. When Butler retired after 2001, Sharper picked up the slack the following season, again being named to the Pro Bowl. Sharper's Green Bay career ended after the 2004 season, when he was allowed to leave as a free agent and sign with the Vikings. In the process, he proved some doubters (who thought his career was over) wrong by making it to yet another Pro Bowl in 2005.

A gang of Packers' tacklers punish Lions' running back James Stewart, forcing a fumble, during the second quarter of Green Bay's 26–13 victory over Detroit on December 10, 2000.
Reuters/CORBIS

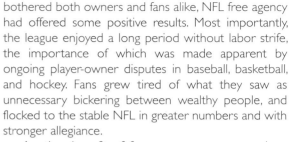

Below: Wide receiver Bill Schroeder, shown picking up 19 yards against the Vikings on December 17, 2000, was a fan favorite in Green Bay. The Wisconsin native became an NFL star against long odds. He was a track star at Division III Wisconsin-La Crosse and played only one year of college football, but went on to play eleven years in the pros.
Reuters/CORBIS

bothered both owners and fans alike, NFL free agency had offered some positive results. Most importantly, the league enjoyed a long period without labor strife, the importance of which was made apparent by ongoing player-owner disputes in baseball, basketball, and hockey. Fans grew tired of what they saw as unnecessary bickering between wealthy people, and flocked to the stable NFL in greater numbers and with stronger allegiance.

Another benefit of free agency was summed up simply as "parity." Because of the more liberal player movement, teams were more evenly matched and the road from the bottom of the league to the top could now be negotiated in but a season or two. Now every fan had hope that their team could be a winner. Free agency, though, proved to be a double-edged sword. Once a team achieved greatness, it was next to impossible to keep the roster intact for any length of time. The new decade became littered with a legacy of Super Bowl teams that failed to even make the playoffs the following season.

NEW COACH FOR A NEW DECADE

As 2000 dawned, the Packers were one of those teams struggling to maintain a high-quality team after winning a championship. Green Bay had fared better than most, keeping the roster strong for two Super Bowl appearances followed by a playoff year. But 1999 had been a huge disappointment. Ron Wolf (and Packers fans) thought the team was still talented; a .500 record and no postseason was not acceptable. He needed a new coach with the skills to quickly turn the squad back into a Super Bowl winner.

Ironically, one of the factors driving the Packers' need to turnaround quickly was the possible retirement of star quarterback Brett Favre. It is unclear exactly when rumors of Favre's retirement surfaced, or who started them, but speculating about how much longer Favre would play became an annual rite for the media and fans. The fact that the quarterback would occasionally talk about the end of his career only fueled these fires, but Favre was still performing at high levels. He entered the decade riding a league-record consecutive start streak for quarterbacks; talking about retirement for one of the game's most durable and exciting players seemed a silly distraction.

More important for the Packers was their new coach, and on January 18, 2000, Ron Wolf surprised most observers when he selected Seattle offensive coordinator Mike Sherman for the job. Sherman had played lineman at little-known Connecticut State College, but never made it to the pros. Instead he started a long career as a college assistant, including two stints at Texas A&M. Sherman broke into

appeared to have a structure that was nearly perfect for continued success.

The other reason for the NFL to be optimistic in 2000 was that it had negotiated the potential minefield of player free agency with relative ease. Though escalating salaries and liberal player movement

"He has healing powers beyond all of us. It's really true. The guy is a freak of nature in regards to his body."
—Mike Sherman, on Brett Favre

professional coaching with the Packers, for whom he tutored tight ends and linemen for two seasons, before following Mike Holmgren to Seattle. With no head

coaching experience and only three years in the NFL, Sherman seemed a curious choice, but Wolf thought he was the right guy for the job—low-key, organized, and very serious about football.

In addition to giving Sherman the head-coaching job, Wolf rewarded him with one of the better drafts of his tenure in Green Bay. Five future starters were selected in the 2000 draft, including tight end Bubba Franks, linebacker Na'il Diggs, defensive end Kabeer Gbaja-Biamila, and offensive tackles Chad Clifton and

Packers' fans love seeing their team beat the Bears, which this quartet of Green Bay defenders—Darren Sharper (42), LeRoy Butler (36), Nate Wayne (54), and Na'il Diggs (59)—made sure of during the Packers' 20–12 win at Soldier Field on November 11, 2001.
John Zich/AFP/Getty Images

Defensive end Kabeer Gbaja-Biamila racks up another sack, this time of Redskins' quarterback Patrick Ramsey, during the Packers' 30–9 win over Washington on October 20, 2002. Selected in the fifth round of the 2000 draft, "KGB" became a terror for NFL quarterbacks thanks to his lightning-quick moves from the end position.
Reuters/CORBIS

end Mark Chmura. The one-time member of the "Three Amigos" (along with close buddies Brett Favre and center Frank Winters) had been rendered ineffective by a neck injury, but an off-the-field incident caused the team more embarrassment. Chmura had been arrested for sexual assault and child enticement after his visit to a post-prom party thrown by the teenage daughter of a friend. He was eventually acquitted of the charges, but the highly publicized trial attracted the attention of a leering media that always seemed on the lookout for bad behavior on the part of pro athletes.

The 2000 season began in sharp contrast to the previous one. Mike Sherman returned discipline to the team, and while it took both him and his team time to adjust to his role as a head coach, there was reason to be optimistic. After dropping their first two games, the team responded with two wins, then seesawed through the schedule to find itself with a 5–7 record going into December. At that point, Sherman showed he was gaining a grasp on his new job by leading his charges to four straight wins to end the season at 9–7. Though in other seasons this might have earned a playoff trip, in 2000 the NFC was loaded with healthy records and the Packers were left out in the cold.

Despite the postseason near miss, fans were relatively pleased with their team. Favre appeared fully recovered from his thumb injury, passing for 3812 yards and 20 touchdowns with only 16 interceptions. Also heartening was the rediscovery of a running game. Ahman Green, obtained in a trade with the Seahawks, rushed for nearly 1200 yards. The former Nebraska star had been dispatched by Mike Holmgren because of his reputation for fumbling, but Packer coaches thought this minor problem was more than offset by his gifts as a runner. Green was adept at both powering into the middle of the line for short yardage and breaking away on the outside with his blazing speed. He quickly became recognized as one of the league's top backs.

HARLAN SELLS SOME AMBITIOUS PLANS FOR LAMBEAU

Mark Tauscher. Gbaja-Biamila (or "KGB" as he became affectionately known) and Tauscher were typical Wolf late-round discoveries. KGB was small for his position but emerged as one of the league's premier speed-rushing ends. Tauscher's intelligence helped him quickly pick up the pro game, and he became a starter his rookie season. Shaggy-haired and bearded, he looks like neither a football player nor a doctoral candidate, but he is both, having continued his graduate studies during off-seasons.

Wolf also shuffled veteran players. Two noteworthy departures were linebacker George Koonce and tight

Just as big a news story in 2000 as the Packers performance on the field was the field itself—Lambeau Field that is. The venerable facility was loved by Green Bay fans, along with people everywhere who cherished the game's traditions, but in 2000 it had fallen far behind other NFL stadiums in how much money it could generate for the team. Bob Harlan was aware of just how important Lambeau Field was to Green Bay fans, but he also had to do what was best for the future of the team. To choose the right course of action, the team initiated feasibility studies to explore various

Above: **All eyes in the huddle are on Brett Favre as he calls a play during a game against the Buccaneers in Tampa Bay. By the 2000s, Green Bay's fortune's rested heavily on the shoulders of their veteran quarterback, who in addition to being the Packers' unquestioned leader remained their most dangerous offensive weapon.**
Cy Jariz Cyr/NewSport/CORBIS

Right: **Kicker Ryan Longwell celebrates even as the ball is leaving his foot: He knows that he has just connected on a last-second 33-yard field goal to give the Packers a 34–31 victory over the Vikings on November 14, 2004.**
Getty Images

options, including building a new stadium. Fans were outraged when they learned Lambeau Field might be replaced, but Harlan deserved credit for his even-handed approach to the problem. What emerged after the studies was a plan that appeared to satisfy, in part, everyone's goals.

Harlan unveiled the plan to the public in January 2000 with a statewide tour. The proposal was visionary: a dramatic expansion and renovation of the stadium that promised to make it a facility on par

RYAN LONGWELL
Kicker
1997–2005

Kickers usually generate little attention (unless they miss a critical field goal), which was the case with Ryan Longwell's career in Green Bay. Over nine seasons with the Packers, he quietly performed as probably the most reliable kicker in the NFL, and when Longwell left the team after the 2005 season, he had most of the team's kicking records in tow. Longwell was not even supposed to make it in the pros. After kicking and punting at the University of California (and graduating with B.A. in English), Longwell was signed as a free agent by the 49ers in 1997, but quickly cut. The Packers picked him up to provide some token competition for Penn State rookie kicking phenom, Brett Conway. Then the unthinkable happened: Conway tore a thigh muscle and was lost for the season. Ryan Longwell—now nicknamed by some "Ryan Longshot"—was Green Bay's kicker. He responded with an outstanding season and people completely forgot about Brett Conway. Longwell's penchant for staying cool in the clutch and his near perfection with games on the line highlighted a Packer career in which he became the team's leader in scoring (1054 points) and field goals (226) and tied the record for longest field goal (54 yards). Longwell became a free agent before the 2006 season and joined the rival Vikings. He ranks as the fifth most accurate field-goal kicker in NFL history—not bad for a guy who was given little chance of even making a pro team.

Linebacker Nick Barnett, shown during the Packers' October 31, 2004, game against the Redskins, turned out to be one of the best Green Bay draft picks of recent years. Selected in the first round in 2003, the former Oregon State star stepped immediately into the starting lineup, providing much-needed speed and toughness in the middle of the Green Bay defense.
Mitchell Layton/NewSport/CORBIS

with—or surpassing—even the gaudiest new NFL stadiums. The highlights of the projects were many:
• Lowering the playing surface to accommodate 6000 new seats around the field
• All-new luxury boxes, increasing the total to 166
• New scoreboards, restrooms, concourses, and concession facilities
• New team offices and training facilities, including an auditorium, gymnasium, and locker rooms

With the expansion, stadium capacity would increase to 72,922, allowing the Packers to offer more tickets to both the general public and some of the thousands on the season-ticket waiting list.

Even with all these improvements, the project's top feature was a five-story, 366,000-square-foot Atrium, which would turn Lambeau Field into a year-round attraction for the community. The Atrium would be filled with restaurants, bars, and space for meetings, weddings, parties, and whatever else the general public desired. In addition, a new and expanded Packer Hall of Fame and Pro Shop would be part of the facility. This promised to be one of the top attractions in the already tourist-friendly state of Wisconsin.

There was one problem: The project was not cheap—it would cost an estimated $295 million—and the Packers would not be able to pay for it themselves. To provide $160 million towards the project, the Packers proposed that residents in Brown County, in which Green Bay is located, pay a half-percent sales tax. Levying the tax would require passage of both legislation in the Wisconsin statehouse and a referendum in Brown County. It was a contentious issue that forced people to wrestle with challenging topics—a tax increase and public support of a private entity—but Bob Harlan did a masterful job of making his case to the people. By persuading the public that the team would provide a huge economic return (estimated at $144 million annually) in return for the small tax increase, Harlan was able to get the legislation signed into law by May, and set the stage for a September 2000 vote in Brown County. The opposition was well organized, but the Packers prevailed by convincing 53 percent of the voters to support their plan.

For their part, the Packers' plan committed the team to making the fifth-largest contribution to a stadium project in NFL history. Most of the $125.9 million raised for the team, city, and league portion of the project came from the 1997 stock sale, as well as a one-time seat license fee for season-ticket holders. Many long-time fans grumbled at the expense (as much as $1400 per seat), and some even dropped their tickets, but most realized it was a worthwhile investment that would help ensure the future of football in Green Bay—again, the fans had come to the rescue. The team officially broke ground on the project in May 2001.

WOLF'S RETIREMENT CAUSES CONCERNS

Concurrent with the excitement surrounding the start of the stadium project came an unexpected and disheartening February 2001 announcement from the Packers' front office: Ron Wolf was retiring. As disappointed as fans were when Mike Holmgren had departed Green Bay, there had been a reassuring sense that things would turn out okay because Wolf was still running the show. He had been the architect

"You'd think that the big news in the locker room this week was the start of preseason, but all everyone could talk about was the new Madden game."
—Ahman Green, on Packers players' obsession with the popular video football game

of the team's return to glory, and as long as he was around, most fans felt optimistic about the Packers' future prospects. Wolf's handpicked successor as general manager turned out to be Mike Sherman. Wolf had been so impressed with the new coach's performance in his first year that he was convinced that Sherman deserved the dual-title role. Most observers were not sure what to make of this development. Sherman seemed to have a good football mind, but was relatively inexperienced in the NFL. Plus, Green Bay had abandoned the combined coach-general manager job in hiring Wolf, and the new structure had delivered the best possible results. Why go back to the old way of doing things?

Wolf and Sherman worked together closely during a four-month transition period that included Wolf's last NFL draft. His performance in that two-day session yielded one of his weaker rookie classes. Five of the six picks stuck with the team, but all were underachievers. Top pick Jamal Reynolds was a certified bust; the undersized defensive end never adjusted to the NFL and barely stepped on the field during his three-year career. Wolf officially retired on June 1, but he continued to help the team in a consulting role. Sherman made smart moves to offset his relative lack of experience by giving more power to talented administrators within the organization, including Reggie McKenzie and John Dorsey, and by hiring Mark Hatley away from the Bears and making him vice president of football operations.

The 2001 season seemed to offer proof that Sherman was more than capable of being both a coach and administrator, and marked a pleasing return to form for the Packers. Relying on largely the same roster as the previous season, the Packers were firing on all cylinders from the opening kickoff, running off three one-sided victories to open the season. Even the terrible terrorist attacks of September 11, which forced a postponement of Week 2 games, proved only a minor distraction for this focused team. Brett Favre looked to be in MVP form again, throwing for 3900 yards and 32 touchdowns with only a modest 16

interceptions. Ahman Green continued as one of the league's elite backs in rushing for 1387 yards and leading the team with 62 catches. The Packers' aggressive defense was especially effective, forcing numerous turnovers and terrorizing quarterbacks with a team-record 52 sacks.

The Packers spaced four narrow losses throughout the season en route to a 12–4 record and a playoff berth, but the road to the Super Bowl would prove challenging. The NFC was packed with great teams, including 12–4 San Francisco, the surprising 13–3 Bears (who captured the Central Division), and the explosive 14–2 St. Louis Rams, who were led by one-time Packers

Green Bay started 2000 with a new coach—former Seahawks offensive coordinator Mike Sherman. The little-known Sherman was a surprising choice, but Ron Wolf seemed to know what he was doing: The Packers were back in the playoffs with a 12–4 record by the 2001 season. *Mitchell Layton/NewSport/CORBIS*

KEY PLAY:
AHMAN GREEN RUNS THE 98 TOSS SOLID BUCK

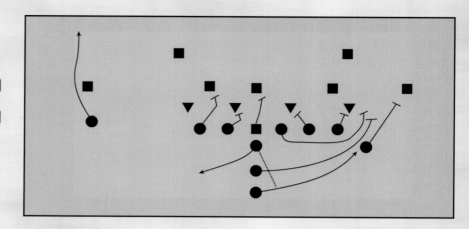

As good as the Brett Favre-led passing game was for the Packers as coached by Mike Sherman, their running game—powered by the talented legs of Ahman Green—was just as effective. This play is a classic power run, not that far removed from the famed Lombardi sweep of the 1960s. The most unique aspect of this formation was the use of backup tackle Kevin Barry (all 330 pounds of him) in the tight end position on the right, with tight end Bubba Franks lining up just outside him as flanker. The backs would line up in the I formation. On the snap, fullback/lead blocker William Henderson would look for the best running lane and put his body on the first defender encountered. Quarterback Favre would turn and make a quick pitch to tailback Ahman Green; after the pitch, Favre would fake a naked bootleg to the left to freeze the defense on that side. Green would follow Henderson as much as possible (usually through the gap between the defensive end and cornerback), but he was free to pick any open spot and explode through it. An interesting twist out of this formation: If the safety on the left cheated up on the run—leaving the wide receiver on that side in single coverage—Favre could audible a pass, often with spectacular results.

Looking for open space after making an upfield cut, Packers' running back Ahman Green looks uncertain as to whether he should put a move on the Eagles' Michael Lewis or simply run over him. The fast and powerful Green is equally as effective at both options.
Frank Polich/Reuters/CORBIS

quarterback Kurt Warner. The Iowan had spent one preseason in Green Bay and then toiled in the Arena League before catching on with the Rams and leading them to a Super Bowl win after the 1999 season.

The Packers faced a familiar foe in their first playoff game in three years, the San Francisco 49ers. A dejected Lambeau Field crowd saw the Packers fall behind 7–6 at halftime, but a timely third quarter interception by cornerback Tyrone Williams turned the tide of the game. Green Bay went on to win 25–15. The following week's trip to St. Louis became one the Packers would soon want to forget. The error-prone Packers committed eight turnovers—including a half-dozen Favre interceptions—and were routed by the

Rams 45–17. It was an emotionally devastating loss, and one that Green Bay would have to work hard to overcome the following season.

DETERMINATION IN THE FACE OF ADVERSITY

Mike Sherman's first draft as general manager yielded a few additions to the roster and two players of note. Wide receiver Javon Walker justified his first-round status by contributing right from the start of his rookie season and leading the team in catches by his third year. Aaron Kampman was a classic late-round steal. A product of tiny Kesley, Iowa, the hard-working defensive end broke into the starting lineup by the end

Fullback William Henderson leaves a would-be Houston tackler on the turf as he turns a short pass into long yardage during Green Bay's 16–13 win over the Texans on November 21, 2004.
Jim Redman/Icon SMI/CORBIS

Wide receiver Javon Walker stretches for a Brett Favre pass during a November 2004 contest in Houston, but the ball is just beyond his fingertips. Walker emerged as Green Bay's top receiver in 2004 with 89 catches, but a serious knee injury in the 2005 opener knocked him out for all of that season, and he was traded to Denver the following year.
Jim Redman/Icon SMI/CORBIS

of his rookie season. He soon developed into one of the league's most reliable defensive linemen and was named to the Pro Bowl after the 2006 season.

Trying to rebound from their playoff humbling at the hands of the Rams, the 2002 team showed grit and determination in the face of adversity. Injuries robbed the team of several starters at various times and threatened to break Favre's growing consecutive start streak. The durable quarterback shook off a midseason knee strain that forced him to the bench during one game, but he rebounded to post respectable passing numbers. The offense was led by the consistently effective Ahman Green, along with emerging receiver Donald Driver, who enjoyed a breakout season with 70 catches. Unfortunately, the Packers struggled to

repeat their defensive dominance of the previous season, and yielded way too many points; nonetheless, the Packers won eight out of their first nine games. They clinched the newly formed NFC North Division (minus Tampa Bay) title with four games left on the schedule.

Needing a win over the Jets in the season finale to wrap up a first-round playoff bye, the Packers looked terrible in losing 42–17. It was not a good way to enter the postseason, though the Packers' first-round game would bring the Falcons to Lambeau Field. Green Bay needed overtime to beat Atlanta in the season's first game, but were a solid favorite for the playoff rematch. What transpired left the Green Bay faithful stunned: From the opening kickoff, Atlanta dominated the

The Green Bay defense—Kabeer Gbaja-Biamila (94), R-Kal Truluck (91), and Hannibal Navies (50) puts a serious hurt on Rams quarterback Marc Bulger on November 29, 2004.

The play was representative of the entire Monday Night contest, in which the Packers crushed St. Louis 45–17. *Allen Fredrickson/Reuters/CORBIS*

Packers' fans celebrate the dedication of the newly renovated and expanded Lambeau Field on September 7, 2003. Unfortunately, Minnesota put a damper on the festivities by beating Green Bay 30–25.
Getty Images

Packers on a snowy Saturday evening that looked tailor-made for Green Bay football. The Packers gave up an early touchdown on a blocked punt and had no answer for athletic Falcon quarterback Michael Vick. Trailing 24–0 at halftime, the Packers never challenged in losing 27–7. It was the first time the Packers had ever lost a playoff game at Lambeau Field.

The traumatic playoff loss probably had a longer-lasting effect than the team wanted to admit. The Packers had long enjoyed a tremendous home-field advantage at Lambeau, and the Falcons' win shattered the air of invincibility that the Packers carried on their home field. After dropping only one home regular season game over the previous two seasons, the Packers would end up losing three home contests in 2003, including a surprising season-opening loss at the hands of the Vikings.

That loss to Minnesota was especially frustrating because the game marked the debut of the renovated and expanded Lambeau Field. The project had gone exceptionally smooth, finishing on time and under budget and not requiring the team to play home games elsewhere, despite the construction site enveloping the stadium. Despite the loss, fans nearly unanimously sang their praises for the new-look Lambeau, especially the incredible Atrium facility. As a result of the successful venture, the Bob Harlan legend continued to grow.

Coming on the heels of back-to-back 12–4 campaigns, the Packers' 10-6 record at the end of 2003 might have been viewed as something of a step backward, but that would have ignored the team's gutsy performance in the season's waning weeks. The Packers were up and down throughout the year, but the offense was generally spectacular, with Favre throwing for 3361 yards (despite another thumb injury) and Ahman Green setting single-season records for rushing (1883 yards) and touchdowns (20).

Trying to make the most of reverse gone awry, Donald Driver leaps over Brett Favre and turns his attention to eluding Bears defenders during Green Bay's December 31, 2006, victory over Chicago at Soldier Field. Driver again finished the season as Green Bay's leading receiver and was rewarded with a well-earned trip to the Pro Bowl.
Tannen Maury/epa/CORBIS

Nevertheless, after the Packers ended November with a 22–14 loss at the hands of the Lions, they were sitting at a mediocre 6–6.

Everything changed with the start of December as the Packers beat the Bears and the Chargers. Then tragedy struck: Brett Favre's much-loved father, Irv—a radio personality in Wisconsin with his insightful and funny post-game commentary—died of a heart attack. The next game, a Monday Night contest in Oakland, ended up being a tribute to Irv as Brett delivered his best performance as a quarterback, throwing for 399 yards and four touchdowns in a 41–7 Packers rout. When Green Bay beat the Broncos in the season finale, they wrapped up another North Division crown.

Green Bay entered the postseason with a head of steam and hosted the Mike Holmgren-coached Seahawks in the first round. The Packers played aggressively in a back-and-forth game, but a late Seattle drive tied the score at 27–27 and forced overtime. After winning the coin toss at the start of the extra period, Seattle quarterback, and former Packer backup, Matt Hasselback declared, "We'll take the ball and we're going to score." Moments later he served up an interception that cornerback Al Harris returned for a touchdown to seal a 33–27 win. The next week's game in Philadelphia did not go as well. The Packers seemingly had the game wrapped up with the Eagles facing a fourth down and 26 yards to go with little time on the clock. The Packers' defense, suspect all season, gave up the first down and the Eagles tied the game with a field goal. Philadelphia then turned a Favre overtime interception into another field goal and an unlikely 20–17 victory.

WHICH WAY ARE THE PACKERS GOING?

Despite the fact that the Packers were performing well on the field, there were concerns about Mike

DONALD DRIVER
Wide Receiver
1999–Present

Donald Driver is one of those football players it is easy to cheer for. On the field, he's a courageous, hardworking, and gifted receiver whose talents are often overlooked because he does not go out of his way to call attention to himself. Off the field, he's one of the NFL's most dedicated players when it comes to community involvement and charitable causes. Many fans still get a lump in their throats remembering Driver's honest tears of joy after he had been rewarded with a generous new contract following his break-out, Pro Bowl season in 2002. His success in Green Bay did not come overnight. Driver was drafted in 1999's second round out of tiny Alcorn State, where he had been better known as a world-class high jumper (many feel that if Driver had focused on track he would have made the 2000 U.S. Olympic team), and spent three seasons playing behind Antonio Freeman, Bill Schroeder, and Corey Bradford. But when that trio was gone by the beginning of 2002, Driver got his chance and delivered a 70-catch, 1000-plus-yard season. After that, he only seemed to get better. The 2006 season was his best; he caught 92 passes for 1295 yards and eight touchdowns, played in his second Pro Bowl, and helped Packers fans believe a return to the playoffs was not far off. With his career still in full swing, Driver is creeping up on the Packers all-time pass-catching lists. His current stats include 421 receptions for 5929 yards and 36 touchdowns.

The ever-enthusiastic Brett Favre celebrates his second quarter touchdown pass against the Rams during Green Bay's 45–17 rout of St. Louis on November 29, 2004. The game marked the 200th consecutive regular-season start for the durable quarterback.
Frank Polich/Reuters/CORBIS

Sherman's performance as general manager. Though he had inherited a talented team, thanks to the efforts of Ron Wolf, fans and media observers questioned the wisdom of some of Sherman's personnel moves. On the free-agent market, Green Bay had not been particularly competitive, and their few signings were relatively disappointing. Former Saints' defensive end Joe Johnson was an especially expensive bust; limited by injuries, he played in only 11 games over two seasons in Green Bay.

Sherman's drafts also left a lot to be desired. Though he had hit on 2003 first-round pick Nick Barnett, who quickly became a fixture at middle linebacker, Sherman had limited success in later rounds, and the Packers' base of young talent started to thin. The 2004 draft was another frustrating one. Though seventh-round pick Scott Wells was an exceptional find who eventually became the starting center, cornerback Ahmad Carroll was another first-round disappointment. Plus, Sherman took considerable heat when he traded up to select punter B.J. Sander in the third round. Not only was it unheard of to pick a punter that high, but Sander never lived up to his reputation and was cut by the Packers before the 2006 season.

So the Packers entered 2004 with a number of questions. Could they rebound after the disappointing playoff loss? Could they maintain their high level of play with what appeared to be an eroding talent base? How much longer could they count on Brett Favre to continue playing and performing at such a high level? As the season began, it looked the answers to these questions might not be ones that Packers fans wanted to hear. After winning their first game, Green Bay stumbled to four straight losses, including three at Lambeau Field. Yet when all looked hopeless, the Packers reeled off six straight wins to pull themselves back into playoff contention.

In the midst of this up-and-down season, Brett Favre was dealing with serious challenges in his personal life. His brother-in-law, Casey Tynes, was killed in an October 6 ATV accident on the quarterback's property in Mississippi. Then, just days later, Favre's wife, Deanna, was diagnosed with breast cancer. The Packers' leader responded to these tragedies by simply playing better. By the end of the season, he had racked up more than 4000 yards passing, thrown for 30 touchdowns, and looked like a quarterback who was a long way from retiring. Helping his cause was the support of another 1000-yard season from Ahman Green and the emergence of the exciting receiving tandem of Donald Driver and Javon Walker.

Despite losing another home game—to the Jaguars—on December 19, the Packers clinched a playoff appearance. Just five days later they traveled to

> **"We are not familiar with losing and that is one thing we stress in this locker room: Don't get familiar with losing, because we never lose games here."**
> **—Donald Driver**

the Metrodome to battle the Vikings for the North Division title. The high-scoring affair came down to a Favre-led 76-yard drive and a last-second field goal try by Packers kicker Ryan Longwell. He made the 29-yard kick and Green Bay captured the division crown by a 34–31 margin.

Two days later, Packers fans were stunned by the unexpected death of retired star Reggie White from a respiratory ailment. Though White had briefly revived his career with the Carolina Panthers, he would always have a special place in the hearts of Green Bay fans and was destined to enter the Pro Football Hall of Fame representing the Packers.

After finishing 2004 with another 10–6 record, Green Bay hosted Minnesota in the first round of the playoffs. The Packers had swept the regular-season games with the Vikings, who barely made the playoffs with an 8–8 record, and were heavy favorites entering the contest. The Vikings ignored the oddsmakers and jumped out to a quick 17–0 lead. The Packers pulled back into the game with 10 unanswered points, but could get no closer in dropping a 31–17 decision. Brett Favre had a particularly poor game, throwing four interceptions. After the contest, Favre fueled more discussion about his retirement when he would not guarantee he would be back the following season and said that he had to spend some time thinking about his future.

TOTAL COLLAPSE AND A COACHING CHANGE

Despite the playoff appearance, the Packers were showing indications of slipping, which led Bob Harlan to strip Mike Sherman of his general manager title and hand the job to Ted Thompson. The former NFL linebacker Thompson was a Ron Wolf disciple who had worked in Green Bay as assistant director of pro personnel for eight years. He moved to Seattle to become the Seahawks' vice president of football operations, but gladly returned to Green Bay as general manager, calling it "a dream-come-true-type job."

Whether Mike Sherman was accepting of this demotion was unclear, but the team received good news in March when Brett Favre confirmed he was returning for the 2005 season. Despite the fact the

Packers' quarterback position was settled, the rest of the roster began to change under Thompson's leadership, and the fans were not happy. Thompson let three popular stars—guards Marco Rivera and Mike Wahle and safety Darren Sharper—leave when he refused to meet their contract demands. Instead of paying aging veterans, Thompson wanted to focus on developing young talent. Yet his first draft choice was a controversial one: quarterback Aaron Rodgers. The former California star seemed to be a bargain where he was selected late in the first round, but observers

Mike McCarthy became the fourteenth head coach in Packers' history when he was hired to take over the team on January 12, 2006. Relatively young and inexperienced, McCarthy nonetheless led the team to a respectable 8–8 record during his first campaign.
Paul Jasienski/Getty Images

questioned the choice with Brett Favre returning and the team having other pressing needs.

As the 2005 season opened, it was obvious the team had some serious problems. The Packers dropped their first four games, in the process losing wide receiver Javon Walker for the season to a knee injury. In fact, injuries decimated the Packers' offense; by midseason

they were also without top running backs Ahman Green and Najeh Davenport. With the offense struggling, Brett Favre did everything he could to carry the load himself, but his risky play carried a heavy cost: He ended up leading the league with 29 interceptions. Receiver Donald Driver stepped up in support of Favre with another outstanding season, and running back Samkon

Opposite: **The Lambeau Leap, 2000s style: Rookie wide receiver Greg Jennings celebrates his first professional touchdown by getting up close and personal with Green Bay fans during the Packers' September 17, 2006, clash with New Orleans.** *Allen Fredrickson /Reuters/CORBIS*

Left: **Despite being a lightly regarded seventh-round pick in 2000, Mark Tauscher earned a starting job his rookie year and became a stalwart on the Packers' offensive line. Here he sets up to pass block during Green Bay's 26–7 victory over the Bears on December 31, 2006, which ended the season on a very upbeat note.** *Getty Images*

Gado emerged as the season's brightest note. The Nigerian-born Gado had not even been a starter at tiny Liberty University, but when given an opportunity because of injuries to other backs, he led the team with 582 yards and 6 touchdowns on the ground.

Throughout this challenging season—which ended with the Packers posting a 4–12 record and finishing in the division cellar—Mike Sherman looked unable to turn around the team's fortunes. So it was not surprising when, on January 2, 2006, Ted Thompson fired Sherman, citing the Packers' need for a change at the top. It was a sad end to a head-coaching tenure in which Sherman had compiled a very good 53–27 record, but critics pointed to his relatively weak 2–4 mark in the postseason and the fact that his teams never made it to the NFC championship game—let alone the Super Bowl.

It promised to be a very trying off-season for Packers fans, who were demoralized by Green Bay's worst season since the Lindy Infante era. In addition, there were strong indications that this season might have been Brett Favre's final one. He said that he would take several weeks, or even months, to make his final decision, citing a need to distance himself from what had been a very tough season and to discuss the decision with his family. And finally there was the question of a new coach, which had become such an important issue to the Packers since Curly Lambeau's departure in early 1950. Was there another Lombardi- or Holmgren-style candidate waiting in the wings? Fans waited breathlessly as Thompson conducted his search.

MCCARTHY—AND FAVRE—GIVE FANS A REASON TO BELIEVE

On January 12, 2006, Ted Thompson introduced his choice for head coach—and it was a surprising one to most observers. Mike McCarthy was a respected NFL assistant (he was offensive coordinator for the 49ers and had served in the same role for the Saints), but he was still fairly young (42) and not necessarily considered one of the elite assistant coaches in the league. On the other hand, McCarthy had extensive NFL experience and was regarded as an expert in the West Coast offense and in working with quarterbacks. In fact, he had served one year as the Packers'

LAMBEAU-STYLE TAILGATING

Green Bay Packers fans did not invent the pre-game tailgate party, but they have been responsible for refining the event into something more akin to a religious experience than a simple act of eating and drinking. On game-day Sundays, when the kickoff is usually scheduled for high noon, the parking lots surrounding Lambeau Field start filling with tailgaters at 8 a.m., or even earlier, no matter how bad the weather. Experienced partiers angle for the best locations, lay out their spreads, and start firing up their grills. The range of tailgate fare is broad to say the least, ranging from bologna to brie, but the menu of most pre-game partiers centers on two key items: beer and bratwurst. Because of Green Bay's strong German and Belgian heritage, it's not surprising that beer is the beverage of choice in Titletown. Bratwurst, as every

Packers fan knows, is a German delicacy whose name means "fry sausage"—but no self-respecting tailgater would fry their brats. They are meant to be grilled, and the mouth-watering aroma of those thousands of grilling sausages fills the air around Lambeau as game time approaches. Meanwhile, music booms from multiple speakers, footballs fly through the air, and a nonstop parade of fans donned in jerseys, cheeseheads, blaze orange (especially near deer hunting season), and an endless array of Packers paraphernalia provides hours of visual entertainment. Then as quickly as the tailgate world came to life, it evaporates as fans head to the stadium for the noon kickoff, leaving a handful of ticketless stragglers who really only showed up for the party.

No Packers tailgate party is complete without bratwurst. Here a generous quantity of the savory sausages get the appropriate grill treatment in the shadow on Lambeau Field before Green Bay's December 24, 1995, game with the Pittsburgh Steelers. *David Stluka/Getty Images*

The tailgate party has become just as important a tradition for Packers fans as attending the games. This group cooks up a feast in the Lambeau Field parking lot prior to an August 2002 preseason game against the Browns.
Jonathan Daniel/Getty Images

A very determined Ahman Green fights through the tackle of Washington tackle Marco Coleman en route to a nine-yard gain during Green Bay's 37–0 shutout of the Redskins on September 24, 2001. *Reuters/CORBIS*

AHMAN GREEN
Running Back
2000-2006

Ahman Green played seven seasons for the Packers and except for an injury-shortened 2005, he rushed for more than 1000 yards every year. That is an amazing record for an NFL running back ... especially one traded away by his first team because they thought he was a "fumbler." Green had a fantastic career at the University of Nebraska, leading the Huskers to three national championships, but he was not selected until the third round of the 1998 draft. Chosen by the Seahawks, Green made little impact during two seasons in Seattle, but he impressed offensive coordinator, Mike Sherman. When Sherman became the Packers' head coach, he helped bring Green to Green Bay, and his career blossomed. Green began a string of four straight Pro Bowl appearances in 2001, and in 2003, he led the league in rushing and set a new Packers' single-season record with 1883 yards. The 2006 season may have been his most impressive, when he returned from a serious injury to re-establish himself as one of the league's top backs. In addition to rushing, Green has always been a big threat catching the ball. He was the Packers' leading receiver in 2001 with 62 catches, and during his years in Green Bay, he snagged 347 passes for 2708 yards and 14 touchdowns. Green became a free agent after the 2006 season, and his Packers' career ended when the Houston Texans made him a rich contract offer that Green Bay would not match.

> **"It's amazing. I will get four- and five-page handwritten letters from fans. How can they possibly have that many questions about one football team? But they do."**
> —*Bob Harlan*

quarterbacks coach (in 1999), during which time he developed a good relationship with Brett Favre.

Elsewhere in the Packers' front office in 2006, inevitable change was in the works. After a long and amazingly successful career, Bob Harlan was planning his retirement. To ensure a smooth transition, Harlan had already been grooming his successor, John Jones, whom he had brought to the club in 1999 from the NFL Management Council. Harlan's plan was to hand the presidency to Jones in May 2006, but to remain with the club as chief executive officer until May 2007. At that time, he would retire and hand the reins of power to Jones. Though fans were saddened by this development, they were grateful for the job Harlan had done, as well as for his efforts to ensure the team would be in good hands after he departed.

Meanwhile, Ted Thompson continued an aggressive remaking of the roster, shifting more to younger athletic players. By the start of the 2006 season, Green Bay had the youngest average age of any NFL club. One notable exception to this youth movement was Thompson's signing of veteran Raiders' cornerback Charles Woodson. Some questioned whether the aging former Heisman Trophy winner and Pro Bowler was worth the money, but he proved any detractors wrong by delivering an outstanding performance in his first year with the Packers, teaming with Al Harris to give the team what arguably was the best cornerback tandem in the league.

Though it's still too early to tell, Thompson's 2006 draft looked like one of Green Bay's best in years. Top pick A.J. Hawk lived up to his billing as the nation's best college linebacker, and started all 16 games for Green Bay. Second-round pick Greg Jennings quickly established himself as the team's number-two receiver. And rookies Darryn Colledge and Jason Spitz shored up an offensive line that had been a problem area for the Packers in 2005. Still, in the days leading up to the draft, one piece of the puzzle was still missing: Brett Favre had yet to make a decision on his future. Finally, three days before draft day, the veteran quarterback agreed to return for at least one more season.

Packers fans were not sure what to think as the 2006 training camp opened. During the preseason, Green Bay looked like a young team with an inexperienced coach, and expectations plummeted. These low expectations were fulfilled when the Bears routed the Packers 26–0 on opening day at Lambeau Field. Another home loss, to the Saints, followed. When the Packers entered the bye week 1–4, the mood in Green Bay was somber. Fans were already questioning the hiring of Mike McCarthy and some were calling for Ted Thompson's job.

When the Packers came out of the bye week with consecutive wins over the Dolphins and Cardinals, fans grudgingly began to admit the team was starting to look different: The young offensive line was adapting to its new zone-blocking scheme despite an ever-revolving lineup thanks to injuries, and the defense was starting to gel into an effective unit. When the Packers hit a three-game skid, including blowout losses at the hands of the Patriots and Jets, any optimism started to disappear. But the McCarthy-coached team proved it was a different one that had been on the field in 2006. Starting with an upset of the 49ers in San Francisco, Green Bay ran off four straight wins to close out the season. The season finale was a 26–7 domination of the Super Bowl-bound Bears, a satisfying turnaround from the teams' meeting in Week 1.

In finishing at a decent 8–8, the Packers kept themselves in the playoff hunt until the final week, ultimately missing out on the wild card due to a tiebreaker. More importantly, the team showed steady improvement throughout the season, and by the end, it looked like one of the NFL's better squads. The defense toughened up as the season progressed, Ahman Green returned from the previous season's serious injury to again rush for 1000 yards, and Donald Driver proved that he was indeed the league's most underrated receiver.

Despite these performances, Packers fans focused, as always, on the quarterback position. Though Brett Favre made a national television audience think he had played his last game, thanks to his emotional interview after the Bears game, he had other plans. Invigorated by a season in which he cut down his interceptions and played like a much younger man, Favre announced during Super Bowl weekend that he would be back in 2007 for his 17th season. With the news, Packers fans were elated. It may have only been an 8–8 season, but Green Bay's love affair with its football team had been rekindled, like it had so many times before. With talk of future playoffs—and maybe another Super Bowl—to sustain them, Green Bay residents could handle the cold and snow of yet another Wisconsin winter. Football season was only a few months away, Brett Favre was coming back, Lambeau Field was still the best stadium in the NFL ... and life was good

Opposite: **Brett Favre has an uncanny ability to avoid sacks—one reason for his amazing durability—but he could not escape the grasp of Minnesota linebacker Ben Leber on December 21, 2006. Despite this minor setback, Green Bay went on to edge the Vikings 9–7 and Favre thrilled fans after the season by announcing he would be back to play in 2007.** *Reuters/CORBIS*

AFTERWORD
BY MARY JANE VAN DUYSE
THE ORIGINAL GREEN BAY PACKERS GOLDEN GIRL

Some of the most memorable moments of my long association with the Green Bay Packers organization occurred during the 1950s and 1960s. For example, on September 29, 1957, during the dedication of the new City Stadium (now known as Lambeau Field), one of the dignitaries in attendance was Vice-President Richard Nixon. After my pre-game show, the vice-president walked out to the 50-yard line to personally congratulate me on my performance.

A few years later, I again met Richard Nixon at a restaurant in Key Biscayne, Florida. He came over to our table and addressed me as "Miss Green Bay Packer." It was a memorable moment and we remained friends for the remainder of his life.

Another special memory was my performance at the 1961 National Football League championship game. The Green Bay Packers played the New York Giants at City Stadium in front of a record crowd—despite the fact that the temperature was 20 degrees at game time and 14 inches of snow had fallen the night before!

I was going to be featured doing my baton-twirling act at midfield during the game, but my baton was so cold that my hands hurt when I moved them. This was a historic day because it was the first championship game to be played in Green Bay. I wore a new red velvet cape that my grandmother had made for me especially for this game. It had eye appeal—and it helped keep me warm. It was quite a day in "Title Town—USA," a name that had been coined by the Green Bay Chamber of Commerce.

I waited to be announced, then ran out onto the field as fast as I could; I reached the 50-yard line at full speed. Nothing could stop me now. I was determined to make this routine as good as possible, so I included a back "fish flop" with my baton. I had to roll backward, then turn over onto my stomach and come up. I felt the ice on the hard, cold ground; it hurt, but the crowd cheered and yelled in approval, so it was worth it.

Another thrilling event in my life as the Green Bay Packers Golden Girl was the 1967 "Ice Bowl" game. The Packers were playing the Dallas Cowboys and the temperature at game time, when we arrived at the field, was 13 degrees below zero. The CBS and NBC television networks had contacted me in advance and told me to have extra girls on the field. Each one would carry a letter; together the girls spelled out the words "MERRY CHRISTMAS AND HAPPY NEW YEAR FROM NBC AND CBS."

We were spread out the length of the field and the whole presentation was very impressive, but it was tough on the Golden Girls. Some of them suffered frostbite on their faces, and one of the girls froze her foot—but the show did go on! My baton was like an icicle. It may have been too cold for spirited routines, but the girls were far from heading home. They bundled up in the stands and huddled on the sidelines until the very last exciting play—in the process earning the respect and admiration of the Green Bay fans.

I want to share with people in my own words what an honor it was working with the Green Bay Packers organization and how much it helped me to this day. In the world of sports, Green Bay is uniquely known because of our superb management. Wherever I have

appeared, people ask me about the team and Lambeau Field, but they also want to hear about the famous team leaders that I have been lucky to know over the years, including Curley Lambeau, Vince Lombardi, and Bob Harlan.

Green Bay may be a small town in a world of large-city franchises, but the Packers will always be the team that fans across the nation root for!

Mary Jane Van Duyse Sorgel
Sturgeon Bay, Wisconsin

BIBLIOGRAPHY

Books

Carlson, Chuck. *Tales from the Packers Sideline: A Collection of the Greatest Stories Ever Told*. Champaign, IL: Sports Publishing LLC, 2003.

D'Amato, Gary. *Stadium Stories: Green Bay Packers*. Guilford, CT: The Globe Pequot Press, 2004.

Goska, Eric. *Green Bay Packers: A Measure of Greatness*, 2nd Edition. Iola, WI: Krause Publications, 2004.

Green Bay Packer Hall of Fame. *The Green Bay Packer Hall of Fame*. Green Bay, WI: Green Bay Packer Hall of Fame Inc., 1995.

Isaacson, Kevin (with Tom Kessenich). *Return to Glory: The Inside Story of the Green Bay Packers' Return to Prominence*. Iola, WI: Krause Publications, 1996.

Kramer, Jerry (ed.). *Lombardi: Winning is the Only Thing*. New York: Crowell, 1976.

MacCambridge, Michael. *America's Game*. New York: Random House, 2004.

Maraniss, David. *When Pride Still Mattered: A Life of Vince Lombardi*. New York: Simon & Schuster, 1999.

National Football League. *The NFL's Official Encyclopedic History of Professional Football*. New York: Macmillan Publishing Co., 1977.

National Football League (foreword by Pete Rozelle). *The Super Bowl: Celebrating a Quarter-Century of America's Greatest Game*. New York: Simon & Schuster, 1990.

Palmer, Pete (ed.) et al. *The ESPN Pro Football Encyclopedia*. New York: Sterling Publishing Co., 2006.

Ross, Alan. *Packer Pride*. Nashville: Cumberland House, 2004.

Starr, Bart (with Mark Cox). *Quarterbacking: Bart Starr*. Englewood Cliffs, NJ: Prentice-Hall, 1967.

Starr, Bart (with Murray Olderman). *Starr: My Life in Football*. New York: William Morrow and Co., 1987.

Sullivan, George. *Pro Football's Passing Game*. New York: Dodd, Mead & Company, 1972.

Whittingham, Richard. *What A Game They Played*. New York: Harper & Row, 1984.

Zimmerman, David. *Lambeau: The Man Behind the Mystique*. Hales Corners, WI: Eagle Books, 2003.

Web Sites

Christl, Cliff. "Lambeau: More than a Name," www.uwgb.edu/voyageur/archive_17_2_lambeau.pdf

Gannett Company. "PackersNews.com," www.packersnews.com/

Green Bay Antiques. www.greenbayantiques.com/

Green Bay Packers Inc. "Lambeau Field," www.lambeaufield.com/

Green Bay Packers Inc. "Packers.com," www.packers.com/

Hickok Sports. "Sports History: Index to Football," www.hickoksports.com/history/footbaix.shtml#hist

Lawrence, Mark. "Football 101," football.calsci.com/

Milwaukee Journal Sentinel. "Packers Plus Online," www.jsonline.com/index/index.aspx?id=44

National Football League. "Official Site of the National Football League," www.nfl.com/

Pro Football Hall of Fame. "Official Site of the Pro Football Hall of Fame," www.profootballhof.com/

Sports Encyclopedia. "Green Bay Packers," www.sportsecyclopedia.com/nfl/gb/packers.html

Wisconsin Historical Society. "Big Bay Blue," www.wisconsinhistory.org/wmh/pdf/autumn05_scotter.pdf

Wisconsin Historical Society. "Packers' Glory Years Go Online," www.wisconsinhistory.org/highlights/archives/2005/09/packers_glory_y.asp?jx=1001

GREEN BAY PACKERS RECORD BOOK

THROUGH 2006 SEASON

* Entries marked with an asterisk are also NFL records

INDIVIDUAL CAREER LEADERS

Passing

Attempts

8,219	Brett Favre, 1992–2006 (15 seasons)
3,149	Bart Starr, 1956–1971 (16 seasons)
2,831	Lynn Dickey, 1976–1977, 1979–1985 (9 seasons)
1,854	Tobin Rote, 1950–1956 (7 seasons)
1,607	Don Majkowski, 1987–1992 (6 seasons)

Completions

5,021	Brett Favre, 1992–2006 (15 seasons)
1,808	Bart Starr, 1956–1971 (16 seasons)
1,592	Lynn Dickey, 1976–1977, 1979–1985 (9 seasons)
889	Don Majkowski, 1987–1992 (6 seasons)
826	Tobin Rote, 1950–1956 (7 seasons)

Completion Percentage (500 or more attempts)

61.09%	Brett Favre, 1992–2006 (5,021—8,219)
57.42%	Bart Starr, 1956–1971 (1,808—3,149)
56.23%	Lynn Dickey, 1976–1977, 1979–1985 (1,592—2,831)
55.32%	Don Majkowski, 1987–1992 (889—1,607)
53.80%	Randy Wright, 1984–1988 (602—1,119)

Yards Passing

57,500	Brett Favre, 1992–2006 (15 seasons)
24,718	Bart Starr, 1956–1971 (16 seasons)
21,369	Lynn Dickey, 1976–1977, 1979–1985 (9 seasons)
11,535	Tobin Rote, 1950–1956 (7 seasons)
10,870	Don Majkowski, 1987–1992 (6 seasons)

Touchdowns

414	Brett Favre, 1992–2006 (15 seasons)
152	Bart Starr, 1956–1971 (16 seasons)
133	Lynn Dickey, 1976–1977, 1979–1985 (9 seasons)
89	Tobin Rote, 1950–1956 (7 seasons)
66	Arnie Herber, 1930–1940 (11 seasons)

Interceptions

271	Brett Favre, 1992–2006 (15 seasons)
151	Lynn Dickey, 1976–1977, 1979–1985 (9 seasons)
138	Bart Starr, 1956–1971 (16 seasons)
119	Tobin Rote, 1950–1956 (7 seasons)
90	Arnie Herber, 1930–1940 (11 seasons)

Passer Rating (Minimum 800 attempts)

85.1	Brett Favre, 1992–2006 (15 seasons)
80.5	Bart Starr, 1956–1971 (16 seasons)
73.8	Lynn Dickey, 1976–1977, 1979–1985 (9 seasons)
73.5	Don Majkowski, 1987–1992 (6 seasons)
72.6	Cecil Isbell, 1938–1942 (5 seasons)

Rushing

Attempts

1,811	Jim Taylor, 1958–1966 (9 seasons)
1,810	Ahman Green, 2000–2006 (7 seasons)
1,293	John Brockington, 1971–1977 (7 seasons)
1,171	Clarke Hinkle, 1932–1941 (10 seasons)
1,025	Tony Canadeo, 1941–1944, 1946–1952 (11 seasons)

Yards Gained

8,207	Jim Taylor, 1958–1966 (9 seasons)
8,162	Ahman Green, 2000–2006 (7 seasons)
5,024	John Brockington, 1971–1977 (7 seasons)
4,197	Tony Canadeo, 1941–1944, 1946–1952 (11 seasons)
3,937	Dorsey Levens, 1994–2001 (8 seasons)

Average Gain (Minimum 750 attempts)

4.58	Gerry Ellis, 1980–1986 (836—3,826)
4.53	Jim Taylor, 1958–1966 (1,811—8,207)
4.51	Ahman Green, 2000–2006 (1,810—8,162)
4.16	Paul Hornung, 1957–1962, 1964–1966 (893–3,711)
4.09	Tony Canadeo, 1941–1944, 1946–1952 (1,025–4,197)

Touchdowns

81	Jim Taylor, 1958–1966 (9 seasons)
53	Ahman Green, 2000–2006 (7 seasons)
50	Paul Hornung, 1957–1962, 1964–1966 (9 seasons)
37	Verne Lewellen, 1924–1932 (9 seasons)
35	Clarke Hinkle, 1932–1941 (10 seasons)

Receiving

Receptions

595,	Sterling Sharpe, 1988–1994 (7 seasons)
530	James Lofton, 1978–1986 (9 seasons)
488	Don Hutson, 1935–1945 (11 seasons, 118 games)
448	Boyd Dowler, 1959–1969 (11 seasons)
431	Antonio Freeman, 1995–2001, 2003 (8 seasons)

Yards Gained

9,656	James Lofton, 1978–1986 (9 seasons)
8,134	Sterling Sharpe, 1988–1994 (7 seasons)
7,991	Don Hutson, 1935–1945 (11 seasons)
6,918	Boyd Dowler, 1959–1969 (11 seasons)
6,651	Antonio Freeman, 1995–2001, 2003 (8 seasons)

Average Yards/Catch (Minimum 150 receptions)

19.72	Carroll Dale, (275 rec, 5,422 yds.)
18.42	Billy Howton, (303 rec, 5,581 yds.)
18.39	Max McGee, (345 rec, 6,346 yds.)
18.22	James Lofton, (530 rec, 9,656 yds.)
16.38	Don Hutson, (488 rec, 7,991 yds.)

Touchdowns

99	Don Hutson, 1935–1945 (11 seasons)
65	Sterling Sharpe, 1988–1994 (7 seasons)
57	Antonio Freeman, 1995–2001, 2003 (8 seasons)
50	Max McGee, 1954, 1957–1967 (12 seasons)
49	James Lofton, 1978–1986 (9 seasons)

Defense

Tackles (1975–2006)

1,020	John Anderson, 1978–1989
1,001	Johnnie Gray, 1975–1983
967	Mike Douglass, 1978–1985
953	LeRoy Butler, 1990–2001
926	Mark Murphy, 1980–1985, 1987–1991

Interceptions

52	Bobby Dillon, 1952–1959 (8 seasons)
48	Willie Wood, 1960–1971 (12 seasons)
39	Herb Adderley, 1961–1969 (9 seasons)
38	LeRoy Butler, 1990–2001 (12 seasons)
36	Darren Sharper, 1997–2004 (8 seasons)

Opponents Fumbles Recovered (1945–2006)

21	Willie Davis, 1960–1969
20	Ray Nitschke, 1958–1972
20	Johnnie Gray, 1975–1983
18	Henry Jordan, 1959–1969
16	Lionel Aldridge, 1963–1971

Sacks (1982–2006)

68.5	Reggie White, 1993–1998
64.5	Kabeer Gbaja-Biamila, 2000–2006
55.0	Tim Harris, 1986–1990
41.5	Ezra Johnson, 1982–1987
36.0	Tony Bennett, 1990–1993

Defensive Touchdowns

7	Herb Adderley, 1961–1969 (7 Int.)	
7	Darren Sharper, 1997–2004 (5 Int., 2 FR)	
5	Bobby Dillon, 1952–1959 (5 Int.)	
5	Doug Hart, 1964–1971 (3 Int., I FR, I blocked FG)	
4	Johnny (Blood) McNally, 1929–1933, 1935–1936 (4 Int.)	

Kicking & Punting
Field Goals
226	Ryan Longwell, 1997–2005
173	Chris Jacke, 1989–1996
120	Chester Marcol, 1972–1980
66	Paul Hornung, 1957–1962, 1964–1966
59	Jan Stenerud, 1980–1983

Field Goal Percentage (Minimum 50 attempts)
81.59%	Ryan Longwell (226/277)
80.82%	Jan Stenerud (59/73)
77.23%	Chris Jacke (173/224)
66.67%	Al Del Greco (50/75)
61.54%	Chester Marcol (120/195)

Points After Touchdown
376	Ryan Longwell, 1997–2005
301	Chris Jacke, 1989–1996
200	Fred Cone, 1951–1957
190	Paul Hornung, 1957–1962, 1964–1966
172	Don Hutson, 1935–1945

Punts
495	David Beverly, 1975–1980 (37.9 yd. avg.)
368	Don Bracken, 1985–1990 (39.7 yd. avg.)
315	Donny Anderson, 1966–1971 (39.6 yd. avg.)
308	Josh Bidwell, 2000–2003 (41.1 yd. avg.)
289	Craig Hentrich, 1994–1997 (42.8 yd. avg.)

Highest Punting Average (Minimum 150 attempts)
42.8 yds.	Craig Hentrich, 1994–1997 (289 punts)
42.6 yds.	Dick Deschaine, 1955–1957 (181 punts)
42.0 yds.	Bucky Scribner, 1983–1984 (154 punts)
41.6 yds.	Max McGee, 1954, 1957–1967 (256 punts)
41.1 yds.	Josh Bidwell, 2000–2003 (308 punts)

Kickoff & Punt Returns
Kickoff Returns
179	Steve Odom, 1974–1979 (4,124 yds.)
153	Al Carmichael, 1953–1958 (3,907 yds.)
120	Herb Adderley, 1961–1969 (3,080 yds.)
77	Travis Williams, 1967–1970 (2,058 yds.)
75	Tony Canadeo, 1941–1944, 1946–1952 (1,736 yds.)

Kickoff Return Yards
4,124	Steve Odom, 1974–1979 (179 ret)
3,907	Al Carmichael, 1953–1958 (153 ret)
3,080	Herb Adderley, 1961–1969 (120 ret)
2,084	Dave Hampton, 1969–1971 (74 ret)
2,058	Travis Williams, 1967–1970 (77 ret)

Average Kickoff Return Yardage (Minimum 50 attempts)
28.16	Dave Hampton, 1969–1971 (74 ret, 2,084 yds.)
26.73	Travis Williams, 1967–1970 (77 ret, 2,058 yds.)
26.69	Roell Preston, 1997–1998 (64 ret, 1,708 yds.)
26.51	Tom Moore, 1960–1965 (71 ret, 1,882 yds.)
25.67	Herb Adderley, 1961–1969 (120 ret, 3,080 yds.)

Kickoff Return Touchdowns
5	Travis Williams, 1967–1970
3	Dave Hampton, 1969–1971
Five players tied with 2 touchdowns	

Punt Returns
187	Willie Wood, 1960–1971 (1,391 yds.)
110	Antonio Chatman, 2003–2005 (903 yds.)
100	Al Carmichael, 1953–1958 (753 yds.)
100	Phillip Epps, 1982–1988 (819 yds.)
87	Walter Stanley, 1985–1988 (720 yds.)

Punt Return Yards
1,391	Willie Wood, 1960–1971 (187 returns)
968	Desmond Howard, 1996, 1999 (70 returns)
903	Antonio Chatman, 2003–2005 (110 returns)
834	Billy Grimes, 1950–1952 (63 returns)
819	Phillip Epps, 1982–1988 (100 returns)

Average Punt Return Yardage (Minimum 50 attempts)
13.8	Desmond Howard, 1996, 1999 (70 ret., 968 yds.)
13.2	Billy Grimes, 1950–1952 (63 ret., 834 yds.)
9.4	Jeff Query, 1989–1991 (76 ret., 712 yds.)
9.2	Jon Staggers, 1972–1974 (50 ret., 460 yds.)
8.9	Steve Odom, 1974–1979 (64 ret., 569 yds.)

Punt Return Touchdowns
3	Desmond Howard, 1996, 1999
2	Billy Grimes, 1950–1952
2	Willie Wood, 1960–1971
2	Jon Staggers, 1972–1974

Service
Most Seasons
16	Bart Starr, 1956–1971
15	Ray Nitschke, 1958–1972
15	Brett Favre, 1992–2006
14	Forrest Gregg, 1956, 1958–1970
13	Buckets Goldenberg, 1933–1945
13	Dave Hanner, 1952–1964

Most Games Played
239	Brett Favre, 1992–2006 (15 seasons)
196	Bart Starr, 1956–1971 (16 seasons)
190	Ray Nitschke, 1958–1972 (15 seasons)
188	William Henderson, 1995–2006 (12 seasons)
187	Forrest Gregg, 1956, 1958–1970 (14 seasons)

Most Consecutive Games Played
239	Brett Favre, 1992–2006 (current)
187	Forrest Gregg, 1956, 1958–1970
166	Willie Wood, 1960–1971
162	Larry McCarren, 1973–1984
151	Rob Davis, 1997–2006 (current)

INDIVIDUAL SINGLE-SEASON LEADERS

Passing
Attempts
613	Brett Favre, 2006
607	Brett Favre, 2005
599	Don Majkowski, 1989
595	Brett Favre, 1999
582	Brett Favre, 1994

Completions
372	Brett Favre, 2005 (attempted 607)
363	Brett Favre, 1994 (attempted 582)
359	Brett Favre, 1995 (attempted 570)
353	Don Majkowski, 1989 (attempted 599)
347	Brett Favre, 1998 (attempted 551)

Completion Percentage (Minimum 140 attempts)
65.39%	Brett Favre, 2003 (308—471)
64.12%	Brett Favre, 1992 (302—471)
64.07%	Brett Favre, 2004 (346—540)
63.74%	Bart Starr, 1968 (109—171)
62.98%	Brett Favre, 1995 (359—570)

Yards Passing
4,458	Lynn Dickey, 1983 (484 attempts)
4,413	Brett Favre, 1995 (570 attempts)
4,318	Don Majkowski, 1989 (599 attempts)
4,212	Brett Favre, 1998 (551 attempts)
4,091	Brett Favre, 1999 (595 attempts)

Touchdowns
39	Brett Favre, 1996
38	Brett Favre, 1995
35	Brett Favre, 1997
33	Brett Favre, 1994
32	Lynn Dickey, 1983

Interceptions
29	Lynn Dickey, 1983 (484 attempts)
29	Brett Favre, 2005 (607 attempts)
25	Lynn Dickey, 1980 (478 attempts)
24	Tobin Rote, 1950 (224 attempts)
24	Brett Favre, 1993 (522 attempts)

Passer Rating
105.0	Bart Starr, 1966
99.5	Brett Favre, 1995
97.1	Bart Starr, 1964
95.8	Brett Favre, 1996
94.1	Brett Favre, 2001

Rushing
Attempts
355	Ahman Green, 2003 (16 games)
329	Dorsey Levens, 1997 (16 games)
316	Edgar Bennett, 1995 (16 games)
304	Ahman Green, 2001 (16 games)
286	Ahman Green, 2002 (14 games)

Yards Gained
1,883	Ahman Green, 2003 (355 attempts)
1,474	Jim Taylor, 1962 (272 attempts)
1,435	Dorsey Levens, 1997 (329 attempts)
1,387	Ahman Green, 2001 (304 attempts)
1,307	Jim Taylor, 1961 (243 attempts)

Average Gain
6.88	Tobin Rote, 1951 (76—523)
5.71	Billy Grimes, 1950 (84—480)
5.49	Gerry Ellis, 1985 (104—571)
5.42	Jim Taylor, 1962 (272—1,474)
5.38	Jim Taylor, 1961 (243—1,307)

Touchdowns
19	Jim Taylor, 1962
15	Jim Taylor, 1961
15	Ahman Green, 2003
13	Paul Hornung, 1960
12	Jim Taylor, 1964

Receiving
Receptions
112	Sterling Sharpe, 1993 (16 games)
108	Sterling Sharpe, 1992 (16 games)
102	Robert Brooks, 1995 (16 games)
94	Sterling Sharpe, 1994 (16 games)
92	Donald Driver, 2006 (16 games)

Yards Gained
1,497	Robert Brooks, 1995
1,461	Sterling Sharpe, 1992
1,424	Antonio Freeman, 1998
1,423	Sterling Sharpe, 1989
1,382	Javon Walker, 2004

Average Yards/Catch (Minimum 24 receptions)
24.88	Don Hutson, (34 rec., 846 yds.)
23.68	Carroll Dale, (37 rec., 876 yds.)
23.22	Billy Howton, (53 rec., 1,231 yds.)
23.17	Max McGee, (30 rec., 695 yds.)
22.41	James Lofton, (58 rec., 1,300 yds.)

Touchdowns
18	Sterling Sharpe, 1994 (16 games)
17	Don Hutson, 1942 (11 games)
14	Antonio Freeman, 1998 (15 games)
13	Billy Howton, 1952 (12 games)
13	Sterling Sharpe, 1992 (16 games)

Defense
Tackles (1975–2006)
194	Nick Barnett, 2005	
180	Mike Douglass, 1981	
166	Rich Wingo, 1979	
165	Mike Douglass, 1980	
162	Mike Douglass, 1983	

Interceptions
10	Irv Comp, 1943 (10 games)	
9	Bob Forte, 1947 (12 games)	
9	Bobby Dillon, 1953 (12 games)	
9	Bobby Dillon, 1955 (12 games)	
9	Bobby Dillon, 1957 (12 games)	
9	John Symank, 1957 (12 games)	

Five other players are tied with 9 during 14- or 16-game seasons

Opponents Fumbles Recovered (1945–2006)
5	Charley Brock, 1945
5	Charley Brock, 1946
5	Paul Lipscomb, 1946
5	Lionel Aldridge, 1964
5	Brian Noble, 1987

Sacks (1982–2006)
19.5	Tim Harris, 1989
16.0	Reggie White, 1998
15.5	Aaron Kampman, 2006
14.5	Ezra Johnson, 1983
13.5	Tim Harris, 1988

Defensive Touchdowns
3	Herb Adderley, 1965 (3 Int.)
3	Darren Sharper, 1997 (2 Int., 1 FR)
3	Darren Sharper, 2004 (2 Int., 1 FR)

Eleven other players are tied with 2 touchdowns

Kicking & Punting
Field Goals
33	Chester Marcol, 1972 (48 attempts)
33	Ryan Longwell, 2000 (38 attempts)
31	Chris Jacke, 1993 (37 attempts)
29	Ryan Longwell, 1998 (33 attempts)
28	Ryan Longwell, 2002 (34 attempts)

Field Goal Percentage (Minimum 1 attempt/game))
91.6%	Jan Stenerud, 1981 (22/24)
88.46%	Ryan Longwell, 2003 (23/26)
87.88%	Ryan Longwell, 1998 (29/33)
86.84%	Ryan Longwell, 2000 (33/38)
85.71%	Ryan Longwell, 2004 (24/28)

Points After Touchdown
52	Jan Stenerud, 1983 (52 attempts)
51	Chris Jacke, 1996 (53 attempts)
51	Ryan Longwell, 2003 (51 attempts)
48	Ryan Longwell, 1997 (48 attempts)
48	Ryan Longwell, 2004 (48 attempts)

Punts
106	David Beverly, 1978 (35.5 yd. avg.)
86	David Beverly, 1980 (38.2 yd. avg.)
86	Paul McJulien, 1991 (40.4 yd. avg.)
85	David Beverly, 1977 (39.9 yd. avg.)
85	Bucky Scribner, 1984 (42.3 yd. avg.)

Highest Punting Average (Minimum 35 attempts)
45.0 yds.	Craig Hentrich, 1997 (75 punts)
44.7 yds.	Jerry Norton, 1963 (51 punts)
44.5 yds.	Jon Ryan, 2006 (84 punts)
44.1 yds.	Boyd Dowler, 1961 (38 punts)
43.5 yds.	Jack Jacobs, 1947 (57 punts)

Kickoff & Punt Returns
Most Kickoff Returns
57	Roell Preston, 1998 (1,497 yds.)
50	Allen Rossum, 2000 (1,288 yds.)
46	Dave Hampton, 1971 (1,314 yds.)
42	Steve Odom, 1975 (1,034 yds.)
41	Harlan Huckleby, 1983 (757 yds.)

Kickoff Return Yards
1,497	Roell Preston, 1998 (57 ret.)
1,314	Dave Hampton, 1971 (46 ret.)
1,288	Allen Rossum, 2000 (50 ret.)
1,034	Steve Odom, 1975 (42 ret.)
927	Al Carmichael, 1956 (33 ret.)

Average Kickoff Return Yardage (Minimum 12 attempts)
*41.06	Travis Williams, 1967 (18 ret., 739 yds.)
33.08	Tom Moore, 1960 (12 ret., 397 yds.)
31.56	Najeh Davenport, 2003 (16 ret., 505 yds.)
29.86	Al Carmichael, 1955 (14 ret., 418 yds.)
29.85	Herb Adderley, 1963 (20 ret., 597 yds.)

Kickoff Return Touchdowns
*4	Travis Williams, 1967
2	Roell Preston, 1998

Punt Returns
48	Desmond Howard, 1996 (875 yds.)
45	Antonio Chatman, 2005 (381 yds.)
44	Roell Preston, 1998 (398 yds.)
41	Charles Woodson, 2006 (363 yds.)
40	Robert Brooks, 1994 (352 yds.)

Punt Return Yards
*875	Desmond Howard, 1996 (58 returns)
555	Billy Grimes, 1950 (29 returns)
398	Roell Preston, 1998 (44 returns)
381	Antonio Chatman, 2005 (45 returns)
352	Robert Brooks, 1994 (40 returns)

Average Punt Return Yardage (Minimum 14 attempts)
19.1	Billy Grimes, 1950 (29 ret., 555 yds.)
16.1	Willie Wood, 1961 (14 ret., 225 yds.)
15.4	Ken Ellis, 1972 (14 ret., 215 yds.)
15.1	Desmond Howard, 1996 (58 ret., 875 yds.)
13.3	Willie Wood, 1964 (19 ret., 252 yds.)

Punt Return Touchdowns
3	Desmond Howard, 1996
2	Billy Grimes, 1950
2	Willie Wood, 1961

INDIVIDUAL SINGLE-GAME LEADERS

Passing
Attempts
61	Brett Favre, vs. SF, Oct. 14, 1996 (28 comp)
59	Don Majkowski, at Det., Nov. 12, 1989 (34 comp)
58	Brett Favre, at ChiB, Dec. 4, 2005 (31 comp)
55	Brett Favre, vs. NO, Sept. 17, 2006 (31 comp)
54	Randy Wright, vs. SF, Oct. 26, 1986 (30 comp)
54	Brett Favre, at ChiB, Dec. 5, 1993 (36 comp)

Completions
36	Brett Favre, at ChiB, Dec. 5, 1993 (54 att.)
35	Lynn Dickey, at TB, Oct. 12, 1980 (51 att.)
34	Don Majkowski, at Det., Nov. 12, 1989 (59 att.)
33	Brett Favre, at Atl., Oct. 4, 1992 (43 att.)
33	Brett Favre, at HouT., Nov. 21, 2004 (50 att.)

Completion Percentage (20 or more attempts)
90.48%	Lynn Dickey, at NO, Dec. 13, 1981 (19—21)
87.10%	Lynn Dickey, at HouO, Sept. 4, 1983 (27—31)
82.14%	Brett Favre, at CleB, Nov. 19, 1995 (23—28)
81.48%	Randy Wright, vs. TB, Sept. 11, 1988 (22—27)
80.00%	Bart Starr, at SF, Dec. 13, 1959 (20—25)
80.00%	Bart Starr, at SD, Oct. 12, 1970 (16—20)
80.00%	Lynn Dickey, at Min., Dec. 16, 1984 (16—20)

Yards Passing
418	Lynn Dickey, at TB, Oct. 12, 1980 (35 comp.)

410	Don Horn, vs. StLC, Dec. 21, 1969 (22 comp.)	
402	Brett Favre, at ChiB, Dec. 5, 1993 (36 comp.)	
399	Brett Favre, at Oak., Dec. 22, 2003 (22 comp.)	
395	Brett Favre, vs. SF, Oct. 14, 1996 (28 comp.)	

Longest Completion
*99 yds.	Brett Favre to Robert Brooks, at ChiB, Sept. 11, 1995
96 yds.	Tobin Rote to Billy Grimes, at SF, Dec. 10, 1950
95 yds.	Lynn Dickey to Steve Odom, at Min., Oct. 2, 1977
92 yds.	Arnie Herber to Don Hutson, vs. ChiC, Oct. 8, 1939
91 yds.	Bart Starr to Boyd Dowler, at LARm, Dec. 17, 1960

Touchdowns
5	Cecil Isbell, vs. ChiC, Nov. 1, 1942
5	Don Horn, vs. StLC, Dec. 21, 1969
5	Lynn Dickey, at NO, Dec. 13, 1981
5	Lynn Dickey, at HO, Sept. 4, 1983
5	Brett Favre, vs. ChiB, Nov. 12, 1995
5	Brett Favre, vs. Min., Sept. 21, 1997
5	Brett Favre, at Car., Sept. 27, 1998

Interceptions
6	Tom O'Malley, vs. Det., Sept. 17, 1950 (15 attempts)
5	Cecil Isbell, at NYG, Nov. 20, 1938 (19 attempts)
5	Jack Jacobs, at NYG, Nov. 23, 1947 (24 attempts)
5	Jack Jacobs, at Phi., Dec. 14, 1947 (36 attempts)
5	Tobin Rote, vs. LARm, Oct. 16, 1955 (40 attempts)
5	Bart Starr, vs. ChiB, Sept. 24, 1967 (19 attempts)
5	Randy Wright, at NO, Sept. 14, 1986 (44 attempts)
5	Don Majkowski, at TB, Oct. 14, 1990 (42 attempts)
5	Brett Favre, at Cin., Oct. 30, 2005 (39 attempts)

Rushing
Attempts
39	Terdell Middleton, vs. Min., Nov. 26, 1978 (110 yards)
33	Dorsey Levens, vs. DalC, Nov. 23, 1997 (190 yards)
33	Ahman Green, at Car., Sept. 13, 2004 (119 yards)
32	Jim Grabowski, vs. ChiB, Sept. 24, 1967 (111 yards)
32	John Brockington, at Min., Nov. 17, 1974 (137 yards)

Yards Gained
218	Ahman Green, vs. Den., Dec. 28, 2003 (20 attempts)
192	Ahman Green, vs. Phi., Nov. 10, 2003 (29 attempts)
190	Dorsey Levens, vs. DalC, Nov. 23, 1997 (33 attempts)
186	Jim Taylor, vs. NYG, Dec. 3, 1961 (27 attempts)
178	Najeh Davenport, vs. StLR, Nov. 29, 2004 (19 attempts)

Longest Runs
98 yds.	Ahman Green, vs. Den., Dec. 28, 2003 (TD)
97 yds.	Andy Uram, vs. ChiC, Oct. 8, 1939 (TD)
90 yds.	Ahman Green, vs. Dal., Oct. 24, 2004 (TD)
84 yds.	Jim Taylor, vs. Det., Nov. 8, 1964 (TD)
83 yds.	James Lofton, at NYG, Sept. 20, 1982 (TD)
83 yds.	Ahman Green, vs. Det., Sept. 9, 2001 (TD)

Average Gain (Minimum 10 attempts)
16.7	Billy Grimes, vs. NY Yanks, Oct. 8, 1950 (10-167)
13.45	Terdell Middleton, vs. Det., Oct. 1, 1978 (11-148)
11.6	Keith Woodside, vs. ChiB, Dec. 17, 1989 (10-116)
10.9	Ahman Green, vs. Den., Dec. 28, 2003 (20-218)

Touchdowns
4	Jim Taylor, at Cle., Oct. 15, 1961
4	Jim Taylor, at ChiB, Nov. 4, 1962
4	Jim Taylor, at Phi., Nov. 11, 1962
4	Terdell Middleton, vs. Sea., Oct. 15, 1978
4	Dorsey Levens, vs. Ari., Jan. 2, 2000

Receiving
Receptions
14	Don Hutson, at NYG, Nov. 22, 1942 (134 yards)
13	Don Hutson, vs. CleR, Oct. 18, 1942 (209 yards)
12	Ken Payne, at Den., Sept. 29, 1975 (167 yards)
12	Vince Workman, vs. Min., Sept. 6, 1992 (50 yards)

Thirteen players tied with 11 receptions

Yards Gained

257	Billy Howton, vs. LARm, Oct. 21, 1956 (7 rec)	
237	Don Hutson, at Bkn., Nov. 21, 1943 (8 rec)	
220	Don Beebe, vs. SF, Oct. 14, 1996 (11 rec)	
209	Don Hutson, vs. CleR, Oct. 18, 1942 (13 rec)	
207	Don Hutson, vs. ChiC, Nov. 1, 1942 (5 rec)	
207	Don Hutson, vs. Card-Pitt, Oct. 8, 1944 (11 rec)	

Longest Pass Reception

*99 yds. Robert Brooks (from B. Favre, at ChiB, Sept. 11, 1995, TD)
96 yds. Billy Grimes (from T. Rote, at SF, Dec. 10, 1950, TD)
95 yds. Steve Odom (from L. Dickey, at Min., Oct. 2, 1977, TD)
92 yds. Don Hutson (from A. Herber, vs. ChiC, Oct. 8, 1939, TD)
91 yds. Boyd Dowler (from B. Starr, at LARm, Dec. 17, 1960, TD)

Average Yards/Catch (Minimum 3 receptions)

49.67 Don Hutson, at Bkn., Nov. 19, 1939 (3-149)
48.67 James Lofton, at Atl. Dec. 26, 1982 (3-146)
47.33 Carroll Dale, vs. SF, Dec. 4, 1966 (3-142)
46.50 Carroll Dale, vs. Atl., Sept. 27, 1970 (4-186)
43.50 Andy Uram, vs. ChiC, Nov. 1, 1942 (4-174)

Touchdowns

4 Don Hutson, vs. Det., Oct. 7, 1945
4 Sterling Sharpe, at TB, Oct. 24, 1993
4 Sterling Sharpe, at DalC, Nov. 24, 1994
Twenty players tied with 3 touchdowns

Defense

Interceptions

*4 Bobby Dillon, at Det., Nov. 26, 1953
*4 Willie Buchanon, at SD, Sept. 24, 1978
Several players are tied with 3 interceptions

Longest Interception Return

99 yds. Tim Lewis, at LARm, Nov. 18, 1984 (TD)
95 yds. Nick Barnett, vs. NO, Oct. 9, 2005 (TD)
94 yds. Rebel Steiner, vs. ChiB, Oct. 1, 1950 (TD)
91 yds. Hal Van Every, at Pit., Nov. 23, 1941 (TD)
90 yds. LeRoy Butler, vs. SD, Sept. 15, 1996 (TD)
90 yds. Mike McKenzie, vs. ChiB, Dec. 7, 2003 (TD)

Sacks (1982–2006)

5.0 Vonnie Holliday, vs. Buf., Dec. 22, 2002
4.5 Bryce Paup, vs. TB, Sept. 15, 1991
4.0 Alphonso Carreker, vs. TB, Dec. 1, 1985
4.0 Tim Harris, vs. Atl., Oct. 1, 1989
4.0 Kabeer Gbaja-Biamila, vs. Chi., Jan. 2, 2005

Kicking & Punting

Field Goals

5 Chris Jacke, at LARd, Nov. 11, 1990
5 Chris Jacke, vs. SF, Oct. 14, 1996
5 Ryan Longwell, at Ari., Sept. 24, 2000
Several players are tied with 4 field goals

Longest Field Goals

54 yds. Chris Jacke, at Det., Jan. 2, 1994
54 yds. Ryan Longwell, at Ten., Dec. 16, 2001
54 yds. Dave Rayner, at Phi., Oct. 2, 2006
Eight players are tied with 53-yard field goals

Points After Touchdown

8 Don Chandler, vs. Atl., Oct. 23, 1966
Eight players are tied with 7 PATs

Punts

11 Clarke Hinkle, at ChiB, Dec. 10, 1933 (407 yards)
11 Jug Girard, at ChiB, Oct. 15, 1950 (418 yards)
11 Jug Girard, at LARm, Dec. 3, 1950 (402 yards)
Ten players are tied with 10 punts

Longest Punt

90 yds. Don Chandler, vs. SF, Oct. 10, 1965
78 yds. Jack Jacobs, vs. ChiC, Oct. 10, 1948

75 yds. Boyd Dowler, at Min., Oct. 22, 1961
75 yds. Boyd Dowler, vs. SF, Oct. 21, 1962
74 yds. Arnie Herber, vs. Det., Oct. 22, 1939
74 yds. Jack Jacobs, vs. LARm, Oct. 5, 1947

Highest Punting Average (Minimum 4 attempts)

61.6 yds. Roy McKay, vs. ChiC, Oct. 28, 1945 (5—308)
54.8 yds. Craig Hentrich, vs. NYJ, Nov. 12, 1994 (6—329)
54.3 yds. Jug Girard, vs. Phi., Oct. 14, 1951 (4—217)
53.3 yds. Boyd Dowler, vs. BalC, Oct. 9, 1960 (4—213)
53.3 yds. Josh Bidwell, at NO, Sept. 15, 2002 (4—213)

Kickoff & Punt Returns

Kickoff Returns

8 Harlan Huckleby, vs. Was., Oct. 17, 1983 (208 yds.)
8 Gary Ellerson, at StLR, Sept. 29, 1985 (164 yds.)
8 Roell Preston, vs. Min., Oct. 5, 1998 (256 yds.)
8 Antonio Chatman, vs. Ten., Oct. 11, 2004 (163 yds.)
7 Steve Odom, vs. Det., Sept. 29, 1974 (160 yds.)
7 Roell Preston, at Ind., Nov. 16, 1997 (211 yds.)
7 Vernand Morency, at Sea., Nov. 27, 2006 (152 yds.)

Kickoff Return Yards

256 Roell Preston, vs. Min., Oct. 5, 1998 (8 ret)
211 Roell Preston, at Ind., Nov. 16, 1997 (7 ret)
208 Harlan Huckleby, vs. Was., Oct. 17, 1983 (8 ret)
194 Dave Hampton, vs. NYG, Sept. 19, 1971 (5 ret)
189 Al Carmichael, vs. ChiB, Oct. 7, 1956 (5 ret)
189 Dave Hampton, vs. NO, Nov. 28, 1971 (5 ret)

Longest Kickoff Returns

*106 yds. Al Carmichael, vs. ChiB, Oct. 7, 1956
104 yds. Travis Williams, at LARm, Dec. 9, 1967
103 yds. Herb Adderley, vs. BalC, Nov. 18, 1962
101 yds. Dave Hampton, vs. Min., Oct. 4, 1970
101 yds. Roell Preston, vs. Min., Oct. 5, 1998

Average Kickoff Return Yardage (Minimum 3 attempts)

50.33 Travis Williams, at StLC, Dec. 10, 1967 (3—151)
44.67 Steve Odom, vs. Det., Oct. 3, 1976 (3—134)
43.33 Del Rodgers, at ChiB, Dec. 9, 1984 (3—130)
43.25 Allen Rossum, vs. Ind., Nov. 19, 2000 (4—173)
42.33 Ike Thomas, at ChiB, Nov. 12, 1972 (3—127)

Kickoff Return Touchdowns

*2 Travis Williams, vs. CleB, Nov. 12, 1967

Punt Returns

8 Phillip Epps, vs. Min., Nov. 21, 1982 (49 yds.)
7 Johnnie Gray, vs. Min., Nov. 21, 1976 (30 yds.)
7 Robert Brooks, at NE, Oct. 2, 1994 (34 yds.)
7 Desmond Howard, vs. SD, Sept. 15, 1996 (118 yds.)
7 Darrien Gordon, vs. Car., Sept. 29, 2002 (43 yds.)
7 Charles Woodson, vs. Min., Dec. 21, 2006 (48 yds.)

Punt Return Yards

167 Desmond Howard, at Det., Dec. 15, 1996
129 Phillip Epps, vs. TB, Oct. 2, 1983
122 Robert Brooks, vs. LARm, Oct. 9, 1994
118 Desmond Howard, vs. SD, Sept. 15, 1996
113 Walter Stanley, vs. Det., Nov. 27, 1986

Longest Punt Returns

95 yds. Steve Odom, vs. ChiC, Nov. 10, 1974 (TD)
94 yds. Mark Lee, vs. NYG, Nov. 8, 1981 (TD)
93 yds. Veryl Switzer, at ChiB, Nov. 7, 1954 (TD)
92 yds. Desmond Howard, at Det., Dec. 15, 1996 (TD)
90 yds. Andy Uram, vs. Bkn., Oct. 12, 1941 (TD)
90 yds. Phillip Epps, vs. TB, Oct. 2, 1983 (TD)

Average Punt Return Yardage (Minimum 3 attempts)

37.0 Mark Lee, vs. NYG, Nov. 8, 1981 (3—111)
36.67 Willie Wood, at ChiB, Dec. 5, 1964 (3—110)
33.40 Desmond Howard, at Det., Dec. 15, 1996 (5—167)
30.50 Robert Brooks, vs. LARm, Oct. 9, 1994 (4—122)
30.0 Antonio Chatman, vs. ChiB, Dec. 25, 2005 (3—90)

TEAM RECORDS, SEASON

League Championships

*12 1929, 1930, 1931, 1936, 1944, 1961, 1962, 1965, 1966, 1967, and 1999

Consecutive Seasons League Champion

*3 1929–1931 and 1965–1967

Most Consecutive Wins

11 1928–1929 and 1961–1962

Most Consecutive Losses

7 1948, 1951, 1958, 1984, and 1988

Single-Season Records

Most Wins, Regular Season

13, 1962, 1996, and 1997

Most Losses, Regular Season

12 1986, 1988, 1991, and 2005

Most Points, Season

456 1996 (16 games)
442 2003 (16 games)
429 1983 (16 games)

Fewest Points, Season

80 1922 (11 games)
85 1923 (10 games)
108 1924 (11 games)

Most Touchdowns, Season

56 1996 (16 games)
53 1962 (14 games)
53 2003 (16 games)

Fewest Points Allowed, Season

22 1929 (13 games)
34 1923 (10 games)
38 1924 (11 games)

Fewest Points Allowed, 16-Game Season

210 1996

Most Points Allowed, Season

439 1983 (16 games)
418 1986 (16 games)
406 1950 (12 games)

Fewest Touchdowns Allowed (Since 1932)

8 1932 (14 games)
13 1935 (12 games)
14 1933 (13 games)
14 1934 (13 games)
14 1936 (12 games)

Fewest Touchdowns Allowed, 16-Game Season

19 1996

Most Touchdowns Allowed, Season

56 1950 (12 games)
55 1983 (16 games)
52 1986 (16 games)

Most Yards Gained, Season

6,357 2004 (1,908 rushing, 4,449 passing)
6,172 1983 (1,807 rushing, 4,365 passing)
5,798 2003 (2,558 rushing, 3,240 passing)

Fewest Yards Gained, Season

2,340 1934 (1,183 rushing, 1,165 passing, 8 laterals)
2,618 1946 (1,765 rushing, 841 passing, 12 laterals)
2,702 1933 (1,513 rushing, 1,186 passing, 3 laterals)

Most First Downs, Season

354 2004 (98 rushing, 228 passing, 28 penalty)

342   1989 (114 rushing, 207 passing, 21 penalty)
340   1983 (99 rushing, 214 passing, 27 penalty)

Fewest First Downs, Season
125   1935
131   1945 (73 rushing, 44 passing, 14 penalty)
134   1938

Most Passes Attempted, Season
630   2006 (350 comp)
626   2005 (383 comp)
609   1994 (375 comp)

Fewest Passes Attempted, Season
134   1932 (48 comp)
178   1946 (54 comp)
197   1934 (74 comp)

Most Passes Completed, Season
383   2005 (626 att)
382   2004 (598 att)
375   1994 (609 att)

Fewest Passes Completed, Season
48   1932 (134 att)
54   1946 (178 att)
74   1934 (197 att)

Most Net Yards Gained Passing, Season
4,449   2004
4,365   1983
4,322   1995

Fewest Net Yards Gained Passing, Season
798   1932
841   1946
1,165   1934

Most Touchdown Passes, Season
39   1995
39   1996
36   2004

Fewest Touchdown Passes, Season
1   1921
3   1922
4   1927
4   1946

Most Times Sacked, Season
62   1990 (16 games)
52   1981 (16 games)
51   1988 (16 games)

Fewest Times Sacked, Season
14   2004 (16 games)
17   1972 (14 games)
17   1974 (14 games)

Most Passes Intercepted, Season
37   1950
34   1953
32   1983

Fewest Passes Intercepted, Season
*5   1966
6   1964
9   1972

Most Rushing Attempts, Season
560   1946
550   1978
544   1972

Fewest Rushing Attempts, Season
283   1982
313   1951
321   1954

Most Yards Gained Rushing, Season
2,558   2003
2,460   1962
2,350   1961

Fewest Yards Gained Rushing, Season
1,081   1982
1,183   1934
1,196   1951

Most Touchdowns Rushing, Season
*36   1962 (14 games)
29   1960 (12 games)
27   1961 (14 games)

Fewest Touchdowns Rushing, Season
5   1922, 1923, 1924, 1977, and 1990

Most Kickoff Returns, Season
79   1983
76   1986
75   2005

Fewest Kickoff Returns, Season
28   1941
28   1943
30   1944
30   1962

Most Yards Kickoff Returns, Season
1,570   2000 (64 returns, 24.5 avg)
1,547   1998 (60 returns, 25.8 avg)
1,546   1971 (58 returns, 26.7 avg)

Fewest Yards Kickoff Returns, Season
381   1940 (11 games)
567   1941 (11 games)
610   1944 (10 games)

Most Touchdowns Kickoff Returns, Season
*4   1967 (14 games)

Most Punt Returns, Season
61   1995
58   1996
56   1997

Fewest Punt Returns, Season
20   1961
22   1965
25   1970
25   1972

Most Yards Punt Returns, Season
*875   1996 (16 games)
729   1950 (12 games)
563   1939 (11 games)
563   1947 (12 games)

Fewest Yards Punt Returns, Season
65   1965 (14 games)
98   1970 (14 games)
137   1973 (14 games)

Most Touchdowns Punt Returns, Season
3   1996 (16 games)

Most Turnovers, Season
57   1950
56   1952
50   1983, 1988

Fewest Turnovers, Season
19   1972
21   1995
22   1994

Fewest Yards Allowed, Season
1,913   1933 (13 games)
2,091   1935 (12 games)
2,299   1937 (11 games)

Most Yards Allowed, Season
6,403   1983 (16 games)
5,782   1980 (16 games)
5,647   1979 (16 games)

Fewest Rushing Yards Allowed, Season
932   1982 (9 games)
1,040   1940 (11 games)
1,112   1943 (10 games)

Most Rushing Yards Allowed, Season
2,885   1979 (16 games)
2,641   1983 (16 games)
2,619   1956 (12 games)

Fewest Rushing Touchdowns Allowed, Season (Since 1932)
4   1932, 1933, and 1962

Most Rushing Touchdowns Allowed, Season
28   1983
24   1950
24   1953
24   1958

Fewest Net Passing Yards Allowed, Season
676   1934 (13 games)
711   1933 (13 games)
837   1935 (12 games)

Most Net Passing Yards Allowed, Season
3,762   1983 (16 games)
3,663   2004 (16 games)
3,640   1995 (16 games)

Fewest Passing Touchdowns Allowed, Season
3   1932 (14 games)
3   1934 (13 games)
6   1938 (11 games)
6   1946 (11 games)

Most Passing Touchdowns Allowed, Season
33   2004 (16 games)
31   1986 (16 games)
28   2000 (16 games)

Most Sacks, Season
52   2001 (16 games)
50   1998 (16 games)
48   1978 (16 games)
48   1985 (16 games)

Fewest Sacks, Season
19   1971 (14 games)
20   1982 (9 games)
25   1973 (14 games)

Most Opponent Turnovers, Season
54   1981 (16 games)
52   1946 (11 games)
51   1943 (10 games)
51   1947 (12 games)

Fewest Opponent Turnovers, Season
15   2004 (16 games)
16   1995 (16 games)
21   2005 (16 games)

Most Passes Intercepted, Season
42   1943 (10 games)
40   1940 (11 games)
33   1942 (11 games)

Fewest Passes Intercepted, Season
8   2004 (16 games)
10   2005 (16 games)
11   1976 (14 games)

Most Interception Return Touchdowns, Season
6   1966 (14 games)

Most Opponent Fumbles, Season
45   1946 (11 games)
44   1975 (12 games)
44   1985 (16 games)

Fewest Opponent Fumbles, Season
12   1995 (16 games)
15   1940 (11 games)
16   2000 (16 games)

Most Blocked Kicks, Season
12   1974 (4 FGs, 4 punts, 4 PATs)

Most Safeties, Season
4   1985 (16 games)

Fewest Penalties, Season
38   1942
41   1955
42   1956 and 1982

Most Penalties, Season
135   1987
128   1986
119   2005

Fewest Yards Penalized, Season
250   1938
259   1939
291   1937

Most Yards Penalized, Season
1,103   1987
1,019   1947
950   2004

TEAM RECORDS, GAME

Most Points Scored, Game
57   vs. Detroit Lions, Oct. 7, 1945 (57–21)
56   vs. Atlanta, Oct. 23, 1966 (56–3)
55   vs. Chicago Cardinals, Nov. 1, 1942 (55–24)
55   vs. Cleveland Browns, Nov. 12, 1967 (55–7)
55   vs. Tampa Bay, Oct. 2, 1983 (55–14)

Most Points Allowed, Game
61   at Chicago Bears, Dec. 7, 1980
56   at Baltimore Colts, Nov. 2, 1958
55   at New York Giants, Dec. 20, 1986

Most Yards Gained, Game
628   at Phi., Nov. 11, 1962 (294 Ru., 334 Pa.)
569   at TB, Oct. 12, 1980 (154 Ru., 415 Pa.)
548   at Oak, Dec. 22, 2003 (156 Ru., 392 Pa.)

Fewest Yards Gained, Game
36   at Cin., Sept. 26, 1976 (71 Ru., -35 Pa.)
61   at BosR, Nov. 4, 1934 (55 Ru., 6 Pa.)
63   vs. DalC, Oct. 24, 1965 (73 Ru., -10 Pa.)
63   at LARm, Oct. 21, 1973 (35 Ru., 28 Pa.)
63   at Det., Oct. 28, 1973 (60 Ru., 3 Pa.)

Most First Downs, Game
37   at Phi., Nov. 11, 1962 (21 rushing, 15 passing, 1 penalty)
32   at TB, Oct. 12, 1980 (11 rushing, 21 passing)
31   vs. TB, Dec. 1, 1985 (12 rushing, 17 passing, 2 penalty)
31   at Det., Nov. 12, 1989 (10 rushing, 19 passing, 2 penalty)

Fewest First Downs, Game
3   vs. Chicago Cardinals, Sept. 18, 1932
3   at Boston Redskins, Nov. 4, 1934 (3 rushing)
3   vs. Chicago Cardinals, Nov. 18, 1934

Most Passes Attempted, Game
61   vs. San Francisco, Oct. 14, 1996 (28 comp)
60   at Detroit, Nov. 12, 1989 (35 comp)
59   at New Orleans, Sept. 14, 1986 (28 comp)

Fewest Passes Attempted, Game
*0   vs. Portsmouth, Oct. 8, 1933
4   vs. Brooklyn Dodgers, Oct. 23, 1932
5   at Chicago Bears, Oct. 16, 1932
5   vs. Detroit Lions, Nov. 1, 1971

Most Passes Completed, Game
36   at Chicago Bears, Dec. 5, 1993
35   at Tampa Bay, Oct. 12, 1980
35   at Detroit Lions, Nov. 12, 1989

Fewest Passes Completed, Game
0   vs. Portsmouth, Oct. 8, 1933
0   vs. Chicago Bears, Sept. 25, 1949

Most Net Yards Gained Passing, Game
423   vs. Chi. Cardinals, Nov. 1, 1942 (27–13–1, 6 TD)
422   vs. StL Cardinals, Dec. 21, 1969 (34–23–1, 5 TD)
415   at Tampa Bay, Oct. 12, 1980 (51–35–2, 1 TD)

Fewest Net Yards Gained Passing, Game
-35   at Cincinnati, Sept. 26, 1976
-18   at Chicago Cardinals, Dec. 5, 1948
-12   vs. Chicago Bears, Nov. 4, 1973

Most Rushing Attempts, Game
64   at Washington, Dec. 1, 1946
63   vs. Pittsburgh Steelers, Oct. 20, 1946
62   vs. Chicago Cardinals, Sept. 12, 1937
62   vs. Cleveland Rams, Sept. 21, 1941
62   at Chicago Cardinals, Nov. 10, 1946

Fewest Rushing Attempts, Game
7   vs. Miami, Sept. 11, 1994
10   vs. Seattle, Dec. 9, 1990
11   at Chicago Bears, Nov. 27, 1988
11   at Denver, Oct. 17, 1999
11   vs. Tennessee, Oct. 11, 2004

Most Yards Gained Rushing, Game
366   vs. Detroit, Oct. 26, 1947 (50 attempts)
312   vs. New York Yanks, Oct. 8, 1950 (40 attempts)
303   vs. Baltimore Colts, Oct. 18, 1953 (56 attempts)

Fewest Yards Gained Rushing, Game
12   at Tampa Bay, Dec. 26, 1999 (12 attempts)
13   vs. Seattle, Dec. 9, 1990 (10 attempts)
17   vs. Boston Redskins, Sept. 17, 1933 (37 attempts)

Most Touchdowns Rushing, Game
6   at Cleveland Browns, Oct. 15, 1961
6   at Philadelphia, Nov. 11, 1962

Most Kickoff Returns, Game
9   Eight different times

Most Yards Kickoff Returns, Game
258   at Dallas Cowboys, Oct. 3, 1993
256   vs. Minnesota, Oct. 5, 1998
245   vs. New York Giants, Sept. 19, 1971

Most Touchdowns Kickoff Returns, Game
*2   vs. Cleveland, Nov. 12, 1967

Most Punt Returns, Game
9   vs. Minnesota, Dec. 21, 2006

Most Yards Punt Returns, Game
167   at Detroit, Dec. 15, 1996
147   at Chicago Bears, Nov. 8, 1959
144, vs. Dallas Texans, Nov. 23, 1952

Most Turnovers, Game
9   vs. Chicago Bears, Sept. 22, 1940
9   vs. Los Angeles Rams, Nov. 12, 1950
9   vs. Detroit Lions, Oct. 26, 1952

Fewest Yards Allowed, Game
33   at Boston Yanks, Nov. 18, 1945
50   vs. Chicago Cardinals, Nov. 18, 1934
54   at Philadelphia, Nov. 11, 1962

Most Yards Allowed, Game
611   at L.A. Rams, Dec. 16, 1956
599   at L.A. Rams, Dec. 8, 1957
594   at Chicago Bears, Dec. 7, 1980

Fewest Rushing Yards Allowed, Game
-7   vs. Philadelphia, Sept. 15, 1940
12   at Boston Yanks, Nov. 18, 1945
12   at Chicago Cardinals, Nov. 10, 1946

Most Rushing Yards Allowed, Game
406   at Chicago Bears, Nov. 6, 1955
375   vs. Chicago Bears, Oct. 30, 1977
323   vs. L.A. Rams, Oct. 21, 1951

Fewest Net Passing Yards Allowed, Game
-6   at Chicago Cardinals, Nov. 29, 1934
-1   vs. Dallas Cowboys, Oct. 24, 1965
0   vs. Chicago Cardinals, Nov. 18, 1934

Most Passing Yards Allowed, Game
442   vs. Minnesota, Oct. 5, 1998
434   at L.A. Rams, Dec. 12, 1954
411   vs. San Francisco, Nov. 4, 1990

Most Passing Touchdowns Allowed, Game
6   at Minnesota, Sept. 28, 1986

Most Sacks, Game
9   vs. Dallas Cowboys, Oct. 24, 1965
9   vs. San Francisco, Nov. 1, 1998
9   at Chicago, Jan. 2, 2005

Most Passes Intercepted, Game
*9   at Detroit Lions, Oct. 24, 1943
7   at Cleveland Rams, Oct. 30, 1938
7   at Cleveland Rams, Nov. 8, 1942
7   at Cleveland Rams, Nov. 12, 1944
7   vs. Los Angeles Rams, Oct. 17, 1948

Most Interception Return Touchdowns, Game
2   nine times

Most Opponent Fumbles Recovered, Game
6   at Pittsburgh Steelers, Nov. 23, 1941
6   at San Diego, Sept. 24, 1978

Fewest Penalties, Game
*0   ten times

Most Penalties, Game
17   vs. Boston Yanks, Oct. 21, 1945
16   vs. Chicago Bears, Nov. 8, 1987
15   vs. Los Angeles Rams, Oct. 5, 1947

Most Yards Penalized, Game
184   vs. Boston Yanks, Oct. 21, 1945
151   at Oakland, Oct. 24, 1976
146   vs. Detroit Lions, Oct. 3, 1948
146   at Los Angeles Rams, Dec. 3, 1950

INDEX